CLAES OLDENBURG

CLAES OLDENBURG

edited by Nadja Rottner

essays and interviews by Joshua Shannon, Yve-Alain Bois, Julia E. Robinson, Ellen H. Johnson, Claes Oldenburg, Benjamin H. D. Buchloh, Cécile Whiting, Robert Pincus-Witten, Barbara Rose, Donald Judd, and Nadja Rottner

OCTOBER FILES 13

The MIT Press
Cambridge, Massachusetts
London, England

This book was set in Bembo and Stone Sans by Graphic Composition, Inc.

Library of Congress Cataloging-in-Publication Data

Claes Oldenburg / edited by Nadja Rottner.
  p.   cm. — (October files ; 13)
Includes bibliographical references and index.
ISBN 978-0-262-01710-7 (hardcover : alk. paper) — ISBN 978-0-262-51693-8 (pbk. : alk. paper)
1. Oldenburg, Claes, 1929-—Criticism and interpretation. I. Oldenburg, Claes, 1929–
II. Rottner, Nadja.
NB237.O42C59   2012
730.92—dc23
2011028991

Contents

OCTOBER Files addresses individual bodies of work of the postwar period that meet two criteria: they have altered our understanding of art in significant ways, and they have prompted a critical literature that is serious, sophisticated, and sustained. Each book thus traces not only the development of an important oeuvre but also the construction of the critical discourse inspired by it. This discourse is theoretical by its very nature, which is not to say that it imposes theory abstractly or arbitrarily. Rather, it draws out the specific ways in which significant art is theoretical in its own right, on its own terms and with its own implications. To this end we feature essays, many first published in *OCTOBER* magazine, that elaborate different methods of criticism in order to elucidate different aspects of the art in question. The essays are often in dialog with one another as they do so, but they are also as sensitive as the art to political context and historical change. These "files," then, are intended as primers in signal practices of art and criticism alike, and they are offered in resistance to the amnesiac and antitheoretical tendencies of our time.

The Editors of *OCTOBER*

Acknowledgments

Joshua Shannon's essay "Claes Oldenburg's *The Street* and Greenwich Village, 1960" was first published in *The Art Bulletin* 86, no. 1 (March 2004), and later appeared in Shannon's *The Disappearance of Objects: New York Art and the Rise of the Postmodern City* (New Haven: Yale University Press, 2009). The text in this volume is a shorter version. Yve-Alain Bois's "Ray Guns" appeared in Yve-Alain Bois and Rosalind E. Krauss, *Formless: A User's Guide* (New York: Zone Books, 1997). Julia E. Robinson's essay "Fetish or Foil: The Caprices of Claes Oldenburg" was first published in the exhibition catalog *Claes Oldenburg* (New York: Zwirner & Wirth, 2005). It has been shortened for this volume. Ellen H. Johnson's article "Oldenburg's Poetics: Analogues, Metamorphoses, and Sources" was published in *Art International* 14, no. 4 (April 1970); it is based on a lecture delivered at Princeton University, November 17, 1969. Claes Oldenburg's "Selected Writings on *The Store* and the Ray Gun Theater" consists of a selection of material from his book *Store Days* (New York: Something Else Press, 1967), together with a previously unpublished text, "Documents of the Ray Gun Theater," written for a talk at the Museum of Modern Art, New York, 1969. Benjamin H. D. Buchloh's "In Conversation with Claes Oldenburg" first appeared as one of a series of interviews with Oldenburg, Andy Warhol, and Robert Morris, entitled "Three Conversations in 1985," in *October* 70 (Fall 1994). Cécile Whiting's "Oldenburg's *Store*" is part of chapter 1, "Shopping for Pop," from her book *A Taste for Pop: Pop Art, Gender, and Consumer Culture* (Cambridge: Cambridge University Press, 1997). Robert Pincus-Witten's interview "The Transformation of Daddy Warbucks: An Interview with Claes Oldenburg" was first published in *Chicago Scene* 4, no. 4 (April 1964). Barbara Rose's "The Theater of Action" first appeared in *Claes Oldenburg* (New York: Museum of Modern Art, 1970). Donald Judd's review first appeared in *Arts Magazine* 38, no. 10 (September 1964); his second text on Oldenburg was part of "Specific Objects," first published in *Arts Yearbook* 8 (1965); Judd's third entry, "Claes Oldenburg," was originally written for an exhibition at the Moderna Museet in Stockholm, *Claes Oldenburg: Skulpturer och teckningar, 1963–1966*, in 1966, but was first published in *Donald Judd: The Complete Writings 1959–1975* (Nova Scotia: Press of the Nova Scotia College of Art and Design, 1975). Barbara Rose's article "Claes Oldenburg's Soft Machines" appeared first in *Artforum* 10, no. 5 (June 1967). Nadja Rottner's essay "Object Lessons" is published for the first time in this volume. Where necessary, the published texts have been minimally edited for consistency and factual accuracy.

The editor wishes to thank Rosalind Krauss for her unwavering support, and the authors for their willingness to participate in this anthology and to rework previously published material. I also owe a special debt of gratitude to this anthology's subject. This book would never have been possible without the generosity and support of Claes Oldenburg. I also wish to warmly thank his staff, Carey Ascenzo and Alexandra Lane, for all their fantastic help along the way. I am especially grateful to Evelyn McElroy for granting publication rights to Robert McElroy's wonderful performance images free of charge. These photographs make this book come alive in a way that would not otherwise have been possible. I was also supported in this endeavor by a Faculty Image Rights Grant from the University of Michigan–Dearborn.

Claes Oldenburg's *The Street* and Greenwich Village, 1960

Joshua Shannon

Pedestrians walking down Thompson Street off Greenwich Village's Washington Square Park in the winter of 1960 were beckoned, by means of a messily painted mural, into the basement of the Judson Church House. The building was the center of the social programs of the progressive Judson Memorial Church, which had presided over the south side of the square for more than a century. The basement of the church house had been converted in the late 1950s into living and studio space for a handful of the neighborhood's many artists, and by the beginning of 1960, it had become the Judson Gallery, a venue for the new urban and quotidian art working to counter the hegemony of abstract expressionism. Those curious enough to descend the stairs that winter found themselves in an exhibition called "Ray Gun." The first room had been converted into an environment called *The Street* by Claes Oldenburg, a thirty-year-old neighborhood artist.

The Street was a visual cacophony of cardboard, paper, newsprint, wood fragments, and black paint. Scraps of trash covered the floor from corner to corner, strips of newspaper hung from the light fixture, and the walls were covered with a sooty-looking cardboard relief. A few freestanding sculptures shared the viewer's own space in the middle of the scrap-strewn floor. There were marks of black paint across the whole work, in places seeming only to give the installation a sullied look, but in others forming letters of the alphabet, defining scorched-looking contours, and identifying facial features. In fact, the careful tearing and cutting of the cardboard, the nailing together of a broad variety of braces and sculptural supports, and the particular—if untidy—application of paint all worked, in their clumsy way, to make a readable representation of an urban environment. Over a period of looking, viewers would have been able to make out at least nine major human figures and four small automobiles, among other forms.

Most of the historical and critical literature on *The Street* has focused on its innovative use of banal materials or its dark representation of human suffering.[1] By contrast, I seek here to understand Oldenburg's odd streetscape as a cogitation on the transformation of New York City under mid-twentieth-century urban renewal. Specifically, I argue that *The Street* applied the problems of recent painting to a representation of New York, identifying renewal's central effort—through the promotion of order, negotiability, and legibility—to produce a newly abstracted city. This close look at *The Street* should allow us to recognize the ways in which the period's debate over the city was fundamentally a debate (at the center of an economic and epistemic shift) over the degree of abstraction desirable in everyday life. *The Street*'s reflection on this transformation was chiefly a negative one, insisting on the obdurate materiality of the city, but it was also complicated, and far from single-minded.

The surviving exhibition photographs, flash-bleached though they are, allow a fairly thorough reconstruction of the original installation (as we shall see, Oldenburg would install it again, a few blocks away, in the spring). Entering the room and facing right, the visitor would have confronted a bearded man in a top hat, slumping behind a shoeshine stand (fig. 1.1, lower right). At the shoeshine man's shoulder was a shop window displaying indefinite goods and a small, illegible sign. Further to the left, but along the same wall, there stood another figure, perhaps holding a gun in outstretched arms (fig. 1.2, at right). As the viewer turned to her left—negotiating the floor's muck of discarded shoes, empty bottles, and scraps of wood and wire—she would have approached a huge silhouetted face looming in the corner, its hair made of scrawled-out words (fig. 1.2, at right). Her passage would have been obstructed, however, by two sculptures standing on the floor of the installation: a striding figure and, beside it, a similarly rendered prominent traffic barricade. Nevertheless, our viewer would have seen a few small forms floating in the undefined pictorial space on the far wall, some describing cars and figures (one, it seems, with a gun), others more ambiguous. Turning left again to face back toward the entrance, the viewer would have seen a few additional large figures, including a talking pair rendered, respectively, in round bulges of paper and angular swaths of cardboard (fig. 1.3).

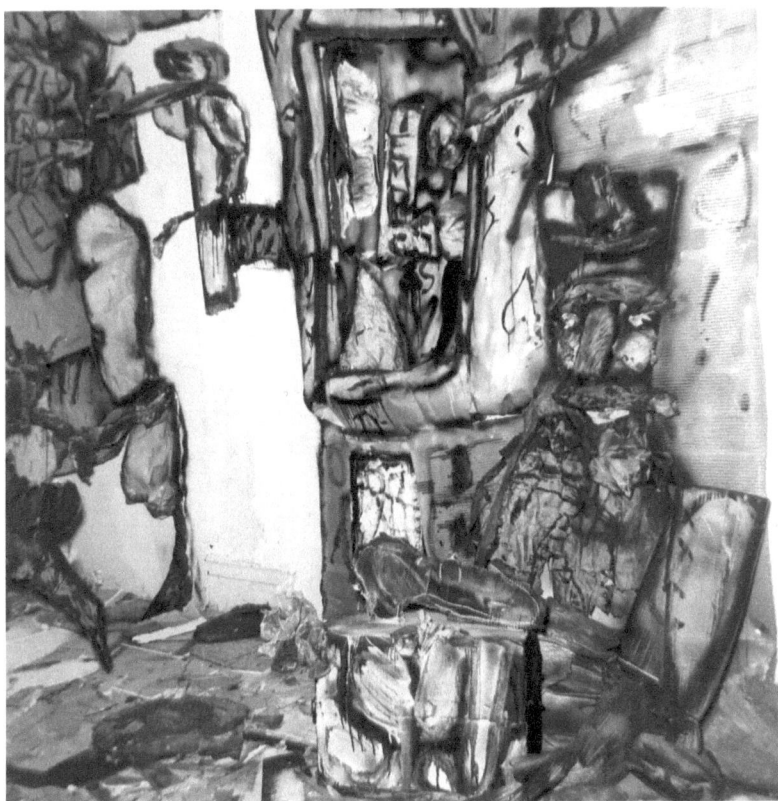

Figure 1.1   *The Street* in "Ray Gun," January 30–
March 2, 1960. Judson Gallery, Judson Memorial
Church, New York. Photo: Charles Rappaport;
courtesy the Oldenburg van Bruggen Studio.

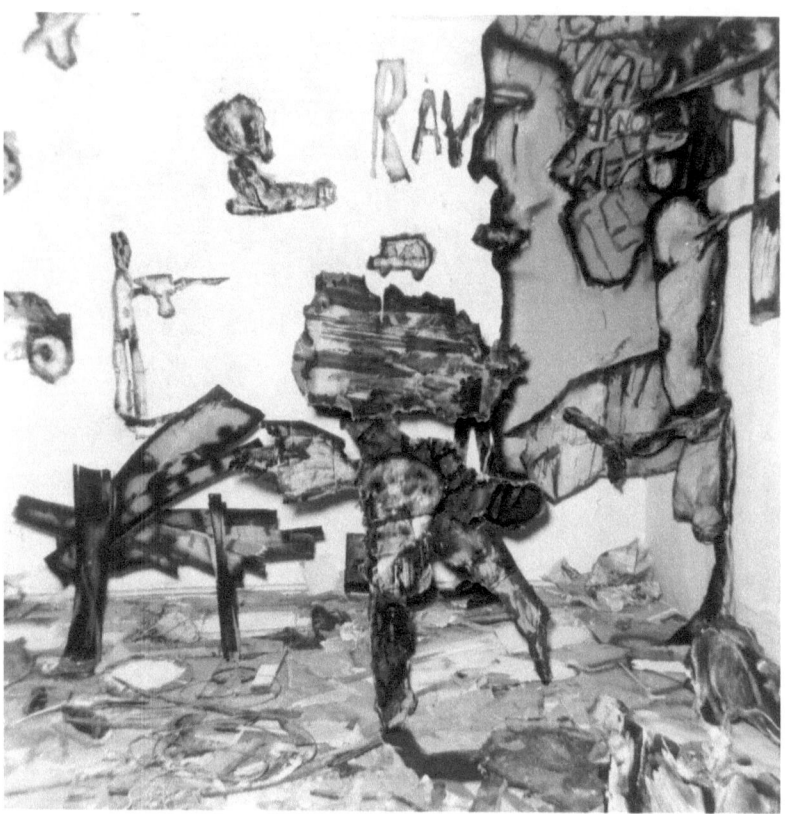

Figure 1.2   *The Street* in "Ray Gun," January 30–
March 2, 1960. Judson Gallery, Judson Memorial
Church, New York. Photo: Charles Rappaport;
courtesy the Oldenburg van Bruggen Studio.

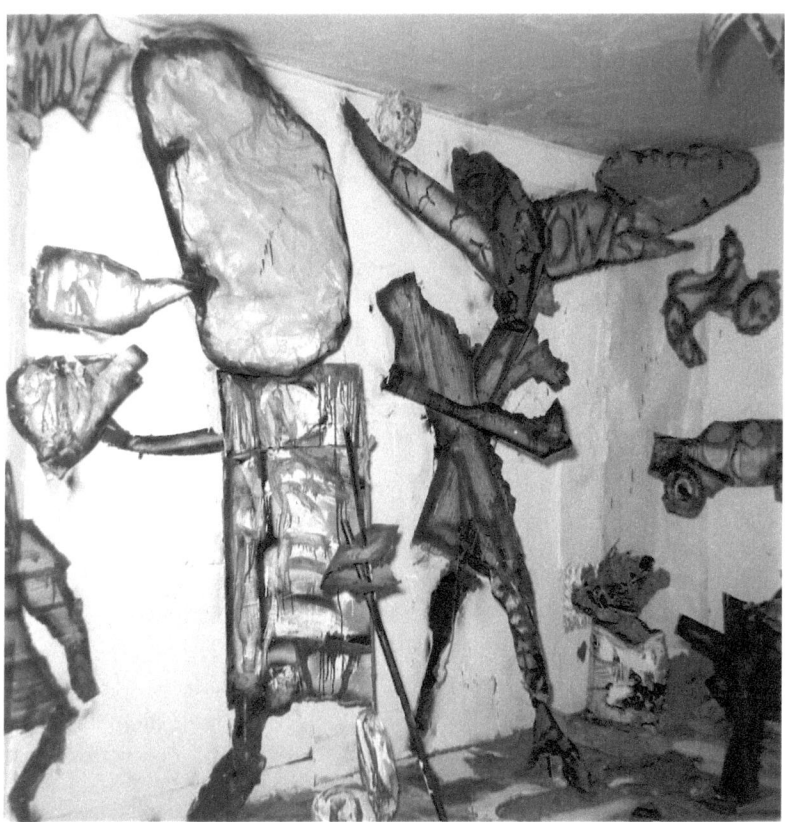

Figure 1.3 *The Street* in "Ray Gun," January 30–
March 2, 1960. Judson Gallery, Judson Memorial
Church, New York. Photo: Charles Rappaport;
courtesy the Oldenburg van Bruggen Studio.

A proper understanding of *The Street* will require us to consider the work in both of its installations, as well as in its various contexts; first of all, it will involve us in a recovery of the earliest clamorous death throes of New York's classic period of urban renewal.

Renewal in New York City

From the 1930s, American urban planning had been shaped by the European modernism of Le Corbusier. In his books *The City of Tomorrow* and *When the Cathedrals Were White*, Le Corbusier had proposed the wholesale destruction of chaotic, dirty old cities such as Paris and New York.[2] In their place would rise gleaming new cities of uniform towers, surrounded by parks and connected by ribbons of high-speed automobile expressways. This sort of urban planning became a kind of official program among Europe's leading architects when, in 1933, the Congrès Internationaux d'Architecture Moderne (CIAM) adopted the Athens Charter, a manifesto for the new city. Meanwhile, in the United States, the means of engineering the new trafficways were being worked out by the German immigrant Fritz Malcher, whose 1935 *The Steadyflow Traffic System* proposed soft curves, dedicated turn lanes, median strips, and separated parking areas in order to promote the ceaseless, signal-free flow of cars across cities.[3] His book, which began by excluding any discussion of sidewalks, formed the foundation of American urban traffic engineering. The tower-in-the-park program and the expressway program became the two chief principles of postwar urban planning.

Although the sheer scale of Le Corbusier's plans made them virtually impossible to adopt completely, at mid-century many governments found ways to incorporate aspects of the Athens Charter in their urban plans. In the United States, such a possibility was opened by Title I of the Housing Act of 1949, which appropriated $1 billion to initiate a national program of urban renewal, and which allowed governments, for the first time, to seize private property in order to offer it, below cost, to private developers. (Often, the developers, who stood to profit neatly when areas were declared blighted, were not under obligation to provide affordable housing in these new buildings.) In New York City alone, $267 million had been spent on Title I housing reconstruction by 1957, twice as much as in all other American cities combined. Alongside this private development were the public projects of the New York City Housing Authority, which, by 1960, had completed fully a third of multiple-dwelling construction in the city since World War II—virtually all of it razing old brick tenements in order to put up neo-Corbusian towers.[4]

Meanwhile, the Federal Aid Highway Act of 1956 established the Interstate system, guaranteeing federal money to cover 90 percent of the cost of the construction of these highways and initially committing $25 billion. Seven thousand miles of urban highways were planned as part of the system, an amount that would more than quadruple total city highway mileage.[5] Greater New York's urban highway boom was particularly robust, with 899 miles existing or under construction by 1964, twice as many as in the runner-up city, metropolitan Los Angeles.[6] A plan adopted in 1951 called for the easing of street traffic as well, and by 1960, Manhattan had converted nearly all of its avenues to one-way flow. Over roughly the same period, the borough narrowed sidewalks on over 450 of its streets.[7]

At the head of virtually all of New York's rebuilding efforts was Robert Moses, who simultaneously held jobs as a city planning commissioner, chairman of the Mayor's Committee on Slum Clearance, and commissioner of parks, among other positions. As director of the extremely lucrative and autonomous Triborough Bridge and Tunnel Authority, Moses bullied governors and mayors—from the 1930s to the mid-1960s—into letting him realize his plans for New York City and its suburbs. His biographer estimates that, counting only the projects executed directly under his authority, Moses built public works costing $26 billion in 1968 dollars and displacing a stunning half-million people.[8] He oversaw the building of the Long Island, Gowanus, Brooklyn-Queens, and Major Deegan expressways, among many others, as well as the construction of towering housing projects from Brooklyn to the Bronx. Renewal and highway construction were also accompanied by subtler methods of controlling urban chaos. The city adopted its first permanent jaywalking law in 1956 and installed its first pedestrian signal lights at the end of the decade. Meanwhile, a major anti-litter campaign resulted in streets that were, by one measure, nearly *seven times* cleaner in 1959 than they had been just four years earlier.[9]

For decades, Moses had enjoyed the press's support, but, in the late 1950s, the fortunes of renewal in New York began to change. In 1956, a group of well-connected citizens defeated Moses's plans for a new parking lot in Central Park. In 1958 *The Exploding Metropolis*—a group of essays irate about renewal, sprawl, and urban trafficways—appeared in mass-market format, echoing arguments that had been available in publications from *Architectural Forum* to the *New Yorker* and *Fortune* for several years.[10] By the spring of 1959, then-United States Representative from New York City John Lindsay had introduced legislation to diminish the secrecy under which Title I renewal was planned, and in the summer, the *New York Times* ran a series accusing the Mayor's Committee on Slum Clearance (which Moses chaired) of corruption.[11]

Even excepting ethical scandal, however, arguments against renewal were growing. In one contribution to *The Exploding Metropolis*, for example, Jane Jacobs—soon to be famous for her invective *The Death and Life of Great American Cities*—argued that cities needed old buildings and small blocks in order to flourish. In Jacobs's view, good planning required "leaving room for the incongruous, or the vulgar, or the strange." She was direct in naming the linchpin of a successful city: "The best place to look at first is the street. One had better look quickly, too; not only are the projects making away with the noisy automobile traffic of the street, they are making away with the street itself. In its stead will be open spaces with long vistas and lots and lots of elbowroom." William H. Whyte called special attention to this point in his introduction to the anthology: "In laying out the superblocks of the huge urban redevelopment projects [many of the people who are redesigning the city] banish the most wonderful of city features—the street." Indeed, the elimination of the street was, in the words of one major proponent of modernist planning, the "first necessity" of future cities.[12] The street, a narrow space used for many purposes, made the city a place of chaos. In its stead, a system of parks and expressways would guarantee order and steady flow in the urban fabric. This hostility toward complex, mixed-use urban space was perhaps nowhere more apparent in 1960 than on Thompson Street, just south of Washington Square Park, in New York City's Greenwich Village (fig. 1.4).

The Streets of Greenwich Village

For over a century and a half, Washington Square Park, in addition to being the unofficial front yard of the Judson Church, had served as the heart of Greenwich Village. Its famous plazas provided "the refuge, the summer vacation place of those who cannot afford to leave the city's heat . . . a meeting place for the elderly men who enjoy their chess and checkers under the great tree [and] above all . . . the children's playground."[13] Since 1900, a modicum of traffic—primarily the occasional bus—had run

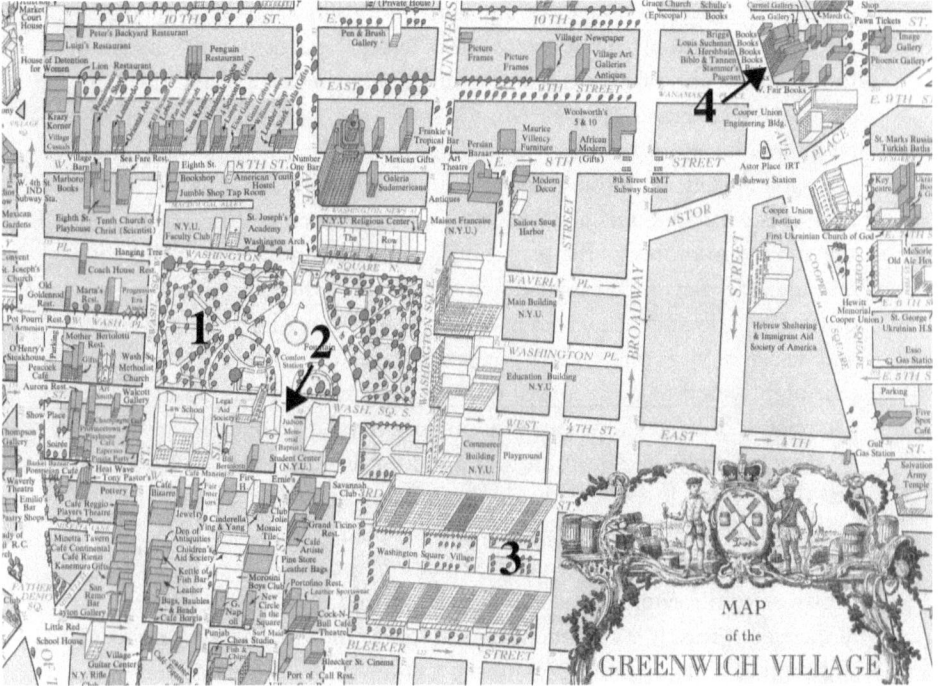

Figure 1.4 Lawrence Fahey, *Map of the Greenwich Village Section of New York City* (detail), 1960. Major buildings are indicated; privately owned buildings are shaded. Numbers added by author: (1) Washington Square Park; (2) Judson Gallery; (3) Washington Square Village; (4) Reuben Gallery. © Map Division, New York Public Library, Astor, Lenox and Tilden Foundations.

across the otherwise tranquil square. During the mid-century renewal and roadway boom, however, the park's open space attracted the eye of civic planners, including Moses, who wanted to ease the flow of downtown traffic. In 1946 and again in 1952, plans to build a more substantial trafficway across the park had failed. In 1958, however, the Board of Estimate and the City Planning Commission both preliminarily approved a proposal to extend Fifth Avenue—which terminated at the north end of the park—across the square, joining it with an existing street to be widened and renamed Fifth Avenue South (see fig. 1.4).

Residents, neighborhood groups, and architectural critics were outraged, fearing the loss of the square. Some believed that Moses had covert plans to use the park as part of a major conduit for carrying traffic right through Manhattan and across to New Jersey.[14] Lewis Mumford called the road an "almost classic example of bad city planning," and the Judson's own Reverend Howard Moody spoke out against it, in testimony and in public letters to both Mayor Wagner and Tammany boss Carmine De Sapio.[15] Although the roadway seemed inevitable, two rallies, a torrent of published letters and opinions, and a petition of thirty thousand signatures also protested the plan. Finally, at a dramatic Board of Estimate hearing, the mayor "brought down the house" when, in consideration of the objections, he canceled his plans to travel to Albany that evening and declared, "It is much more important to me to be here."[16] The board that night voted to delay a final decision, and when it met again in late October, it ordered a temporary closing of even the small existing road in Washington Square. The study was a success: in the spring of 1959, the board voted to close the park permanently to all traffic. Villagers held a celebration that June, burning a mock car in effigy.[17]

During the long battle, the press had often called the project an expressway, while Moses objected that it was merely "a wide avenue."[18] Whatever it was, it was certainly not a street. Indeed, the very point of the project had been to upgrade the trafficways in the neighborhood, mitigating the complexity and obstructions caused by the diverse uses of true streets. Had the project gone ahead, circulation in the area would have been defined not by multiuse public spaces fringed with sidewalks and old facades, but rather by a constant flow of automobiles through a freshly widened roadway. The symbolic outcome of the Washington Square battle was a triumph for traditional paved public space over efficiency of travel. "Progress" was stopped, and to this day the square blocks and fractures the flow of traffic at the foot of Fifth Avenue.[19]

Despite their victory over the Washington Square roadway, opponents of renewal in Greenwich Village were not so fortunate in other respects. Built one block from the Judson Gallery between 1957 and 1960, Washington Square Village, for example, is a mammoth Title I development that demolished "191 old stores and lofts" and replaced them with a superblock (now Greenwich Village's biggest) of privately owned apartments (fig. 1.4, bottom).[20] The project comprises two seventeen-story buildings (three were originally planned), each running the entire length of what had been three blocks. Between them is a large courtyard with trees, benches, and—of course—parking. The project's addresses deny any relationship to the surrounding neighborhood, refusing ordinary street numbers. In a Herculean achievement of Corbusian order, 148 distinct street addresses on seven separate streets were replaced simply by numbers one through four, Washington Square Village.[21]

And Washington Square Village was only one of many major new building projects in the neighborhood; at the end of 1957, the *New York Times* counted ten active construction sites within about 1,500 feet of Washington Square.[22] New York University's Title I renewal, for example, razed several blocks along the south side of the square. These developments included even the property directly facing the entrance to the Judson Gallery, which remained an open lot during the run of "Ray Gun."

This local rebuilding faced criticism throughout the late 1950s, but it was in the spring of 1959 that local opinion decidedly turned against the new construction. John Lindsay argued in March that Washington Square Village would never have been built if the public had known more about it in advance. In April, the *Voice* ran an editorial asserting that Greenwich Village was threatened by the current building boom; in July, the paper bemoaned the neighborhood's "vanishing local color"; and in August, it ran a lengthy letter charging that the "orgy of destruction" was neutralizing the physical character that attracted artists and intellectuals to the neighborhood.[23] The letter ended imperatively: "Save the Village!" By October, the Save the Square Committee had been formed to "preserve the present architectural character and scale of Greenwich Village," and a "Save the Village" petition had been launched "to preserve the character of the area 'from obliteration by spreading apartment projects.'"[24]

Of course, there were many reasons for this backlash in the Village against renewal. Corruption and high rents were high among them. But what is striking about the objections is how often they centered on rhetorical claims that the simplicity and uniformity of the new buildings threatened the cultural fecundity of the neighborhood. Perhaps the most sustained example came very early, in the eulogistic article which appeared on the front of the *New York Times*'s real estate section on December 8, 1957: "New Projects Will Change the Face—and the Character—of the Washington Square Area: Bohemian Flair Fades in Village."

The article mentions rising rents and the arrival of the bourgeoisie, but the real threat to writers and artists, it would seem, came from the new "curtain of blue-green glass" punctuating the neighborhood. In the article's final paragraph, its author, Ira Henry Freeman, describes in vivid terms exactly what was disappearing from the Village: "There are now under construction, or soon will be, in the Village at least eight modern apartment buildings where crooked studios with smoky fireplaces used to huddle. There won't even be an ailanthus tree and a broken fountain in the back yard."[25] This is a particular kind of nostalgia, leaning heavily on terms such as "huddle," "smoky," and "crooked." The denotative accuracy of these terms is questionable, but their force is clear: the longing is for disorganization, irrationality, and excess matter in the face of the plans for an ordered and sensible new city.

Oldenburg and the Judson Gallery

Soon after arriving in New York, in 1956, Claes Oldenburg moved into an apartment on Ninth Street, a few blocks northeast of Washington Square. Asked in 1973 about these quarters, he stressed one salient quality: "At that time they were tearing down a big building there called Bible House so that in my room I could only see the flames and the wreckage. . . . It's where Cooper Union has now built a new building."[26] The artist soon moved to an apartment at 330 East Fourth Street, just east of Greenwich Village. He offered very similar recollections of this place, where he lived while making *The Street*: "When I lived in the Lower East Side there was a great deal of tearing down going on, especially between where I lived and where I worked. So I could pass through all these ruins all the time."[27]

Oldenburg's keen awareness of the urban renewal surrounding him turned, in at least one case, to harsh critique. In an absurdist poem he wrote at the time, renewal is associated with class-based oppression, as a public official shouts: "Civic improvement, plazas, malls, centers, ports, projects, projects, projects. Got two heads full! Cut the folks up, cut up the plain folks, trim em like trees, saw em to size, make bricks of em, beams, pile em up, seal em to each other by their juices. Build Build Bld [*sic*]."[28]

With "plain folks" literally sacrificed to urban building projects, this is grim satire indeed. Taken as a whole, however, Oldenburg's thoughts about renewal were complicated and even contradictory. He seems to have had an aesthetic appreciation of "the flames and the wreckage" around him, as well as a satisfaction in the fact that he "could pass though all these ruins all the time." At around the time of *The Street*, he wrote delightedly in one of his notebooks, "The city is a landscape well worth enjoying—damn necessary if you live in the city. Dirt has depth and beauty. I love soot and scorching."[29]

Oldenburg was clearly attentive to the changing form of the city around 1960, but his investment was not that of a partisan in the political battles. Rather, the changes in New York formed the environment in which the artist viewed his own creative production. The new slabs everywhere supplanting lower Manhattan's tenements, the recent roadway fight—these were symptoms of the postwar vision of an ordered, negotiable, and legible city. This dream (and its antonyms) deeply interested Oldenburg: "Ray Gun" and *The Street* were, among other things, his complicated response. "A new definition of NY is needed you see," Oldenburg wrote, "and that is why New York will be renamed Ray-Gun."[30]

The installation of *The Street* at the Judson Gallery was a carefully constructed mess. Its discards and other banal materials covered every surface, and even the grandest sculptures in the installation were made of trash—cardboard, crumpled package paper, and broken slats of wood. Oldenburg had liberally dirtied the whole scene with black paint. Scale and representational mode were inconsistent, and the parts floated in an unordered pictorial space, with tiny cars jostling against giant silhouetted heads. Indeed, the whole "Ray Gun" exhibition was conceived and directed by Oldenburg as a festival of disorder. The other fixture of the show was Jim Dine's similarly chaotic installation *The House*, which was made from newspaper, children's paintings, a ripped umbrella, and other scraps, and which was overpainted with nonsensical expressions such as "Yes eggs" and "Goo." The exhibition also hosted several happenings, or "Ray Gun Spex": one performance each by Oldenburg, Dine, Red Grooms, Al Hansen, Dick Higgins, Allan Kaprow, and Bob Whitman. These, like most happenings, were characterized by a conspicuous lack of narrative sense.

All the untidy abjection at the "Ray Gun" exhibition made at least some viewers recoil sharply, sensing an attack on order and logic. Perhaps the *Village Voice* critic stretched slightly in claiming that some people—square uptowners, presumably—"feel that ['Ray Gun'] must be stamped out or that civilization will be in peril," but the show did certainly garner efficient dismissals in the mainstream publications that deigned to review it.[31] The tiny review in *Art News* described "Ray Gun" as "varied junk," and *Time* magazine, discussing the happenings, concluded sarcastically: "It was beat, man, though up-beat, and it was, like, existential. Real children might do it better."[32]

These are easy, and empty, clichés. But *Time*'s invocation of children, even in sneering disapproval, speaks to something of the exhibition's deliberate refusal of logic, its carnivalesque delight in disorder and nonsense. Notice, for example, the hair of that imposing silhouette in the far corner of *The Street* (see fig. 1.2); the ambiguous words "YEAH," "WELL," and "TELL" join, in a Dada nursery rhyme, with the nonsense expressions "HYNO" and "GURB." Look, too, at the careful ambiguity of the form to the left of the silhouette, suspended beside the word "RAY." Here we have the most illegible of objects, representing, we might guess, a human figure, an automobile, or even an airplane. If any art in New York in this period deserved the label neo-Dada, *The Street* is it—a kind of *Merzbau* of the sidewalk, rendered in trash.

In part, *The Street* was an attack on sense and order; in the place of logic and legibility, it offered a kind of passionate insanity. Years later, Oldenburg described the work, affirmatively, as "my ravings." In the 1960s, Oldenburg wrote, "This country is all bourgeois down to the last deathtail [*sic*]," and he remarked in an interview, "It sounds too crazy when you speak the truth. The truth is too crazy."[33] Oldenburg was not alone in aiming Dada-like nonsense at Eisenhower culture. The Beats had also lauded irrationality in the face of a conformist mainstream, and a questioning of common sense was endemic to Greenwich Village around 1960. A 1959 *Village Voice* advertisement soliciting subscriptions, for example, pictured a figure holding a sign reading: "Help To Stamp Out Mental Health!" When the Judson Gallery launched *Exodus*, its own journal, the *Voice* ran a warm news piece about the publication, citing its inclusion of entries called "The Insanity Bit" and "Poem of Holy Madness," as well as Bud Scott's description of it as "a way-out magazine."[34]

The struggle over the Washington Square roadway and the shape of Greenwich Village was itself cast as a struggle between logic and nonsense. In a statement about the expressway plans published both in the *New York Times* and the *Village Voice*, Robert Moses twice invoked "common sense" in defense of the project, saying that the result of not building it would be a "mess" and an "absurdity." An essay in the *Voice* satirically urged support for Moses and every "right thinker" under him. Another piece run in the same publication argued against the new campaign of issuing tickets for littering: "It seems to take us all one giant step nearer to that ideal society envisaged by the prophets of pure order."[35]

The value of Greenwich Village was said to depend on the illogic of its landscape. An essay about the character of the neighborhood linked "a magic in Greenwich Village" to the fact that "West 11th Street crosses West 4th." A prominent New York politician remarked in a similar vein, "City planners who would probably straighten out Morton and Gay Streets or widen MacDougal Alley . . . have shown no appreciation for what a community is." And a letter in the *Voice* argued that the Village's "community" and the fact of its housing "the most creative theatre in the country" depended on its being a "holdout from the nineteenth century," a "crazy patchwork of streets and buildings."[36]

It would be easy, then, to see the celebration of illogic in "Ray Gun" as a volley in a war between the reason of postwar planning and a culturally motivated refusal of order. Certainly this is part of what was going on. But to simplify the exhibition as an attack on the new vision of urban order would mean covering up the violence and destitution everywhere bound to the show's chaos. *The Street*, after all, does not picture the delightfully quirky city of Jane Jacobs. It continually emphasizes dirt, poverty, and violence. Remember, for example, the patina of soot covering the figure slumped behind the shoeshine stand, as well as the unhappy ploy for respectability signaled by his anachronistic facial hair and top hat (see fig. 1.1). As Barbara Rose has noted, Oldenburg associated *The Street* with *Guernica*, the century's most conspicuous painting of misery, even noting that his subject was "everyday agony."[37]

The double-edgedness of disorder in *The Street* is nowhere more apparent than in its ambiguous evocation of gun violence. In addition to the gun carried by Oldenburg in *Snapshots from the City*, there are the guns in the hands of two of the figures on and near *The Street*'s back wall (see fig. 1.2). The name of the exhibition, however, suggests that these guns, like those of science fiction, might not be purely deadly. As Oldenburg said later: "The idea was Ray Gun was shooting something other than a lethal blast." At the time, Oldenburg wrote in his notebook, "When Ray Gun shoots, noone [*sic*] dies."[38] Oldenburg and Dine had also written that the "slogan" for the "Ray Gun" exhibition was "Annihilate-Illuminate," a phrase that appeared in the show's advertisement in the *Voice*, the Judson Gallery's spring calendar, and Oldenburg's own notebooks, among other spots.[39] The phrase bespeaks *The Street*'s two-sided nature as a city of both fecundity and destruction.

The postwar planners envisioned an open, airy, and peaceful city—a clean and ordered system of smooth, white walls and seamlessly flowing traffic. *The Street*, by contrast, is a hyperbolic representation of the city as it had been (and—despite the incursions of renewal—as it continued to be); it exaggerates not only the exciting disorder and density of the existing city, but also its dirt, desperation, and confusion. Above all, *The Street* offers an image of the city as a place of unruly matter, of obdurate stuff refusing to be abstracted into order or legibility. These are the qualities we need to understand if we are to make sense of this conflicted representation of New York.

The chaos of *The Street* made it very difficult to "read" in any conventional sense. Recall the visual and interpretive opacity that marks our first experiences of the work. Look again, for example, at the wall to the right of the doorway—the one with the two large, standing figures (see fig. 1.3). Although we can be fairly certain that we see two human figures here, we cannot be sure what that form might be against the ceiling in the far corner, or what is on the floor below it. Also, we are not certain if the long horizontal forms extending from the head of the large figure on the right are ears, hair, speech bubbles, or perhaps somehow all three. Even where there is clearly a speech bubble—attached to the figure at left—its only contents are a dripping squiggle of paint. The unclear identities of the triangular form in the figure's hand and of the odd stick at its side further underline this illegibility in *The Street*, this blockage of interpretation.

Look also at the biggest nonfigurative element in the installation, that freestanding sculpture of the scorched traffic barricade (see fig. 1.2). Much of *The Street*'s account of urban experience is condensed into this one apparently senseless tool of blockage. An ordinary barricade depends for its utility on the legibility of its bright colors, bold lettering, and deliberate placement, but Oldenburg's sooty version, pointlessly dense with overlapping wood slats, lacks any institutional authority. Its awkward placement at the center of this odd streetscape leaves even its very purpose ambiguous: Is it meant to stop the flow of automobile traffic or—by blocking pedestrians—to foster it? Then there is also the ambiguity of the sooty finish. Has this barricade been darkened by the dirt of the old city? By the fires of renewal? All these difficulties of interpretation cue us to what these boards really do insist upon, namely their identity as trash, as materiality beyond or at the fringes of representation. What is blocked by the particular material excess here, therefore, is not simply physical movements, but also meaning.

The rhetoric in the "Battle of Washington Square" had explicitly pitted "flow" against a kind of blockage. One activist attacked the notion that "we must accommodate everything else to easing [traffic's] flow." An architectural critic, too, had said that Greenwich Village was "inhabitable" only because of "its jaywalkers, who slow up a confused and intermittent traffic," and Washington Square Park Committee Chair Shirley Hayes had argued that the neighborhood depended on the fact that traffic "winds" around the square—emphasizing that "winding is a good word for it."[40]

The barricade does a lot to make *The Street* a place where traffic (both corporeal and intellectual) must do a lot of "winding." There is no easy flow here; our experience and understanding of this work might well be characterized as "confused and intermittent." The sense of diversion, blockage, and fracture imitates the ways traffic might be diverted, blocked, or fractured at a barricade line or around a city park. For Oldenburg, one of the effects of his work was specifically a blockage of meaning. He typed a note about this effect a few years later: "My art is the constant enemy of meaning . . . or you could say I have aimed at neutralizing meaning (which is unexpungable). . . . To eliminate appearances seems to me impossible and therefore artificial. . . . Simply grasp them and show how little they mean."[41] *The Street* shows the city locked in a stunted transformation, where paper, cardboard, wood, and trash are used literally, as street debris, at least as much as they are used in the service of representation. The obdurate matter of the city clogs up renewal, traffic, and representation itself.

The Reuben Installation

Although it opened only a few weeks after the Judson show came down, the Reuben Gallery incarnation of *The Street* was vastly different (fig. 1.5). In fact, the whole of the Judson show's chaos seems to have been jettisoned for a quality of finish. The floors are bare, and each piece of the new installation is mounted separately, surrounded with sufficient space for individual contemplation. In this second version of *The Street*, Oldenburg has allowed himself to make several individual characters with their own titles. (*Lorraine*, for example, occupies the foreground of fig. 1.5.) This crystallization of *The Street* into discrete sculptures evolved over a series of sketches the artist seems to have made between the two shows. From the first, the drawings suggest a desire to try out making more legible units. Oldenburg writes on one sheet, for example, "FACES against black floor ea. a picture."[42] After all the resistance to representation at the Judson, Oldenburg is having a try at making pictures.

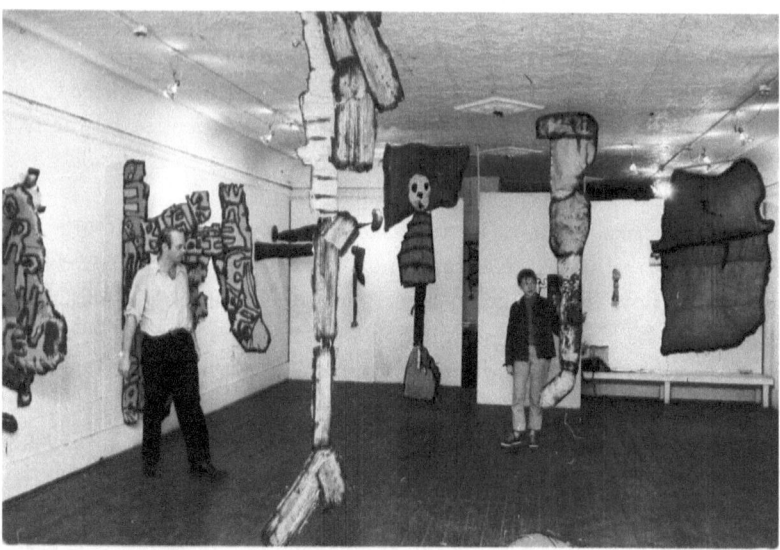

Figure 1.5 *The Street*, May 6–19, 1960. Reuben
Gallery, 61 Fourth Avenue, New York. Installation
view with Oldenburg and Anita Reuben. Photo:
Charles Rappaport; courtesy the Oldenburg van
Bruggen Studio.

For all its new order, however, the Reuben installation of *The Street*
is still very much an image of trash, poverty, and confusion. Like the
Judson version, it is rendered all in brown and black, a reduced color
scheme evocative both of city pavement and of aging social documentary photographs. The figures' lack of arms and their ragged clothes
(see, for example, the repaired shoes worn by *Street Chick (Big)*, at the
rear of fig. 1.5) also communicate a general desperation. As at the
Judson, the whole work here is executed in plain materials, including
paper, muslin, burlap, and cardboard. And here, too, all the forms are
edged in a scorched-looking contour line. This singeing effect suggests that the Reuben installation is a snapshot of renewal just at the
moment when it actually adds to the dirt and chaos of the city, just as
the seams and the material excess it aims to eliminate are most visible.
This moment was everywhere manifest in Greenwich Village in the
winter of 1960; look, for example, at the unfinished southern section of
Washington Square Village, as it appeared in the *Village Voice* on January 27 (fig. 1.6).

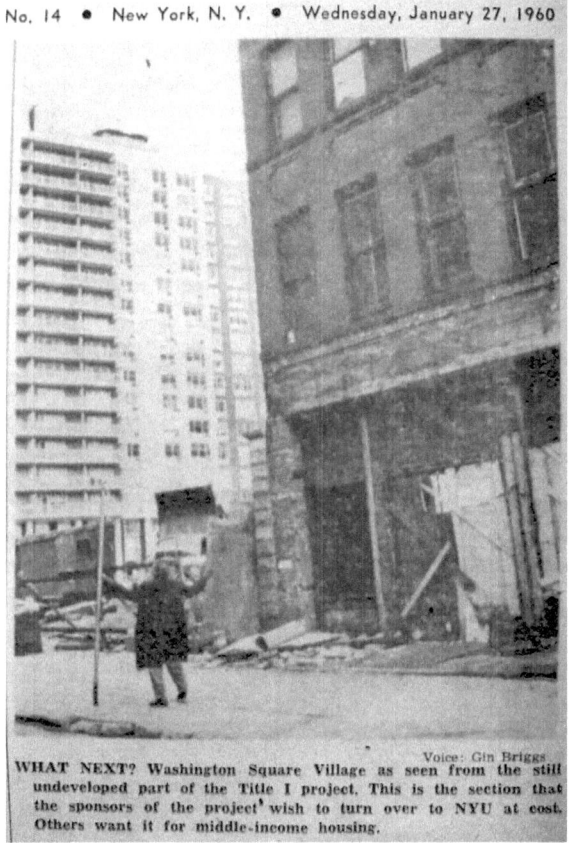

No. 14 • New York, N. Y. • Wednesday, January 27, 1960

Voice: Gin Briggs
WHAT NEXT? Washington Square Village as seen from the still undeveloped part of the Title I project. This is the section that the sponsors of the project' wish to turn over to NYU at cost. Others want it for middle-income housing.

Figure 1.6   Site of the planned extension of Washington Square Village. From the *Village Voice*, January 27, 1960, p. 1. Photo: Gin Briggs.

At first appearance, of course, the Reuben *Street* seems far easier to read than its predecessor. In the place of that continuum of chaos, we have newly discrete objects. But one effect of this change is that the work offers neatly framed studies of varying degrees of legibility. Representation nearly evaporates altogether, for example, in works such as the enormous and ambiguous *Street Head I ("Big Head"; "Gong")*, in which the title underscores the interpretive flexibility of the form. In fact, the childish stick-figure quality of the whole installation might be understood as a careful rendering of the streetscape in a language of reduced representation, where the elements threaten not to cohere, not to mean.

One of the most significant differences between the two installations is the inclusion, at the Reuben, of several prominent signs, occupying as much space as the figures and surrounding them on all sides (see fig. 1.5, beside and behind Oldenburg, for example). An untidy black lettering crawls all over at least four such signs, overpacking them with percussive, ambiguous syllables. The variety of forms taken by the letters of the alphabet stresses their materiality: some are merely painted, others are shaped out of bits of nailed-on cardboard, and still others are defined by scraps attached as negative space. Orientation is insecure, so some forms resolve alternatively as *Z* or *N* or as *E* or *M*. A few expressions are generally emphatic ("YA," "NOW"), while others seem simply nonsensical ("ZY," "KIG"); some passages fail to resolve into letters at all. In a notation that seems to address the *Street Signs*, Oldenburg made explicit his interest in noncommunicative lettering: "Where I use writing, I should like to provoke a physical effect of enunciation . . . certain letters are missing . . . the writing loses its sign character."[43] The signs in *The Street* are made so as to short-circuit communication in favor of an insistence on their own materiality and their own occupation of space in the city. If "physical," however, these signs still offer an "effect of enunciation," an emphatic call for the possibility of representation.

In particular, careful scrutiny reveals that most of the letters in the *Street Signs* do in fact work as fragments of one of two words: "ORPHEUM" (which appears as "ORPHM," "ORPH," "HEUM," "EUM," and "HUR") and "EMPIRE" ("EPRIRE," "EMPIRIS," "EM," and "EMPIRS"). It seems likely that Oldenburg was drawn to "Orpheum" as a term for the *Street Signs* by the fact that it recalls Orpheus, a figure of both artistic power and failure. But he might also have been drawn to it because it was the name of three corset shops, a Greenwich Village playhouse, and two movie theaters in Manhattan alone.[44] "Empire" had even more associations, evoking the nickname of New York State (and its most famous building), and naming over a full page of businesses in the Manhattan phone book. The Empire Theater was joined by the downtrodden Empire Diner as well as hairdressers, printers, and parking garages; packing, oil, and shipping companies; and four separate listings for the Empire Mfg. Co. Also listed were both an Empire Display Co. and an Empire Display Mfg. Co.[45] In the *Street Signs*, then, urban representation is frustrated not only by heaping, nonsensical forms, but also by constant multiplication of meanings and ambiguities of reference.

Even the most legible of the *Street Head* works, the giant, burlap *Street Head III (Profile with Hat)* (fig. 1.5 at right; fig. 1.7) is a far more ambiguous object than its title would suggest. Many of the black marks across both sides of it, for example, seem randomly and meaninglessly applied; it is only after a comparison of front and back that we can clearly recognize the eyes, mouth, and sideburns indicated on both sides. And, even though expressive content emerges immediately (the lips appear pursed, almost cute), these legible marks remain at the brink of meaninglessness, quite small compared even with marks (such as those across the back of the hat) that really are haphazard and nonspecific.

That this work may have had implications specifically for *The Street*'s consideration of the urban landscape is emphasized by Oldenburg's careful painting of a Manhattan street address right across the face of the sculpture. Barbara Rose suggests that *Street Head III* was made from a "burlap garbage bag," and Oldenburg has recently repeated this assertion,

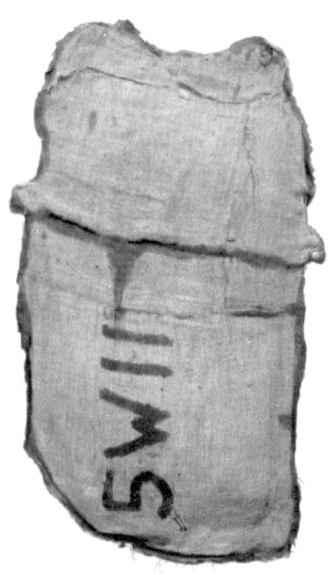 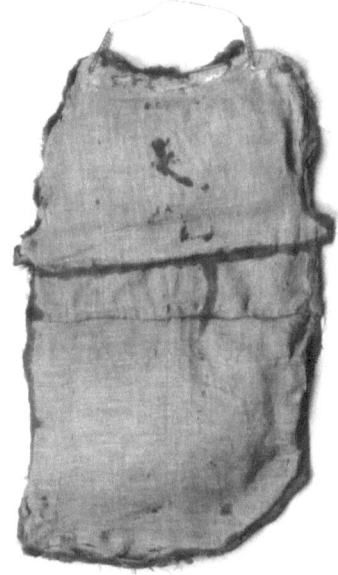

Figure 1.7   *Street Head III (Profile with Hat)*, 1960.
Burlap stuffed with newspaper, painted with
casein, 76 × 46 × 7 in. (193 × 116.8 × 17.8 cm).
Collection Museum Ludwig, Cologne, Germany,
Ludwig Donation, 1984.

adding that "5 W 11" was painted on the bag when he found it, indicating that it belonged to 5 West Eleventh Street.[46] However, the color, texture, and width of the brushstrokes in the address match those of the sculpture's outlines so closely that it seems more probable that Oldenburg added the address himself. This possibility seems all the more likely when one considers that there is no 5 West Eleventh Street in Manhattan and that there has not been since at least 1893.[47]

If Oldenburg did in fact paint on this address, one can imagine that he selected the address he did for the ambiguity of its figures: the number five looks like the letter *S*, and the number eleven could be mistaken for two *L*s or *I*s. Perhaps—West Eleventh Street being less than a five-minute walk from the Judson—Oldenburg even selected "5 W 11" specifically because he knew it was a sign with a phantom referent. In any case, the doubt about his account of the address also calls into question the claim that he collected the burlap from the streets at all. It seems at least as likely that Oldenburg purchased the burlap, which he might have done six blocks from his home in the Lower East Side, at a business called the Empire Burlap Bag Company.[48]

Street Head III does not merely stress its own materiality at the expense of particular readings. It also enacts elaborate failed representation—communications begun but stalled. Its marks might or might not form facial features. Its lettering might or might not signify an address. Representation is not merely obstructed here; it is performed as ever-present possibility followed by slippage, meaninglessness, failure. Meaning is always suggested but then bungled by particular material fact.

Early in 1960, the Reuben Gallery, no less than the Judson, was surrounded by rebuilding. The gallery, on the block of Fourth Avenue between Ninth and Tenth streets, was bordered on the south and the west by whole-block construction projects, both of which were completed that year. The project to the south was Cooper Union's engineering building, the very site Oldenburg had observed being cleared a few years earlier, from one of his first homes in New York. The other project was an upscale apartment tower, which shunned the street in the typical modernist fashion, with a virtually unbroken wall along the entire length of Wanamaker Place.

The Reuben Gallery, by contrast, was a third-floor walk-up in a small, aging building. Not only the ceilings but even the walls on which the art was hung were made of stamped metal, a hallmark of New York prewar construction (see fig. 1.5). With an awkwardly exposed utility meter plainly visible in the room and even an old heating stove, the space would have registered as an antiquated antonym to the development of the neighborhood. It might just have qualified as one of the "crooked studios" Ira Henry Freeman had eulogized in the *New York Times*.

In its second incarnation, then, *The Street* again appeared in the context of competing visions of the city. It is specifically in this context that Oldenburg again represented the city with a collection of carefully rendered but emphatically unruly and illegible detritus. The installation at the Judson had presented a city refusing order, negotiability, and legibility. The city presented in the Reuben reinstallation—now superficially tidied—appeared to offer these values a potential foothold. Instead, the Reuben *Street* offered only elaborately bungled gestures at communication—an excess of saying, with little clearly said. If this was an urban space imagining the possibility of coherent abstraction, its material particularity frustrated that possibility at every turn.

The Post-Abstract-Expressionist City

In part, Oldenburg conceived *The Street* as a reaction against abstract expressionism, which had dominated New York art for over a decade. At a symposium he helped to organize in 1959, he complained of the movement's painters, "They want everything to happen on the picture plane. My impulse is to make it come to life—to be an actual living thing." Even as he introduced a corrective return to figuration and to social subject matter, however, Oldenburg saw himself continuing to develop the formalist interests of abstract expressionism: "[My art is an] instance of the human image which has a strong formal guise," he remarked. "[It] carries art definitely forward."[49]

Oldenburg's reading of abstract expressionism owed a great deal to Allan Kaprow and specifically to "The Legacy of Jackson Pollock," an *Art News* article in which Kaprow made predictions about the directions art would take following Pollock's recent death. In the essay, Kaprow characterized the previous seventy-five years of painting not as a high modernist effort (per Picasso or Mondrian) to question and sharpen *representation*, but rather as a gradual (but ultimately Pollockian) move toward materiality per se: "Strokes, smears, lines, etc. became less and less attached to represented objects and existed more and more on their own, self-sufficiently." Kaprow then argued that the contemporary situation required an investigation of quotidian experiences and substances: "The young artist of today," he declared, "will discover out of ordinary things the meaning of ordinariness." He declared that "Objects of every sort are materials for the new art: paint, chairs, food, electric and neon lights, smoke, water, old socks, a dog, movies, a thousand other things." All these ordinary things were to be presented as they were, untransformed by transcendental or even metaphoric impulse: "Only their real meaning," Kaprow wrote, "will be stated."[50]

Oldenburg was so excited by Kaprow's manifesto that he sought out the author in person. In his own notebook, Oldenburg made similar declarations: "Art should literally be made of the ordinary world; its space should be our space; its time our time; its objects our ordinary objects."[51] In making *The Street* (think of the talking pair at the Judson, for example, or *Street Head III*), Oldenburg clearly aimed to let the world in both pictorially and materially. *The Street* was insistent both about picturing and about resisting that picturing with an excess of untidy, interpretation-resistant substance.

The emphatic materiality of *The Street* (and the corollary cost to easy legibility) was not especially new in avant-garde art. Some thought it had been Pollock's defining feature. Dada, too, had gathered ordinary scraps in works that frustrated or deflected meaning, and Dubuffet had piled on extraordinarily thick impasto in his own primitivist, faux-naïf art. What was particular to Oldenburg was his use of this emphatic materiality (and its resistance to legibility) to consider the nature of the urban environment. Oldenburg's materiality—in a complicated, even self-contradictory way—was marshaled against postwar renewal's aims of abstracting the city.[52]

One day in the middle of the "Ray Gun" show's run at the Judson, the *Village Voice* published a photograph of an old butcher's shop (fig. 1.8). The caption read: "Remember when Heymann's historic meat market graced the corner of West 4th Street and Sixth Avenue. The butcher's blocks and the uniforms remain, but the decor is different. The considerably more discreet sign on the window now reads: O. Henry's."[53] One in a periodic and informal series of front-page pictures about changes in the neighborhood, this picture eulogized Heymann's vibrantly cacophonous and unruly signs. In the photograph, blaring numbers and letters cover the shop's every vertical surface, even plastering the door and reaching to the sidewalk. This kind of overloaded urban signage was becoming less fashionable at mid-century, in favor of a more efficient and ordered kind, the kind that would not deflect easy reading

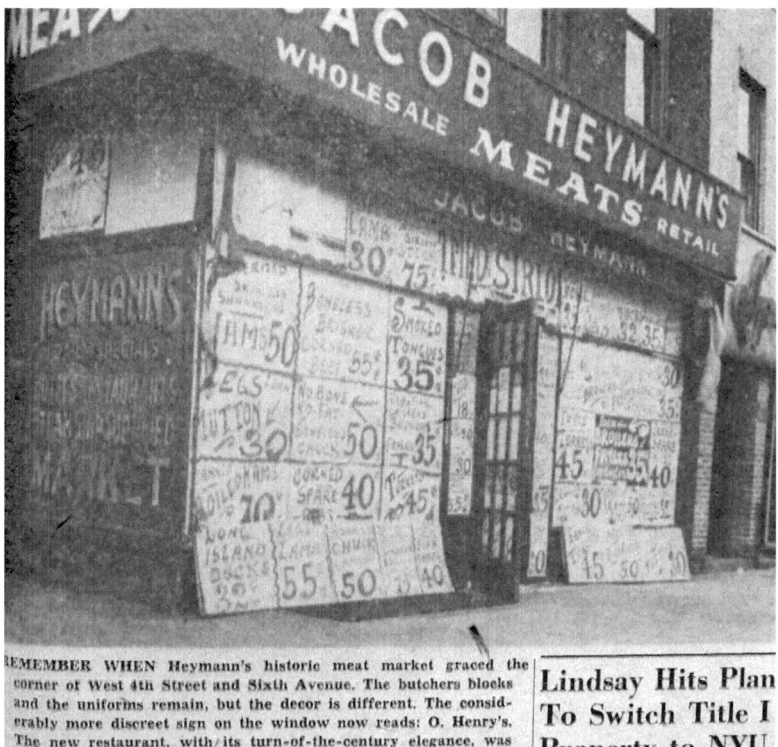

REMEMBER WHEN Heymann's historic meat market graced the corner of West 4th Street and Sixth Avenue. The butchers blocks and the uniforms remain, but the decor is different. The considerably more discreet sign on the window now reads: O. Henry's. The new restaurant, with/its turn-of-the-century elegance, was inspired in a modest way by its meat-dispensing predecessor.

Lindsay Hits Plan To Switch Title I Property to NYU

Figure 1.8   Jacob Heymann's Meats. From the
Village Voice, February 3, 1960, p. 1.

with too many material particularities to take in. (It was this change that J. B. Jackson, editor of *Landscape* magazine, lamented in a short commentary called "Signs of Life." Jackson defended "raucous billboards" over the ideal of "the discreet, non-hortatory sign . . . [the] whispered . . . neatly lettered 'Please!'")[54]

Also in the year of "Ray Gun" and the *Voice* photograph, Kevin Lynch, an MIT theorist of urban design, published his landmark study *The Image of the City*. Reporting on the accuracy of residents' mental maps of Boston, Jersey City, and Los Angeles, Lynch argued that cities were successful insofar as they lent themselves to strong mental images that could diminish unpleasant feelings of disorientation and chaos. Three years later, the author led a graduate seminar with Donald Appleyard specifically about urban signage. The professors published the work of their students as a book called *Signs in the City*, which they introduced with a photograph of a too-chaotic Boston streetscape and a statement of their goal: to find ways to augment the "clarity, congruence, and visible meaning of the environment." Lynch, Appleyard, and their students were hardly apologists for postwar renewal, but they shared its conviction that the city had to be made less chaotic, more negotiable and legible as a whole.[55]

All planning is of course a form of representation, an attempt to get the city to hew to an image of itself. Modernist planning in particular, however, was distinguished largely by its abstraction, its drive to make the entire city cohere as a single giant sign. Particularity is eliminated in favor of a hope that city dwellers (or at least planners with their bird's-eye views) might be able to read the ordered system of the whole city all at once. Consider Le Corbusier's famously crisp models, or the relative simplicity of Washington Square Village, reducing those 148 street addresses to the simply legible four (see fig. 1.4). The French art and architecture critic Françoise Choay rightly calls this kind of planning "monosemic."[56]

In exploring the connections between legibility in the city and legibility in art, *The Street*—at least as we look at it in retrospect—also helps us to understand why urban renewal was such a terrible failure.[57] The complexity of city life (its particularities, its disorder, even its nonsense) cannot be made to fit within a unified, abstract scheme of order. It is partly for this reason that single-style, high-rise public housing was dynamited in the 1990s to make way for more varied, low-rise developments. Nevertheless, it must also be remembered that *The Street* was not made simply as a polemic against the flow of the Washington Square Park roadway or against the monosemic new construction projects. It certainly could not be said to be valorizing its image of the chaotic city, nor to be blaming its depravity wholly upon renewal. On the contrary, the dirt, violence, and poverty in *The Street* all beg for some ordering of chaos, just as the unruly cardboard and burlap beg for pictorial readings. In *The Street*, a dialectic always buzzes between the need for order, negotiability, and legibility (even the *inevitability* of them), and the material facts that seem always to escape or exceed them.

Oldenburg's *The Street* was not so much a protest against the abstraction of the city as an insistence that no such effort could ever be entirely successful. It shows the city forever "los[ing] its sign character." Its insistence on disorder, blockage, and illegibility ought to be understood as an equivocal negation of a material environment apparently becoming ever more abstract. The work responded to the growth of an ordered, negotiable, and legible system of exchange, which seemed more and more to be trumping the world of material particularities.

The Street documents the changes in the city around it, lingering on the moment in which the effort to bring order and legibility to all that material chaos seemed to bring only more particularity and more chaos. This hyperbolic documentation suggests that the fight about the future of New York was fundamentally a fight about the limits and possibilities of abstracting the material world—of making it cohere in an ordered and flowing system. *The Street* at once begs for that impulse and insists that such an impulse must (and should) allow for the inherent disorder of material fact, for the inevitability of blockage and chaos. If abstract expressionism had been animated by doubt over the legibility or abstractability of matter (if, we might say, it had been a negative response to earlier modernists' quests for seamless representation), then Oldenburg brought that same doubt to bear on the urban terrain. In *The Street*, the planner's desire to systematize the city—like the modernist painter's desire to perfect representation—inevitably gives way, at least partially, to failure.

Notes

1. Barbara Rose's chapter on *The Street*, written over forty years ago, is still the most comprehensive overview of the work: Barbara Rose, *Claes Oldenburg* (New York: Museum of Modern Art, 1970), pp. 37–50. See also Robert E. Haywood, "Heretical Alliance: Claes Oldenburg and the Judson Memorial Church in the 1960s," *Art History* 18, no. 2 (June 1995), pp. 185–212.

2. These works were originally published as *Urbanisme* (Paris: G. Crès, 1924), available in English by 1929, and *Quand les cathédrales étaient blanches* (Paris: Plon, 1937), available in English by 1947.

3. Fritz Malcher, *The Steadyflow Traffic System* (Cambridge, Mass.: Harvard University Press, 1935).

4. Title I figures are from Robert A. Caro, *The Power Broker: Robert Moses and the Fall of New York* (New York: Vintage Books, 1975), p. 12. Housing Authority figures are from McCandish Phillips, "City Marks Birth of Public Housing," *New York Times*, December 4, 1960.

5. Francis Bello, "The City and the Car," in *The Exploding Metropolis: A Study of the Assault on Urbanism and How Our Cities Can Resist It*, ed. Editors of Fortune (Garden City, N.Y.: Doubleday, 1958), p. 34. Robert Caro puts the total figure at 6,700 miles (*Power Broker*, p. 704).

6. Caro, *Power Broker*, p. 940.

7. On traffic change, see Irving Spiegel, "Two One-Way Shifts Go Smoothly," *New York Times*, July 18, 1960. On the narrowing of sidewalks, see Jane Jacobs, *The Death and Life of Great American Cities* (New York: Vintage, 1961), p. 364.

8. Caro, *Power Broker*, pp. 9, 20.

9. On jaywalking and pedestrian signals, see coverage in the *New York Times* on May 3, June 15, August 8, and November 17, 1958, and on March 31 and June 15, 1959. On litter, see the *New York Times*, March 30 and October 6, 1959.

10. Bello, *The Exploding Metropolis*.

11. "Lindsay Acts to Take Secrecy Wrap off Title I," *Village Voice*, April 1, 1959, p. 1; major articles on the Slum Clearance scandal appeared in the *New York Times* that summer on June 21, 22, 24, and 30; July 1, 2, 4, 14, and 15. In the fall, a special issue of the *Nation* addressed the Title I scandal among other controversies: Fred J. Cook and Gene Gleason, "The Shame of New York," *Nation* (October 31, 1959).

12. Jane Jacobs, "Downtown Is for People," in Bello, *The Exploding Metropolis*, pp. 168, 143 (see also Jacobs, *Death and Life*); William H. Whyte, Jr., introduction to *The Exploding Metropolis*. It was Sigfried Giedion who saw the elimination of the street as a necessity: Giedion, *Space, Time and Architecture: The Growth of a New Tradition* (Cambridge, Mass.: Harvard University Press, 1941), p. 559.

13. Laura Benet, letter to the editor, *New York Times*, April 7, 1958.

14. Charles Grutzner, "Strategy Revamped on Washington Sq.," *New York Times*, March 30, 1958.

15. "Mumford Hits Plan for Washington Sq.," *New York Times*, March 10, 1958. Moody's actions were reported in Daniel Wolf, "Moses Hints 'Retreat' on Sq. Owing to Village Pressure," *Village Voice*, May 21, 1958, p. 3; "Washington Square Traffic Plea," *New York Times*, February 4, 1959; and "Close 'Square' Permanently; Take It Out of Politics," *Village Voice*, January 14, 1959, p. 3.

16. Charles G. Bennett, "'Village' Protesters Led by De Sapio," *New York Times*, September 19, 1958.

17. See especially coverage in the *New York Times* on October 24, 1958, and on April 10 and June 13, 1959. See also Robert Fishman, "Revolt of the Urbs: Robert Moses and His Critics," in *Robert Moses and the Modern City: The Transformation of New York*, ed. Hilary Ballon and Kenneth T. Jackson (New York: W. W. Norton, 2007), pp. 122–129.

18. "Statement of Robert Moses Regarding Washington Square," *Village Voice*, January 1, 1958, p. 15.

19. Robert Moses had championed the roadway project as "progress" (ibid.), while two *New York Times* editorials arguing against the road had used the same word in distancing quotation marks (November 5, 1958; April 11, 1959).

20. "'Village' Housing Dedicated Here," *New York Times*, December 11, 1957.

21. This change is made apparent by a comparison of the situation today with a 1955 fire insurance map, *Manhattan Land Book of the City of New York* (New York: G. W. Bromley, 1955). For an encyclopedic treatment of Washington Square Village and related development, see "Catalog of Built Work and Projects in New York City, 1934–1968," in *Robert Moses and the Modern City*, pp. 244–248.

22. Ira Henry Freeman, "New Projects Will Change the Face—and the Character—of the Washington Square Area," *New York Times*, December 8, 1957, section VIII.

23. "Lindsay Acts," p. 1; William W. Brill, "Zoning for Survival," editorial, *Village Voice*, April 29, 1959, p. 4; "Vegetables and Art," photograph caption, *Village Voice*, July 29, 1959, p. 1; Lester Dreizen, letter, *Village Voice*, August 19, 1959, p. 4, p. 12.

24. "'Save the Village' Wins Sq. Association Support," *Village Voice*, October 14, 1959, p. 3; "'Save the Village' Drive Seeks Local Volunteers, 10,000 petition signers," *Village Voice*, October 28, 1959, p. 3.

25. Freeman, "New Projects Will Change the Face."

26. Claes Oldenburg, interview with Paul Cummings, 1973–1974, tape recordings, Archives of American Art, Smithsonian Institution, Washington, D.C., transcript, p. 70. Courtesy Claes Oldenburg.

27. The Fourth Street address is indicated in Rose, *Claes Oldenburg*, p. 199; the Oldenburg quotation is from the interview with Cummings, p. 116.

28. Claes Oldenburg, "A Card from Doc: Postscript," in *Injun and Other Histories (1960)* (New York: Great Bear, 1966), p. 13.

29. Quoted in Barbara Rose, "The Origins, Life and Times of Ray Gun: 'All Will See as Ray Gun Sees . . . ,'" *Artforum* 8, no. 3 (November 1969), p. 53.

30. Claes Oldenburg, *Store Days: Documents from The Store (1961) and Ray Gun Theater (1962)*, ed. Claes Oldenburg and Emmett Williams (New York: Something Else Press, 1967), p. 7; excerpts reprinted in this volume.

31. Suzanne Kiplinger, "Ray Gun," *Village Voice*, February 17, 1960, p. 11.

32. A[nne] S[eelye], "Reviews and Previews: New Names This Month: Ray Gun," *Art News* 59, no. 1 (March 1960), p. 18; "Up-Beats," *Time*, March 14, 1960, p. 80.

33. Claes Oldenburg, telephone interview with the author, June 15, 2000; Oldenburg, *Store Days*, p. 8; Claes Oldenburg, interview with John Jones, tape recordings B6, Archives of American Art, Smithsonian Institution, Washington, D.C., transcript, p. 5. Courtesy Claes Oldenburg.

34. "Help To Stamp Out Mental Health!" advertisement, *Village Voice*, April 22, 1959, p. 12; J. H. Livingston, "The Search for a Way Out by a Way-Out Magazine," *Village Voice*, April 29, 1959, p. 3.

35. "Statement of Robert Moses," p. 1; Jean Shepherd, "Bring on the Concrete, We're Behind You, Bob," *Village Voice*, April 22, 1959, p. 12; John Wilcock, "All Right, Men, Go Out and Police the Area," editorial, *Village Voice*, April 30, 1958, p. 4.

36. John Wilcock, "Greenwich Village, 1927–1957: How Many Times Have They Buried Its Bohemians?," *Village Voice*, January 1, 1958, p. 16; "Abrams on the Village: Sameness Is a Bore, Variety a Strength," *Village Voice*, February 19, 1958, p. 1; David McReynolds, "Save the Village," letter to the editor, *Village Voice*, March 23, 1960, p. 12.

37. Rose, *Claes Oldenburg*, p. 38.

38. Oldenburg, telephone interview with the author; Oldenburg, *Store Days*, p. 44.

39. Jim Dine and Claes Oldenburg, "Spring Calendar at the Judson Gallery" [1960], transcript, Judson Church archives, n.p.; "Ray Gun" advertisement, *Village Voice*, January 27, 1960, p. 11; Rose, "The Origins, Life and Times of Ray Gun," pp. 51, 54.

40. Raymond R. Rubinow, quoted in Grutzner, "Strategy Revamped"; Douglas Haskell quoted in "Village Hears Gibe at 'Traffic Hounds,'" *New York Times*, April 1, 1958; Shirley Hayes, letter, *Village Voice*, April 9, 1958, p. 4.

41. Claes Oldenburg, typed notebook page, a copy of which is held in the Ellen H. Johnson Papers, Archives of American Art, Smithsonian Institution, Washington, D.C. The note was probably made in 1963. Ellipses in original.

42. See Rose, *Claes Oldenburg*, p. 41.

43. A copy of this notation, dated 1963, is held in the Ellen H. Johnson Papers.

44. *Manhattan Telephone Directory* (New York: New York Telephone Company, 1958–1959); and "Orpheum Theatre," advertisement, *Village Voice*, December 24, 1958, p. 19.

45. *Manhattan Telephone Directory*, p. 483.

46. Rose, *Claes Oldenburg*, p. 43; letter from Oldenburg's studio, signed Anu Vikram, November 10, 2000; Claes Oldenburg, letter to the author, November 20, 2000.

47. In that year, the current First Presbyterian Church of New York was built, stretching west from Fifth Avenue and occupying the place where 5 West Eleventh Street would lie. It is remotely possible that Oldenburg simply misremembered the address where he found this bag, and that what we see is only a fragment of 115 West Eleventh Street or some other longer address.

48. In 1960 Oldenburg lived at 330 East Fourth Street (Rose, *Claes Oldenburg*, p. 199), and the Empire Burlap Bag Company was located at 231 East Ninth (*Manhattan Telephone Directory*, p. 483).

49. "New Uses of the Human Image in Painting" (symposium at the Judson Gallery, December 2, 1959), transcript, pp. 4, 1, Judson Church Archives.

50. Allan Kaprow, "The Legacy of Jackson Pollock," *Art News* 57, no. 6 (October 1958), pp. 26, 56–57.

51. Rose cites Oldenburg's seeking out Kaprow (*Claes Oldenburg*, p. 25); she gives the quotation (without citation) on p. 53.

52. For a consideration of the relevance of the Situationist International, see the fuller versions of this essay, "Claes Oldenburg's *The Street* and Greenwich Village, 1960," *Art Bulletin* 86, no. 1 (March 2004), pp. 136–161, reprinted in the author's *The Disappearance of Objects: New York Art and the Rise of the Postmodern City* (New Haven: Yale University Press, 2009).

53. *Village Voice*, February 3, 1960, p. 1.

54. J. B. Jackson, "Signs of Life," *Landscape* 14, no. 2 (Winter 1964–1965), p. 1.

55. Kevin Lynch, *The Image of the City* (Cambridge, Mass.: MIT Press, 1960); *Signs in the City*, ed. Kevin Lynch and Donald Appleyard (Cambridge, Mass.: MIT Press, 1963), p. 76.

56. Françoise Choay, "Urbanism and Semiology," in *Meaning in Architecture*, ed. Charles Jencks and George Baird (New York: George Braziller, 1970), p. 34.

57. See Peter Blake, *Form Follows Fiasco: Why Modern Architecture Hasn't Worked* (Boston: Little, Brown, 1977).

Ray Guns

Yve-Alain Bois

Trash collection is the business of public sanitation; recycling, the very height of capitalist alchemy, turns everything into grist for commodification's mill. But it is also a strategy of aesthetic sublimation that, according to Thomas Crow, is internal to modernism (he has analyzed the cyclical aspect of this in terms of the incorporation of the "low" by the "high").[1] In this matter of artistic recycling, the work of Dubuffet and of pop art represent two examples from the two extremes of a huge gamut of possibilities. Dubuffet tried to "rehabilitate dirt," as he said himself in 1946. After listing the materials in the *Hautes Pâtes* shown in his "Mirobolus, Macadam & Cie" exhibition ("very vulgar and cost-free substances such as coal, asphalt, or even dirt")—materials whose shock effect at the time we now find surprising—Dubuffet wrote: "In the name of what—except perhaps the coefficient of rarity—does man deck himself out in necklaces of pearls and not of spider webs, in fox furs and not in fox innards? In the name of what, I want to know? Don't dirt, trash, and filth, which are man's companions during his whole lifetime, deserve to be dearer to him, and shouldn't he pay them the compliment of making a monument to their beauty?"[2]

Pop art, which is perhaps more nostalgic than it seems, takes the inversion covertly carried out by the capitalist economy as its starting point: commodity itself (and the kitsch of the culture industry) is the contemporary cast-off, and it is this very throwaway that pop art seeks to redeem.

Claes Oldenburg started off from Dubuffet (along with Céline, this was the major reference of his early work), and he ended up with pop.

Between these two points of his itinerary came the invention of the "ray
gun" (fig. 2.1). It first put in a timid appearance, in the scrap heap of
Oldenburg's first exhibition, *The Street* (January to March 1960), among
the torn silhouettes pinned to the walls and hanging from the ceiling,
and took the form of notes that the visitor could read. These notes are
Dubuffet "applied" to the urban theme: "The city is a landscape worth
enjoying—damn necessary if you live in the city. Dirt has depth and
beauty. I love soot and scorching. From all this can come a positive as
well as a negative meaning."[3] Given the fact that it is urban, the trash is a
little less aestheticized than in Dubuffet's work. The silhouettes were cut
out, with a blowtorch, from material gathered in the street (lots of corru-
gated cardboard, and newspapers), and the Judson Gallery itself—where
a series of happenings also took place—became a kind of trash can: the
ground was littered with detritus of all kinds; bums hung out there. But it
was still an aestheticization of trash (which was even more obvious in the
second exhibition of *The Street*, at the Reuben Gallery two months later,
made from the rarefied residues of the first show).

Secluded in the country after these two exhibitions, Oldenburg
drew this lesson from them: "A refuse lot in the city is worth all the
art stores in the world."[4] At this point he began seriously elaborating
the figure of the ray gun, while he was preparing the objects he would
soon sell intermittently between 1961 and 1963 in his studio-shop *The
Store*—ostensibly slapdash and oversized "replicas," made of cloth soaked
in plaster and garishly colored, of perishable foodstuffs or of tiny objects
of contemporary mass consumption.

The two projects were related (*The Store* was even placed under the
rubric "Ray Gun Manufacturing Company," as indicated in the poster
announcing its opening): their essential stake, the question of recycling.
The Store's idea took off from the premise that all avant-gardist daring is
assimilable, recuperable by middle-class culture ("The bourgeois scheme
is that they wish to be disturbed from time to time, they like that, but
then they envelop you, and that little bit is over, and they are ready for
the next").[5] The projected solution to this dilemma: skip over the illusory
stage in which art pretends to escape commodification. Art objects "are
displayed in galleries, but that is not the place for them. A store would be
better (Store—place full of objects). Museum in b. [bourgeois] concept
equals store in mine."[6] *The Store* would thus function like any other,
each piece sold being immediately replaced on the shelves by another,

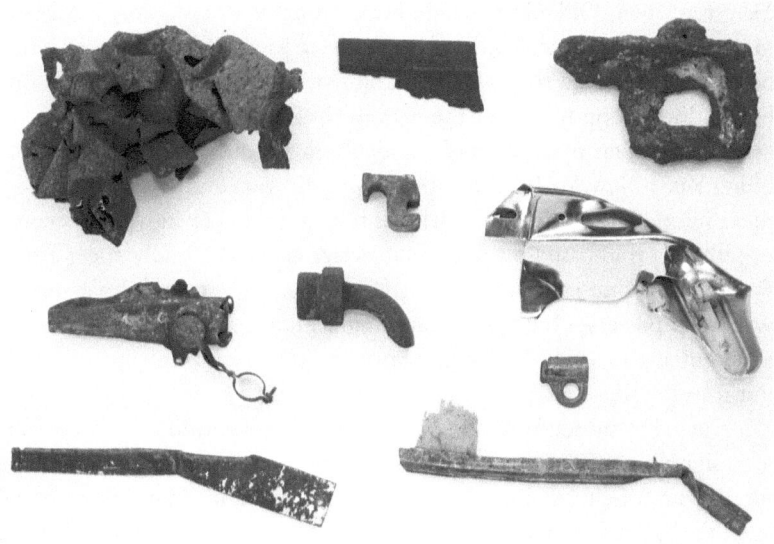

Figure 2.1   Detail of a vitrine from *Mouse Museum/Ray Gun Wing*, 1965–1977. Metal fragments resembling guns. Ludwig Collection, on permanent loan to Museum Moderner Kunst, Vienna, Austria. Photo courtesy the Oldenburg van Bruggen Studio.

often made on the spot (but this is not to say that the prices, even though modest, would be those of the corner grocery: it was not a matter of "democratizing" art, but of avoiding the detour of its aesthetic sublimation). "Store is cloaca; defecation is passage," Oldenburg wrote.[7] The solution was provisional, and Oldenburg knew very well that the objects he sold in his store would end up in a museum; it is from that end that the ray gun attacks the problem of recycling. At the outset (in *The Street* show), it was a question of a parodic science-fiction toy, whose image Oldenburg took over by simplifying it. But he quickly saw that it took little to make a ray gun: any right angle would suffice, even blunted, even barely perceptible. The ray gun is the "universal angle": "Examples: Legs, Sevens, Pistols, Arms, Phalli-simple Ray Guns. Double Ray Guns: Cross, Airplanes. Absurd Ray Guns: Ice Cream Sodas. Complex Ray Guns: Chairs, Beds."[8] Mondrian didn't need to reduce everything to the right angle: almost everything is already a right angle. During the time *The*

Store was open, Oldenburg made huge numbers of ray guns (in plaster, in papier mâché, in all kinds of materials, in fact), but he soon saw that he didn't even need to *make* them: the world is full of ray guns. All one has to do is stoop to gather them from the sidewalks (the ray gun is an essentially urban piece of trash: Oldenburg produced their anagram as "Nug Yar": New York). Even better: he did not even need to collect them himself; he could ask his friends to bring them to him (he accepted or refused a find based on purely subjective criteria). Finally, there are all the ray guns one cannot move—splotches on the ground, holes in the wall, torn posters—but which one might photograph. The "inventory" is potentially infinite. And what should be done with this invasive tide? Put it in the museum.

But what museum would want such a proliferation of objects (objects signifying, for all that, nothing but their very proliferation)? Only a simulacrum of a museum could be imagined. The idea for one emerged in 1965 but would not be achieved until 1972, for Documenta V, in Kassel, Germany. A selection of ray guns was presented in a special wing of Oldenburg's *Mouse Museum* (a kind of giant Duchampian *Boîte en valise*, whose ground plan was in the schematic shape of Mickey Mouse's head—a "Double Ray Gun," it should be remarked in passing)[9] and decorously classified in various vitrines according to whether they had been made by the artist, simply altered by him, made by others, or only found (without being altered). The *Mouse Museum* was reconstructed in 1979. Since then, ray guns have once again been piling up on the shelves of Oldenburg's studio.

But Oldenburg was not the only one to have cruised the city's trash cans. In France, beginning in 1949, this practice had been pursued by the *décollagistes*. Oldenburg was countering abstract expressionism's pathos (which had become purely rhetorical); for their part, the *décollagistes* (Raymond Hains, Jacques Villeglé, and François Dufrêne, to name a prominent few) weighed in against Art Informel and its metaphysical pretensions. But they were also turning against what had, in its own day, been one of the most radical modernist inventions, and which had since become rather anodine (as early as 1930, Carl Einstein had noted in *Documents:* "There was a time when collage played the part of the acid thrower, [when it was] a means of defense against the happy chance of virtuosity. Today it has degenerated into easy riddles and is in danger of lapsing into the fakery of petit-bourgeois decoration").[10] No need for virtuosity, no need for glue, it is enough to strip off posters from the hoardings where they have accumulated, themselves already partially lacerated by anonymous vandals. This is important (it constitutes the difference between the position of the French *décollagistes* and that of the Italian, Mimmo Rotella, who wanted the privilege of being the sole lacerater for himself):[11] the stripped-off poster is only fragmentarily legible, at best. Moreover, we are not dealing with one poster but a veritable mattress of posters, myriad skins whose identity has been destroyed by irregular tearing (carried out over time): the strata merge into one another; the lettering grafts together; the words cannibalize one another; information is little by little reduced to undifferentiated noise. The *décollages* are like Arman's *Poubelles* (particularly effective when they showed that nothing would remain from linguistic exchange but a little pile, as in *L'affair du courrier* of 1962): they declare that all activity, but above all human communication, finishes up as uniform cinders.

This type of entropic deliquescence of language had been exploited by Dubuffet in 1944, in his exceptional series *Messages*, which were made on newspaper, imitating the little notes that one tacks to a friend's door when he or she is not home. But even if it is with difficulty, one can still recover enough linguistic matter (and even sentences) from these scribbled snatches to be able to imagine various scenarios ("I will wait for you until 8:00. Come back," "The key is under the shutter. Wait for me," "That will teach you"). Nothing of the sort from the *décollagistes* (who probably did not know these relatively obscure works by Dubuffet and could not bear the rest of his production). With them entropy is even redoubled, since the advertising poster belongs to "noise" even before being attacked: torn, it simply becomes a more ridiculously evident vanity. As for Dufrêne, he only bothers to show its reverse side: it's six of one, half a dozen of the other.

Notes

1. Thomas Crow, "Modernism and Mass Culture in the Visual Arts" (1983), in *Modern Art in the Common Culture* (New Haven: Yale University Press, 1996), pp. 3–37.

2. Jean Dubuffet, "L'auteur répond à quelques objections," reprinted in *Prospectus et tous écrits suivants*, vol. 2, ed. Hubert Damisch (Paris: Gallimard, 1967), pp. 61–62. This text was first published in the catalog of the exhibition "Mirobolus, Macadam & Cie, Hautes Pâtes," at the Galerie René Drouin in 1946, then republished many times, notably under the title "Réhabilitation de la boue."

3. Claes Oldenburg, quoted in Barbara Rose, *Claes Oldenburg* (New York: Museum of Modern Art, 1970), p. 46.

4. Ibid., p. 191. Notes dated "Provincetown, 1960."

5. Claes Oldenburg, Notes from 1961, in Claes Oldenburg, *Store Days: Documents from The Store (1961) and Ray Gun Theater (1962)*, ed. Claes Oldenburg and Emmett Williams (New York: Something Else Press, 1967), p. 8.

6. Ibid.

7. Claes Oldenburg, quoted in Rose, *Claes Oldenburg*, p. 33. The list of prices can be found in Oldenburg, *Store Days*, pp. 31–34. Items were rarely under $100, even going up to $899.95 (mimicking retailers' avoidance of round numbers).

8. Claes Oldenburg, notes dated "New York, 1961," reprinted in Coosje van Bruggen, *Claes Oldenburg: Mouse Museum/Ray Gun Wing* (Cologne: Museum Ludwig, 1979), p. 24.

9. Ibid., p. 67.

10. Carl Einstein, "Exposition de collages (Galerie Goemans)," *Documents* 2, no. 4 (1930), p. 244.

11. On this point, as on the movement as a whole, see Benjamin Buchloh, "From Detail to Fragment—Décollage Affichiste," in *Décollage: Les Affichistes* (New York: Zabriskie Gallery, 1990), p. 7.

Fetish or Foil: The Caprices of Claes Oldenburg

Julia E. Robinson

The radical morphology Claes Oldenburg introduced into the field of "sculpture" at the turn of the 1960s calls for entirely new terms that would redefine that long-standing category of art. The work's vital, all-over animation of the objects that are his subjects enacts a startling oscillation between resolute banality and cryptic specificity. That the former is enigmatically and implacably recoded by the latter in Oldenburg's hands requires from the observer a special agility, a capacity to shift between the two states, just as the artist does himself.

If the birth of happenings in 1959–1960 catapulted painterly means outward, into the space of spectatorial apperception, Oldenburg's critical role in this activity would shape his sculptural production immediately thereafter. That inventive activation of actual space and real time imbued the work that emerged from this moment with new traits, making new demands on its "audience." The first demand was that the subject relinquish the armor that would distance him or her from the artwork and create a safe and separate space, enforcing the automatic, passive, and contemplative role of mere spectator. The drawings through which Oldenburg theorized the objects' unimaginable process of formation contributed to their startling address, to his definition of his spectators as psychologically complex subjects rather than benign, unknowable masses. Arriving at a peak moment of burgeoning postwar consumer culture, Oldenburg's strange new objects contested the conditions already forced upon the subject by the vast, preexisting field of visual stimuli—from the mass media, advertising, and entertainment. Stimulating a retooled perception, Oldenburg's objects exhorted the subject to mobilize an intimate knowledge of his or her own corporality—its strangeness, its robust obstinacy, and its alarming fragility; they exhorted one to come to the work sensitized and open to the surprise of Oldenburg's utterly original morphological language, to return its disarming and vulnerable subjectivity—its strangely profound generosity—with one's own.

The decade beginning in 1960 encompasses many of the foundational criteria of Oldenburg's career; it rehearses the forms and subjects that make the rest legible. Registering as so many imagoes—the visual manifestations that constitute the psychic blueprint of childhood—a set of figments and forms begins here and recurs compulsively, with altered perspectives, establishing the *ur*-terms for an implacable inquiry, elaboration, and exploration that now spans more than half a century. *The Store* (1961), Oldenburg's sited work of art, has gained the status of a landmark in the advanced art of the twentieth century; and yet it retains the sense of a still-cryptic laboratory, still ripe for theoretical speculation and decipherment. Visible to onlookers on Manhattan's East Second Street, it was a place of womblike creativity for the artist (a metaphor elaborated in the extensive sketches for the project) where the familiar and the uncanny intersect. Meanwhile, the fantastic, acerbic vulgarity of the soft and hard objects initiated in the mid-1960s—based on common, industrially produced items from daily life, such as light switches, household appliances, and bathroom fixtures—further complicate our understanding of the foundational concepts charted at the outset of the decade.

Of course what Oldenburg called his "objective expressionism"— that barricade of fetishes he pitted against the foils of "object pornography"—reads quite differently today.[1] The morphological and conceptual relays between the condition of art and that of the everyday object, the address to subjective desire, and the paradox of empathetic abjectness are inflected by an exponentially altered commodity world, omnipresent visual stimuli, and escalated technologies. As we begin to consider the ways in which Oldenburg's object language was shaped by a now distant condition of commodification, his art historical and morphological field of reference also connects to a conceptual framework that is much more a part of the last century, indeed perhaps of modernism, than of our contemporary moment. It is this spectrum of reference, these forceful psychic and physical articulations of a particular space and time, which will focus the work of bringing Oldenburg's extraordinary contribution to late-twentieth-century sculpture once more, profoundly, within our grasp.

I like to imagine a man suddenly faced with [*Los Caprichos*]. . . . An enthusiast, an amateur, who . . . will experience a sharp shock at the core of his brain. . . . [I]n works which spring from profoundly individual minds there is something analogous to those periodical or chronic dreams with which our sleep is regularly besieged. That is the mark of the true artist—who always remains firm and indomitable even in those fugitive works, which are, so to speak, hung upon events. . . .

. . . I mean a love of the ungraspable, a feeling for violent contrasts, for the blank horrors of nature and for human countenances weirdly animalized by circumstances. . . .

Goya's great merit consists in having created a credible form of the monstrous. His monsters are born viable. . . . No one has ventured further than he in the direction of the possible absurd. All those distortions . . . are impregnated with humanity. . . . In a word, the line of suture . . . between the real and the fantastic is impossible to grasp; . . . such is the extent to which the transcendent and the natural concur in his art.

—*Charles Baudelaire*[2]

In the many notebooks that have always accompanied Oldenburg's practice as an artist—paralleling his artwork like a kind of dialogic doppelgänger—he has reflected upon modern artists who seemed to have had certain interests at heart, interests very much like his own. Chief among these is the compulsion to make the formal structure of the art palpably take on the load of conveying its significance. In each case, what emerges is a new mode of realism, an urgent evocation of the contemporary "real," to which Oldenburg and his heroes in modern art found themselves resolutely committed.

This new realism sought gritty immediacy and contested the instrumentalization of painting and sculpture by fundamentally literary functions. Such acts of taking form and medium into one's own hands were disposed toward the *story* rather than the *history*, the idea that art could be subjective, even eccentric, and still communicate. Attendant upon this mode of artistic rebellion was the sense that the small documentary truths of daily life were all that could imaginably be represented. One grand, if distant, figure Oldenburg admired in this kind of approach to form and representation in art was Francisco de Goya. As the above excerpts from the review by Baudelaire suggest, Goya's work tore through the programmatic veneer of painterly convention with an unrivaled savagery. But it is the precise terms Baudelaire uses that are primarily at stake for us here, in thinking about the coincidence of pathos and aggression in Oldenburg's own formal approach. Baudelaire describes an art reminiscent of the raw and involuntary images of dreams, "fugitive works" which are "hung upon events." He speaks of an art whose form seems to erupt from real conditions, from the immanence of a contemporary imperative: "nature . . . weirdly animalized by circumstances."

So many of Baudelaire's observations—voiced in a critical language long since lost, a language equal to its subject—proffer ideas that could fairly be used to characterize the baffling strangeness of Oldenburg's *Store* objects: a watch in its case that resembles a bloody, gaping mouth regurgitating a glutinous lump of partially digested, unidentifiable food; underpants that would betray their wearer by releasing, with impunity, all the fluids the abdomen can possibly produce, virtually *constituted* in this unwieldy release—the "possible absurd" in Baudelaire's terms. We will return to these pieces in relation to *The Store*. For now it is simply important to consider the powerful work that the willful assertion of a kind of failure of form—its collapse or devolution—at its best, can produce. It thus seems crucial to trace the foundations of such a vocabulary in Oldenburg's work, to seek out sources for that oddly omniscient morphological address of which all his objects are possessed.

Looking at a succession in Oldenburg's early drawings—from his bust profiles of 1954 to the self-portraits of 1956 to 1958, through to an extraordinary series of 1960 flag studies, which translate almost logically into the object morphologies he creates as "notes" to envisage *The Store* in 1960–1961—what emerges is not only an all but unfathomable, seismographic equivalence between subjects and the emotions that attach themselves to them, but a search for essence through specific media (charcoal, watercolor, crayon, and graphite). It was through this self-imposed, rigorous training of his hand and his media that Oldenburg learned the evanescent fluency with which he would come to imbue all his future media (charcoal as painting, watercolor as drawing, canvas as sculpture, and their numerous permutations through cardboard, vinyl, plastic, etc.).

The forging of a subject via the medium, as well as the use of the profile—as a kind of subjective eye, countering the putative objectivity of frontality—recalls another artist beloved by Baudelaire, the painter, draftsman, and caricaturist Honoré Daumier. In his drawings of *saltimbanques* and clowns—a subject Oldenburg took on and materially enacted—and in the ineffable "Don Quixote" series, Daumier distills optimism and pessimism, the tender and the pathetic, into essences of crayon, graphite, and watercolor. Conversely, Daumier's critique of human beings brutalized by their own hypocrisy was built up in plaster whose scabrous surface treatment, in each case, almost demonstrates, morphologically, the character of each person's particular violation of humanity. If Daumier's critique addressed shifting *subject* relations, Oldenburg developed such manipulations, more than a century later, to address a changing sphere of *object* relations.

Several other modernist projects seem foundational to a precise grasp of the calculated caprices that pulse through Oldenburg's oeuvre. Paramount in this is the development and the concomitant refunctioning of the genre of *nature morte*.[3] Our capricious use of the term "realist" for Oldenburg is doubled in the urge to characterize him, likewise, as a still-life artist, from the moment of *The Store* onward. It is a willful eccentricity that seems justified and at the same time estranged by the device of scale that reorients our relation to his subjects—up and down, near and far, by turns—throughout his oeuvre.

One might cite Paul Cézanne as the founding modernist who pushed the still life—the genre the Salon least valued—into a realm of *protest* that would pit the low against the high in order to counter an ailing litany of rules about proper painting. Conflating genres, Cézanne's favorite subject, *Mont Sainte-Victoire* and its forceful, surrounding terrain, seem present in a ginger pot nestled in the rumpled topography of a common tablecloth.[4] Cézanne's utter concretism with respect to objects did not, of course, arrive fully intuited; it was no doubt in part inherited (from precursors in quotidian concreteness such as Chardin), as Oldenburg's is too. But in his formative period Cézanne also made works that now seem almost aberrations in his oeuvre, which would seem to reveal the dawning primacy of integral subjectivity in modern art.

One phenomenon we might consider to be at stake here is an almost compulsive need for a "primal scene" in the early career of an artist, along with the attempt to kill off heroes or heroines in order to be able to move on, to accede, as psychoanalysis would have it, to "proper

Oedipality." Before he could define himself as an artist—a figure ultimately inducted as a founder of modern art—Cézanne made two inordinately strange paintings, both of which seem to have "doubles" in
Oldenburg's early formation. One was called *The Murder* (c. 1867), a
dark scene with two murderers and one victim; but, as with all unconscious constellations, one is prepared to read it in reverse (fig. 3.1). Perhaps this image came from a notion of one protagonist, the artist himself,
and two victims: Cézanne's historical imperative to murder Goya and
possibly Daumier as well, by working through their formal achievements,
and moving on, to find his own.

   In Oldenburg's work, too, there is an early drawing that is truly "uncanny" (in the full sense of the term) called *Street Event—Woman Beating
Child* (1958) (fig. 3.2). The overt subject matter is at one level a literal
depiction of violence—and the gestures here are as aberrant in Oldenburg's oeuvre as those in Cézanne's *Murder*, of which they are almost a

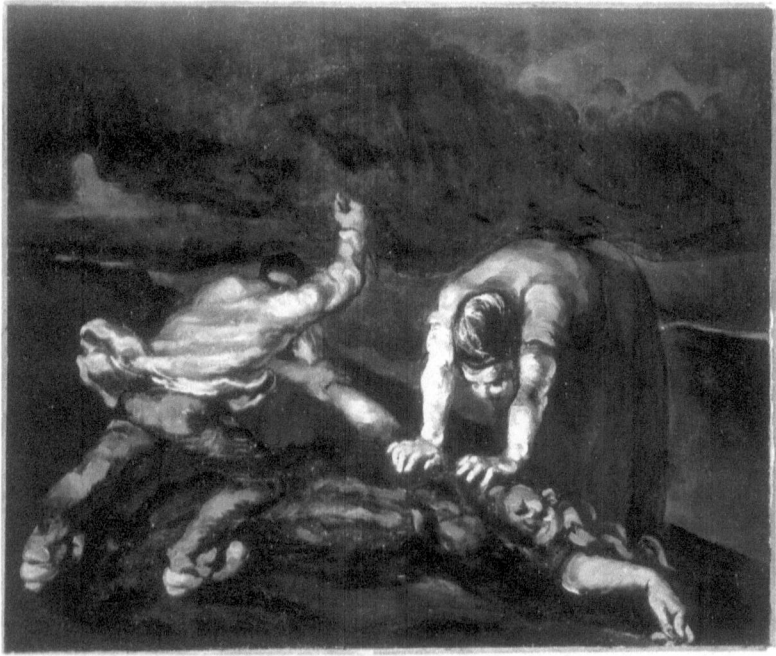

Figure 3.1   Paul Cézanne, *The Murder*, c. 1867.
Oil on canvas, 25¾ × 32 in. (65.4 × 81.3 cm).
Walker Art Gallery, Liverpool, Great Britain.
© National Museums Liverpool.

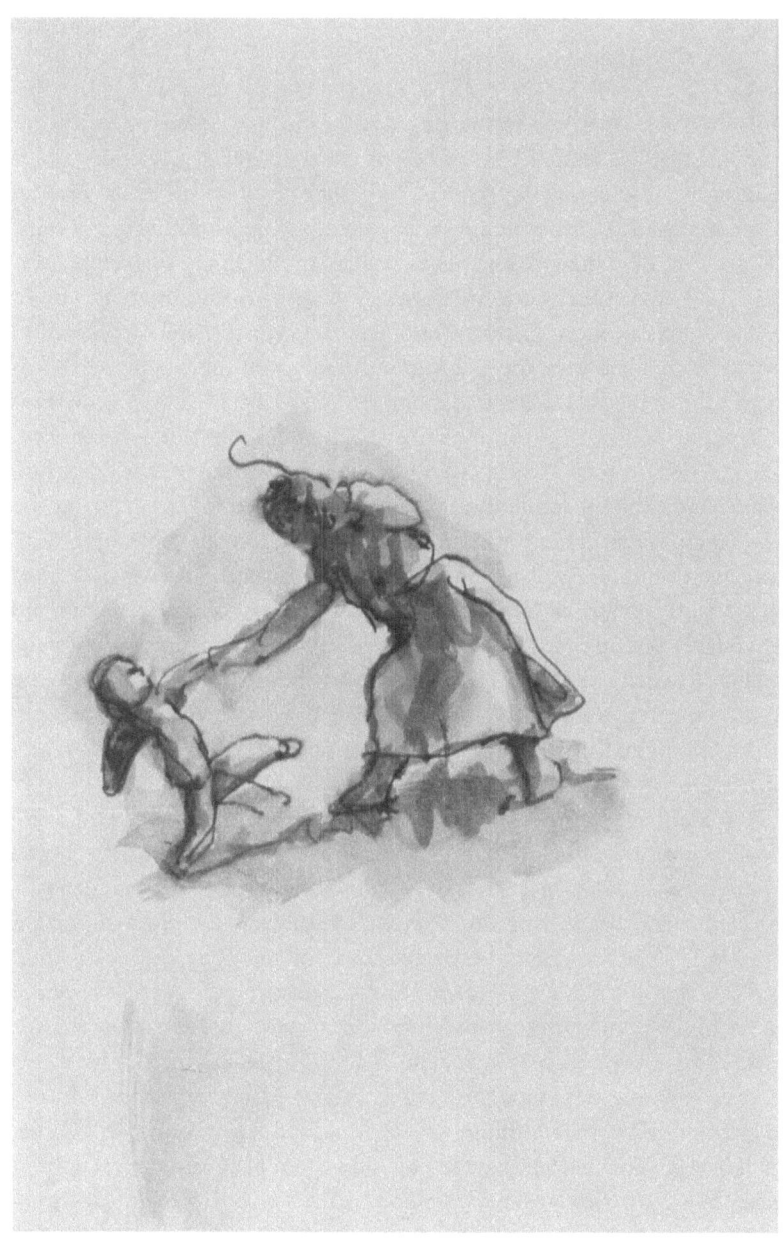

Figure 3.2 *Street Event—Woman Beating Child,*
1958. Felt pen and watercolor, 7½ × 5 in.
(19.1 × 12.7 cm) on sheet 10⅞ × 8⅜ in.
(27.6 × 21.3 cm). Collection Claes Oldenburg
and Coosje van Bruggen. Photo: D. James Dee,
New York; courtesy the Oldenburg van Bruggen
Studio.

mirror image. One of the strangest aspects of the Oldenburg drawing is the insistent doubling of the left leg of the child, which pretends to be a palimpsest in the drawing process, but clearly endows the child with an oversized phallus, for which he is apparently being threatened and punished. This drawing will emerge as crucial in Oldenburg's development.

The other touchstone in Cézanne that seems to illuminate one of Oldenburg's most enigmatic works and the artists' shared appreciation for an assault on form (here through the figure of the phallic female) is a painting called *The Eternal Feminine* (c. 1877). I am thinking here of Oldenburg's emblem of brutalizing, phallic femininity, the *Bride Mannikin* (1961) (fig. 3.3). She is emblematic in the loosest sense because she dictates the morphological paradoxes grounded in sexuality and the unconscious that characterize, as we shall see, all the *Store* objects, the soft and hard sculpture and beyond.[5] Cézanne's *Eternal Feminine* batters its subject (in paint) back to the crudest possible evocation of femininity and therefore, perhaps, its psychic archetype. The ruddy painterly enforcement of sexual ambiguity is doubled in a barrage of phallic forms—the bishop's miter and staff, the strong man's pulsing forearm, the musicians' instruments, and, anchoring it all, the rear view of a bald head, front and center in the composition.

Oldenburg's *Bride Mannikin*—whose very name is *unformed*, misspelled so that it can embody the male within the female, the artist's own double, and the dressmaker's fake body used for display and commerce— exacerbates a split in language, and a riven subjectivity.[6] Propped up on its stand in the back of the crowded scene of *The Store*, the *Bride* stood like *the light at the end of the tunnel*, or cave, charging the space where the artist himself could be seen making more pieces, discovered in the process of creating, by any voyeur who chanced upon the scene. She stands for the *ur*-terms of psychic formation, a body consumed by the phallus— a concept rather than a thing, a symbol rather than an organ, which we will have to define with greater precision in order to read it properly in Oldenburg's object vocabulary once we arrive at *The Store*. Her projectile arms and their lumpen substructure seem to fuse the automaton with the messy organicity of real bodies: the mess we picture ourselves as in the most troubling of dreams. Cézanne's sculptural painting and Oldenburg's painting-ravaged sculpture evoke the ambiguity with which the unconscious represents the world to us. And like the space of the unconscious, they set the subjects in a scene: evoking a subjective *architecture*, the timeless edifice of erectness that instantiates the reality of our

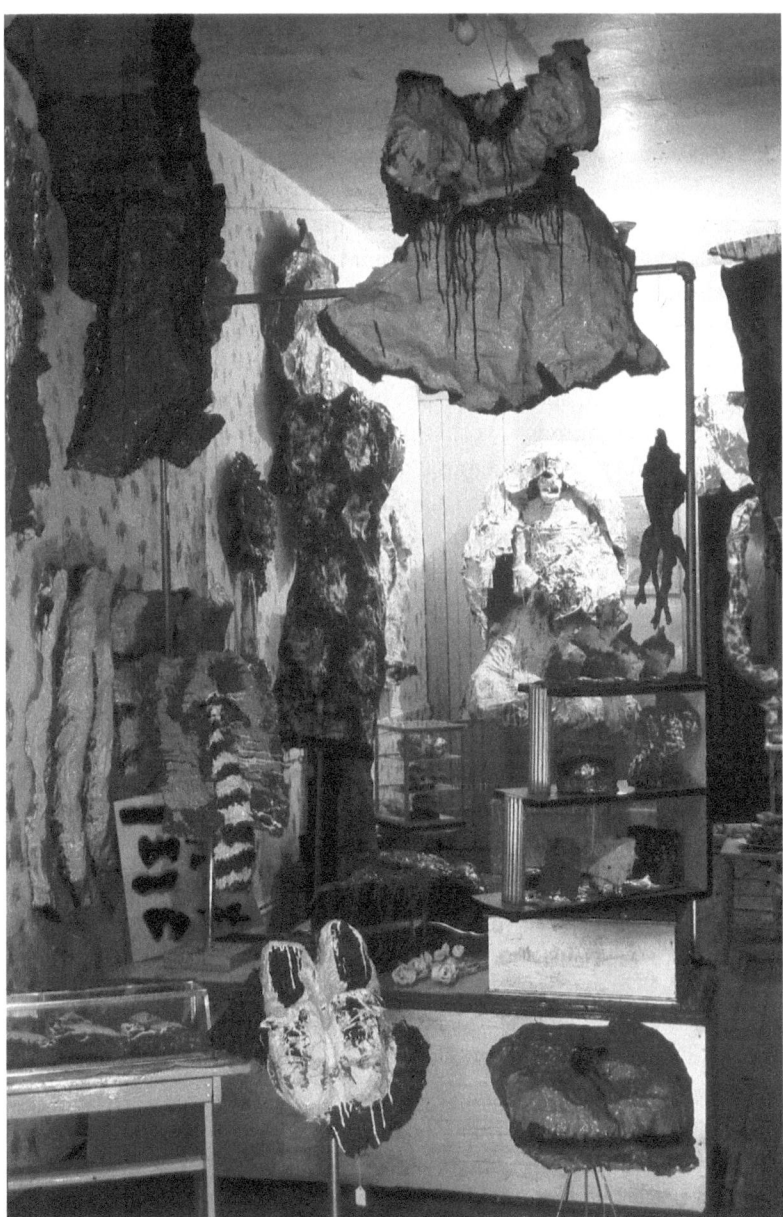

Figure 3.3 *The Store*, December 1, 1961–January 31, 1962. 107 East Second Street, New York. Installation view with *Bride Mannikin*. Photo © Robert McElroy/Licensed by VAGA, New York, NY; courtesy the Oldenburg van Bruggen Studio.

own implacable (carnal) otherness. The chronological separation not-withstanding, it seems almost logical to draw a line between Cézanne's *Eternal Feminine* and Oldenburg's monstrous *Bride Mannikin* (mounted as if forming the altarpiece of *The Store*) in the incremental solidification of the *wound* in which subjectivity is founded, as elaborated in the history of modern art.

The last crucial precursor figure in our prelude to Oldenburg is Édouard Manet—another "founding father" of modernism, of unform-ing, fragmentation, and the still life, who thought particularly about the impact of the commodity world upon this genre and others. Any discus-sion of the reforming and renewal of the still life, its beguiling projection into the sites of modernity, its singularization and unexpected fragmenta-tion—doubling the fragmented violence experienced by the body of the modern, urban subject—and the undoing of form by matter or medium, can hardly be developed without Manet.

If the unfathomable creation of Oldenburg's *Store* might never be fully defined by language—and that is certainly its point—clearly it shares traits with those "sets" constructed by Cézanne and, quite differ-ently, by Manet. The spectacular modern shop counter captured in Ma-net's *A Bar at the Folies-Bergères* (1881–1882) illuminates the persistent enigma of *The Store*. Femininity is posited as the site of exchange—a female figure sutured to the scene, marking the commercial encounter. As the subject, she is another double of the artist. She becomes one with her setting: a frozen commodity no different from the objects around her, though apparently communing with them in a battle for subjective animation. Manet marks her apparent loss of individuality through the painterly inscription of the indistinct female double in the mirror behind her, who enacts an actual social exchange with a male figure, while not seeming to match the woman who faces us. A final self-identification in this scene is Manet's mode of coldly equating his own facture with commercial manufacture—incorporating the signature that says "Manet" within a bottle label, as just one more brand name. At the same time, he underscores his capacity to convert this bottle-commodity into a painted bottle, that is to say, a work of art by Manet. In this sense, we might think of Manet's painted signature as the *material*, facture-invested precursor to the performative gesture of the Duchampian readymade, as well as to Oldenburg's later *performance of painting*.

If the scene at the *Bar* prefigures Oldenburg's self-suture to *The Store*, so too does Manet's extraordinary mode of singularization of the still life, his concept of removing it from its setting, as if somehow (even if momentarily) to assert the *subjecthood* of that one element. A lump of ham, *Le Jambon* (c. 1875–1878), in its blunt facticity, defies the narrative of an even slightly greater elaboration of context that would locate the work more squarely within that genre (fig. 3.4). Instead, it seems to call for a new definition of the still life. It is hard not to think of it alongside Oldenburg's lump of meat, *Roast* (1961), hanging in *The Store*, more visceral than Manet's ham but its equal in unapologetic, blatant *this-ness* (fig. 3.5).

Perhaps most extraordinary of all, as we consider Oldenburg in the context of Manet's foundational recognition of the still-life object's commodity status—and the commodity's pernicious trafficking in subjective desire—is one painting that becomes two: Manet's *Bunch of Asparagus* (1880) and the subsequent, single *Asparagus* (1880). The robust corporeality of the bunch of asparagus, in the first instance, its "here-ness" and

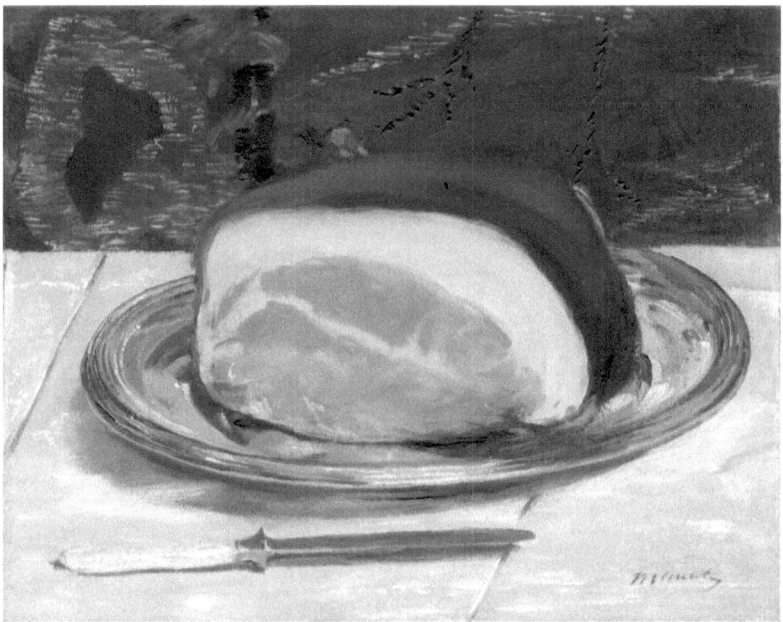

Figure 3.4 Édouard Manet, *Le Jambon* (Ham), c. 1875–1878. Oil on canvas, 12¾ × 16¼ in. (32.4 × 41.3 cm). Glasgow Museums, The Burrell Collection. © Culture and Sport Glasgow (Museums).

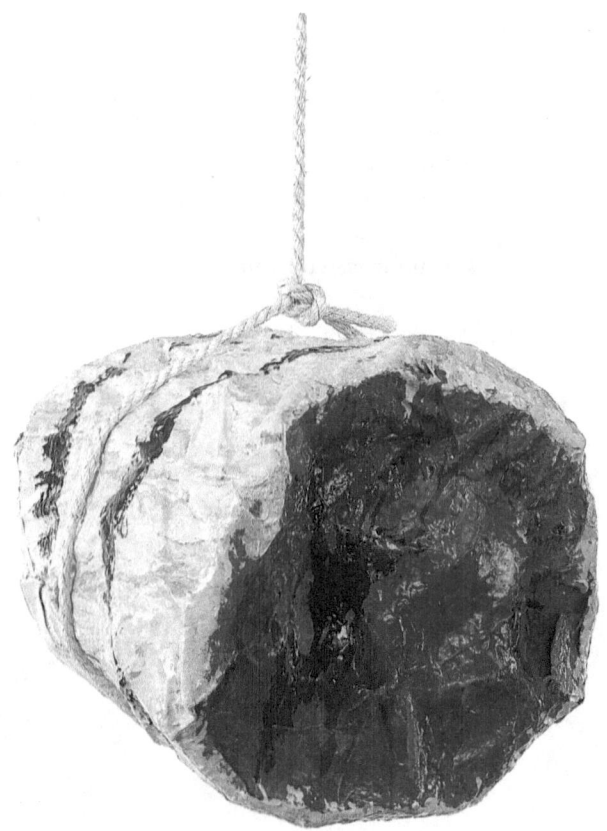

Figure 3.5   *Roast*, 1961. Muslin soaked in plaster
over wire frame, painted with enamel, with
rope, 14 × 17 × 16 in. (35.6 × 43.2 × 40.6 cm).
Sonnabend Collection. Photo courtesy David
Zwirner.

facticity, is reiterated in the polymorphously lumpen objects of Oldenburg's *Store*, such as the *Red Cap*, for example—that monstrous, spelunker garage for the brain. Manet's bunch of asparagus appears to have landed there with no apparent need to explain itself. The reeds below, apparently vestiges of the old accoutrements of the conventional still life, there to set the scene, themselves enact a material transformation. As pure painting—more brushstroke than reed—they prop up the "noses" of the asparagus, asserting, perversely, the triumph of painterly instantiation over convention.

The single asparagus, on the other hand, which was painted later as Manet's response to his sense that the collector had paid more than he should have for the first painting, was conceived in and out of lack. Suddenly, a single asparagus spear justified itself as the entire subject; it stood for the difference between painting and value, facture and finance. Tenderly imbued, brushstroke by brushstroke, with an ambiguous phallic presence, it is the embodiment of desire, the material trace and instantiation of the *always missing*. In the event of this painting and this gesture of generosity on the part of the artist, the phallus as the symbol of lack was thematized in modern art. Such oscillation between the presence of the humble object brought into being as a subject through pure facture—painterly desire pitted against commodity-coded desire—will be as essential in Oldenburg as it was in Manet.

A 1996 exhibition on the subject of the *informe* in the history of modern art—conceived by Rosalind Krauss and Yve-Alain Bois for the Centre Georges Pompidou—developed a lineage that began with Manet and ran though surrealism, Dubuffet, Pollock, Oldenburg, and beyond. Its theme, drawn from the work of Georges Bataille, sought to engage the idea of "the formless" less as a trait than as a kind of agency, an "operation," as Bataille called it. The primary site (or "institution") for Bataille's merciless critique was language, and the "institution" through which he chose to attack it was the dictionary. What interested Krauss and Bois in their elaboration of the *informe* were those "*operations* [that] split off from modernism, insulting the very opposition between form and content."[7]

This exhibition explored an idea that had long been present in Oldenburg's thinking, which, in fact, may have been one of the most important factors in the development of his art. That is to say, it sought to pinpoint the relationship between the demise of a certain precision in language and its implications for art: how art responded with a vast array of "anti-forms" in the effort to remake a field of object relations founded on exceptions rather than rules. However, for Oldenburg, it was not Bataille's *baseness* that was most important but that of two other "Frenchmen"—Louis-Ferdinand Céline, and Jean Dubuffet.[8]

Language's Eclipses and Ellipses . . .

To sensitize language so that it pulses more than it reasons, that is my goal.

—Louis-Ferdinand Céline[9]

The thing is, creative writing begins only at the point where words are no longer used in their strict meaning (this dimension of words only allows them to operate on an impoverished register for stating simplistic thoughts) but with art, the way jugglers convert objects like hats, eggs, handkerchiefs, through a new optic, into things other than head apparel, omelets or nose wipers. Using words in this way enables one to create a new keyboard for transmitting raw, vital thought. Hence Céline's inauguration and his progress . . . [using his means] in such a way as to break the immediacy of their tie to the direct transcriptions of objects. . . . The painter [or writer, when it's Céline] . . . obliges the viewer or reader to make continual substitutions which soon brings him to read not the lines themselves but between the lines. The work is thus endowed with a third dimension comparable to relief.

—Jean Dubuffet[10]

Oldenburg's long-standing admiration for Dubuffet and through him, *with him*, for the acerbic polemicist novelist Céline, has been alluded to often in the literature on the artist. Two key works from 1959, the ink drawing *DUBUFFET—CÉLINE—FRENCHMEN* and the magisterial, newspaper-based, painted sculpture *C-E-L-I-N-E Backwards*, prompted these references, without necessarily provoking the deeper analysis they insist upon. Why these "Frenchmen"? And what is the connection between the scarified cave wall that the lettering *DUBUFFET—CÉLINE—FRENCHMEN* leans upon *and doubles* as it shifts schizophrenically between three types of lettering, three subject positions, and the works that followed? *C-E-L-I-N-E Backwards* then enacts a double rewriting of (1) drip painting and (2) the use of newspaper as ground, to recode the "flat" (modernist) field, causing it to splutter and protrude into corporeal excess as if in a process of self-anthropomorphization. And what does all this have to do with the invention of the *"Empire" ("Papa") Ray Gun* in the very same year (fig. 3.6)?

A more focused look into how Céline and Dubuffet functioned for Oldenburg still seems lacking. The death of "Papa-Pollock" and a series of painterly recodings, or unravelings, of Pollock's apparently insurmountable, *ne plus ultra* example of painting—by Rauschenberg, Johns, and Twombly in quick succession—posed an urgent (Oedipal) imperative for the next generation. It was at this moment that Oldenburg chose "fathers" who were not Americans but *Frenchmen.*

Oldenburg's consistent recourse to notebooks, with the process of writing always running parallel to the process of making art, suggests the importance of the functions of language to the development of the consuming morphological "language" that confronts us in his work. For everything else they do, Oldenburg's objects, in their plenitude, acknowledge loss: the hemorrhaging of meaning that has been visited upon objects forced into the system of circulation that defines the commodity world. Their plenitude is his resistance to this loss and the alienation it engenders. Céline was critically important for Oldenburg because he attacked, violently, a similar loss in language, a loss he marked by three dots: the almost compulsive use of ellipses. And he overwrote written language with spoken language, a strange variation of argot, to give it a paradoxical crypticness and immediacy, the kind we also find in Oldenburg's art. Céline's famous ellipses, which asserted themselves most forcefully in his book *Mort à credit*, made a deep impression on Oldenburg. Ultimately the three dots—the mark of loss or lapsus—found their way into Oldenburg's own writing. Like plastic interruptions jubilantly animating sentence fragments, observations from life, insults, and non sequiturs, they appear throughout his notebooks, performance notes, and numerous "statements" on his art.

It was Dubuffet, however, who asserted the connection between Céline and what might be possible in art: the idea that "form determines the effectiveness of the work."[11] He tested this himself in sculptural paintings renewing and revitalizing the very definition of that term via an intransigent mode of philosophical brutality. Dubuffet knew the imperative for painting—which he felt was already well ahead of writing

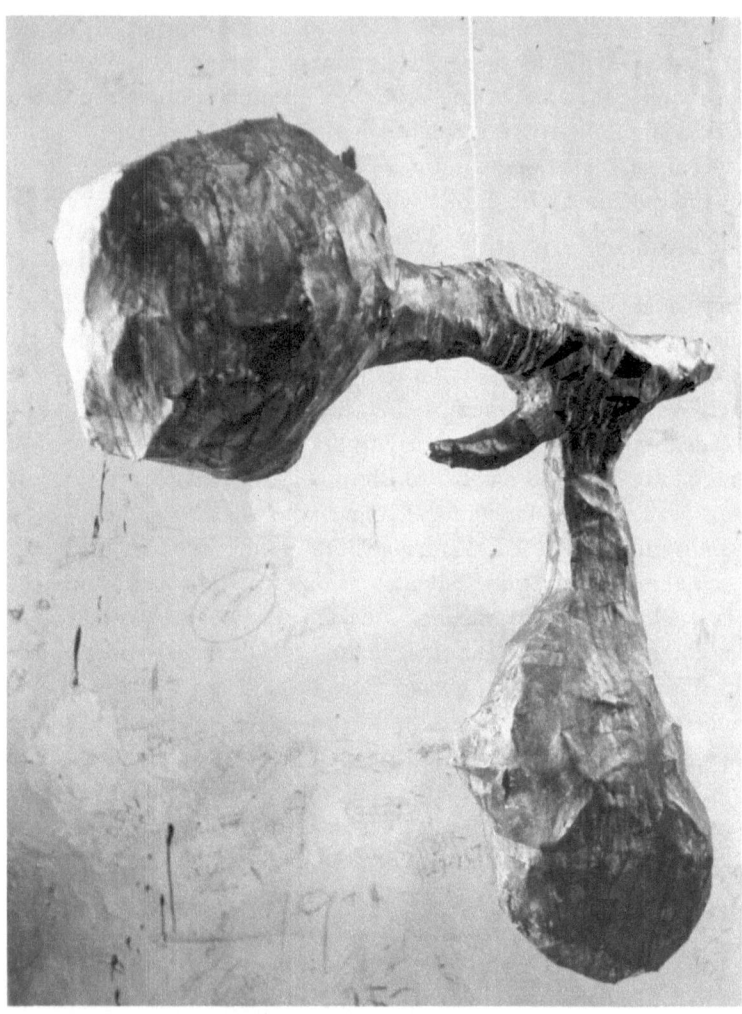

Figure 3.6 *"Empire" ("Papa") Ray Gun*, 1959.
Newspaper soaked in wheat paste over wire
frame, painted with casein, 35⅞ × 44⅞ × 14⅝ in.
(91.1 × 114 × 37.2 cm). Collection The Museum
of Modern Art, New York.

in its level of directness—was at bottom a linguistic imperative, and he wrote about it as such in his article "Céline Pilote":

> Painting believed for a long time that its business was to confer upon its Christs and its virgins ingeniously reworked expressions. But when it took it into its head to replace all that with apples, absinthe glasses, and packages of tobacco then it had created its revolution. The latter was to bear not just on the object to be drawn but on the means and materials brought into the work, the methods of transcription, the syntax.[12]

Oldenburg ultimately understood, better than Dubuffet, that it was not the media—whether letters, typeface, paint, or dirt—that required another revolution but the *syntax*: a pernicious and fugitive metastructure that not only changes as quickly as does culturally coded apperception, but is utterly reformed and newly grasped by each new subject experiencing these larger "macro" conditions. Such was/is the double writing of experience, the vexing problem that asks the subject to invent a *doubleness* of his or her own, just to survive. And the "revolution," the rebellion that constitutes subjective desire and draws energy from all the forces of repression shaping subjectivity, could not be founded in any simple regression (for Dubuffet, back to the primitivism forged by the historical avant-gardes). Rather than a *cultural* regression, what had to be mobilized were the resources of actual psychic regression, the kind that psychoanalysis uses to save the ailing subject. This meant generating a field of "symbols," or useful, *protective fetishes*, in order to counter the fraudulent foils (of the commodity fetish), which were leaning on the salutary functions of psychic fetish and leeching agency from subjective desire. This saving double—doppelgänger—was also crucial to remake art, to sever it from its conventions and to forge a truly original form. It was this apparently unbearable load that was taken on by Oldenburg's *"Empire" ("Papa") Ray Gun.*

Oldenburg's engagement with the work of Freud in the late 1950s and his project of self-analysis and free association—using friends as surrogates for his past selves in his own psychic formation—is well documented.[13] This is the period in which he made *Street Event—Woman Beating Child* (1958) (which rendered visual Freud's source for his development of the concept of the uncanny), and the Céline, Dubuffet, and *"Empire" ("Papa") Ray Gun* works, which came the year after.[14] While

Woman Beating Child expresses quite clearly the role of the sudden appearance of the phallus as a protective agent—via the enigmatic graphic palimpsest in the drawing that endows the mother's infant victim with an impossible third leg—the *"Empire" ("Papa") Ray Gun* renders such a prospect, such a materialization, in three dimensions. It also incorporates the complex role of language in this mix. The presence of the Ray Gun, then, clarifies a through line in Oldenburg's work, from the early drawing, through the Céline and Dubuffet works, and the Ray Gun itself, to the polymorphous field of *The Store*.

Oldenburg himself spoke ambiguously about the role of the symbol in his work; he even contradicted himself on this score. At one point he protested: "I reject symbolism as an artificial imposition which violates the truth of perception." And at another moment: "I am making symbols of my time through my experience."[15] This is no doubt because the word "symbol" is so loaded with all that he wanted to reject in art history, as well as being the actual mode through which each subject represents the world to him- or herself. Oldenburg didn't want "symbol" as that old thing called "iconography" (dog = faithfulness, lily = death); he wanted "symbolization" as the psychic distortions that shape the strangeness of the world into a strangeness we can recognize because it is of our own making. This is the fantastic, productive work of the unconscious. It is also the reductive, repressive work of language. And finally, perhaps most unpalatably, it is the work of distortion by which advertising converts the things of the world into the shape of our desire, or at least, a desire that it invents for us. By addressing these three conditions at once, Oldenburg accomplished a body of work that could be utterly subjective and, paradoxically, universal enough to speak to all of us as subjects while critiquing the quotidian operation of commercial desire-making machines.

Psychoanalysis has given us the clearest definition of this mode of the "symbolic"—the enlightenment that turned Oldenburg's two-dimensional illustration of Freud into a massive (phallic) signifier inserted into the real world, called *"Empire" ("Papa") Ray Gun*, borne by the engagement with language, which ran parallel with his art. This clarification of the loaded term "symbolic" was delivered in Jacques Lacan's amplification of Freud.[16] The very title *"Empire" ("Papa") Ray Gun* itself doubles the extraordinary object it defines—by pitting the first double-syllabic utterance of the child (*pa-pa*) against the totalizing force of repression/"civilization" (*empire*), and converting this potent mix of desire and loss into a boundless resource for creative production.[17]

These are the determinations of the "symbolic" that illuminate Oldenburg's extraordinary invention of the Ray Gun as the life force that singularizes and universalizes the forest of symbols that constitutes his oeuvre. The Ray Gun's enigmatic presence—the "papa" as well as his numerous offspring (the extensive ray gun "collection" Oldenburg generated subsequently)—embodies the split between what we see and feel, and the forms available to us to represent these impulses. For most of us, the form is language; for some, it is art. The *"Papa" Ray Gun* does not try to tame its manifest weirdness, or to discipline its phallic/testicular presence into anything we can bear to look at in the automatic, contemplative mode of model spectator; it challenges that system-wide repression that would (over-)determine what we think of as "art."[18] *"Papa" Ray Gun* establishes a paradigm for the *Store* objects and the soft and hard permutations of the everyday industrial production that follow, by constituting, in its very form, the difference between impulse and "proper" representation, enacting, as it does, the paradoxical devolution of that civilizing process analysts characterize as "repression."

The split at the heart of representation, manifested most obviously in language—in that arbitrary and differential relation between signifier and signified—is an element that Lacan pulled from structural linguistics (and from Freud) to characterize the operative mechanisms of the unconscious. In *The Signification of the Phallus*, an essay pertinent to our focus on the primacy of the Ray Gun for all of Oldenburg's future work, Lacan explained this complex field in the following terms:

> [I]t is Freud's discovery that gives to the signifier/signified opposition the full extent of its implications: namely, that the signifier has an active function in determining certain effects in which the signifiable appears to be submitting to its mark, by becoming through that passion the signified.[19]

In other words, signifiers—like the phallus that inspired Oldenburg's *"Papa" Ray Gun*, which was one signifier he chose from many possibilities—can have agency in diverting the habitual, formal rules of meaning construction. This process which the originating term goes through in order to be read by a subject, *to mean*, is what Lacan calls "the passion of the signifier." For Lacan, this process, this passion, now becomes a new dimension of the human condition in that it is not only man who speaks, but in that man and through that man that it speaks (*ça parle*), that his nature is woven by effects in which is to be found the structure of language, of which he becomes the material.[20]

Situating the operation of repression inherent in the (Oedipal) formation of subjectivity, Lacan defined desire as generated in "the deviation of man's needs from the fact that he speaks," wherein that primal need gets returned to the subject as something alienated:

> That which is thus alienated in needs constitutes a . . . primal repression, an inability, it is supposed, to be articulated in demand, but it reappears in something it gives rise to that presents itself in man as desire. . . . The phenomenology that emerges from analytic experience is certainly of a kind to demonstrate in desire the paradoxical, deviant, erratic, eccentric, even scandalous character by which it is distinguished from need.[21]

Woman/mother and the phallic are conflated because the child needs and the mother is invested with all the power to satisfy that need. Our need is always irreducible to form; the object world as we experience it can never be represented as an absolute. Herein lies the difference between the apparently mad morphology of Oldenburg's *Store* objects, to which we will now turn, and their real referents in life, the commodity world from which he draws. The Ray Gun was the "symbol" of this split, this difference, this unavoidable loss that plagues all representation. The potency of its revelations made possible the extraordinary vitality and originality of Oldenburg's future forms (and their profound critique of the world from which they deviated). Functioning as symbol, not a thing, the phallus for Lacan operated as the Ray Gun did for Oldenburg, as "the bastard offspring of this signifying concatenation"—a monument to ineffable loss, which was also a catalyst to a remaking.[22]

The Store: Performing Making

> The Store . . . a collection of psychological statements which exist concretely . . . nature altered toward psychology . . .
>
> The fragments are different as to scale and time, though they are all related. You are to imagine the missing, that is, what is called

negative space or absent matter, counts for something. These are rips out of reality, perceptions like snapshots, embodiments of glances. This elevation of sensibility above bourgeois values . . . will (hopefully) destroy the notion of art and give the object back its power.

—*Claes Oldenburg*[23]

I have imitated, parodied, certain professions—all taken more seriously in the U.S. than the profession of art; f. ex. the house painter, the sign painter, the advertising artist. Also the manufacturer, the pastry cook.

—*Claes Oldenburg*[24]

The poster Oldenburg made for *The Store* resembles the kind of poster one might find outside a theater, announcing a play or performance. The drawing from which it was conceived, *The Store, Study for a Poster* (1961), gives us much more information. In its layers of facture, a cloudy white painterly ground projects at least five different kinds of "writing," whose *difference*—part graphic, part affective—is destined to be erased when it is turned, inevitably, into the typeface of mechanical reproduction. If the top textual banner, "Ray Gun Mfg Co," seems almost comic in the painterly study, apparently standing in for the name of the *theater* that will host the performance of that *play*, "The Store by Claes Oldenburg," the printed version will normalize these role-playing words, reducing their many meanings to a kind of collision of "brands."

The exception to this is the second banner of text, a rupture in the reign of the English language that says "DICIEMBRE 1 AL 31"—waving the wonderful flag of ethnic specificity by alluding to a truth of a real neighborhood, where the posters were fabricated, signaling a sense of place—which still does this work in the final poster. Otherwise, inevitably, in the space between the handmade and the machine-made, information will be lost. It will be mostly information of a plastic kind, such as the largeness of the word "STORE"; as a textual index calibrated to the artist's attachment to his subject, it could not be clearer. This element operates in stark contrast to the script below, whose illegibility diverts our interest away from reading, toward the action of a hand trying to "write" with a paintbrush. This latter element, the automatic writing scrawled cursorily in the lowest section of the drawing—providing mandatory factual information like hours, and yet another "affiliation" for the project, the "cooperation" of "The Green Gallery"—will be normalized as it accedes toward the alienated format of "advertising."

One of the most profound aspects of *The Store* is just this simultaneity of plastic and semantic performance, which is reiterated physically, humanly, by Oldenburg's steady presence at the heart of a site of real making, on view through the frame of a shop window on East Second Street. The idea that his objects/subjects are commodity forms that become "relics" after their use locates the artist's process of making as particularly vital and charged by temporality. To appreciate fully the instantaneity, the cacophony, the spluttering and uttering still palpable in the *Store* objects, we need to consider how this special context defined their deep purpose—the intersection of site and process that brought them into being.

It is in *The Store* that "the uncanny," which was the theme of Oldenburg's *Street Event—Woman Beating Child*, is materialized in actual space and time. For psychoanalysis, uncanny objects are familiar elements made strange by repression: the process of incremental "civilization" of the subject and his or her relation to the things of the world.[25] Oldenburg's operation in *The Store* is to manhandle this process of object (re-)formation, to try to reexperience regression, in order to mark out a path back from alienated object relations.

Crucial here is the idea of "art." Oldenburg has recoiled from comparisons to the different modes of his peers, which would suggest that the concept of a "store" meant he was just selling normal things, merely dissolving art into life. On the contrary, *The Store*'s tension and historical relevance is founded upon Oldenburg's insistence that in it he was always making art. Specifically, he was *performing this making*—which he compared to numerous other forms of making—masochistically, and redemptively. It was that time-honored trait of modern art—that is, its lack of function, its status as a "nonfunctional commodity"—that had to be present in order for Oldenburg to make his case.[26] And he needed the veracity of a real storefront to assert his point with the urgency and pathos that drove him to this performance. If art was supposedly the exempt realm of production in which the handmade object was still vaunted with almost religious devotion, this was the myth Oldenburg needed in order to expose the reality of his time.

The rapid development and sexualization of functional-objects-for-sale emerging to colonize human desire and all subject/object relations was constituted in the first decades after the Second World War by a newly violent abuse of human psychology. The form it took was the commodity (or what Marx had called the "commodity fetish"); objects were marketed and projected with escalating mediatic means and ever more sophisticated strategies into a field of inexorable fraudulence: that mode of "representation" benignly known as advertising. Oldenburg realized *The Store* as a kind of triage site, contending with this all but invisible violence with a visible violence. *The Store* became a frame in which he could engage in a trauma of the object in order to accomplish something almost unimaginable: that is, *to pathologize the commodity*. Working at announced hours in the lit space at the back of *The Store*, the artist himself was on view, reduced to *representing making* as an almost caricatured performance of his own extraordinary creative capacities. Like a latter-day Goya, Oldenburg was acutely conscious of the power of art to project this manifest state of horror at which "culture" and human experience had now arrived. And as he noted, polemically, excess is easy to assimilate:

> The imagination of horror exceeds the experience of horror . . . or is a disguise for something else (like a nightmare). The representation of horror is not necessarily connected with what is being represented. Horror in reality is too impersonal and the natural body is too quick to protect itself . . . imagined horror is absolutely limitless . . . the experience of staring into the abyss . . . the vision of horror . . . is personal and abstract. . . . Before I close the door, before I try to put it all together, I go a little further than most. This accounts for the ugliness of my work, which is easy to overcome. Man can get used to anything.[27]

It is this nexus between the "personal" and its display that unlocks some of the sphinxlike mystery attached to the site of *The Store*. It is also what makes its "products" communicate as extraordinary works of art and not simply private ideas. In thinking of this field of critical, protective fetishes (or counterfetishes), the ones invented by the self rather than by the system, we might recall Baudelaire speaking of Goya and say that Oldenburg's insanely polymorphous *Store* objects are *born viable*. Moreover, they share a raison d'être with Goya's monsters, grounded as they are in unwavering humanism. "I feel my purpose is to say something about my times" said Oldenburg: "for me this is a recreation of my vision of the times . . . my reality, or my drama reality, and this demands a form of a theatrical nature."[28]

As a kind of vestige from the exploratory indeterminacy of his earlier flag studies, there appears in *The Store* a *Plate of Meat* that seems to
take the form of a flag (fig. 3.7).[29] There are no stars, and the stripes
are redirected and reshaped, now signifiers for fat (or stripes as strips of
bacon?). The blue "background" looks less like a plate than one of those
polystyrene trays one finds under shrink-wrapped meat in the supermarket. Has the floating flag now found a gutsy identity? Is this the meat of
America? Such are the free associations—that foundational technique
psychoanalysis induces to generate and mend the (self-)expressive capacities of the subject—which Oldenburg galvanized into an artistic strategy.
This was the meat of his primal form-making. As a directed mode of
masochism, contrasting interestingly with the more emulative version of
his peer Andy Warhol, who said, "I want to be a machine," Oldenburg
stated with equal and opposite profundity: "I am a sausage-maker."[30]

In his 1961 statement repeating the line "I am for an art that . . . ,"
and following with a litany of images utterly opposed to conventional
ideas of art, Oldenburg generated an array of radical new functions for

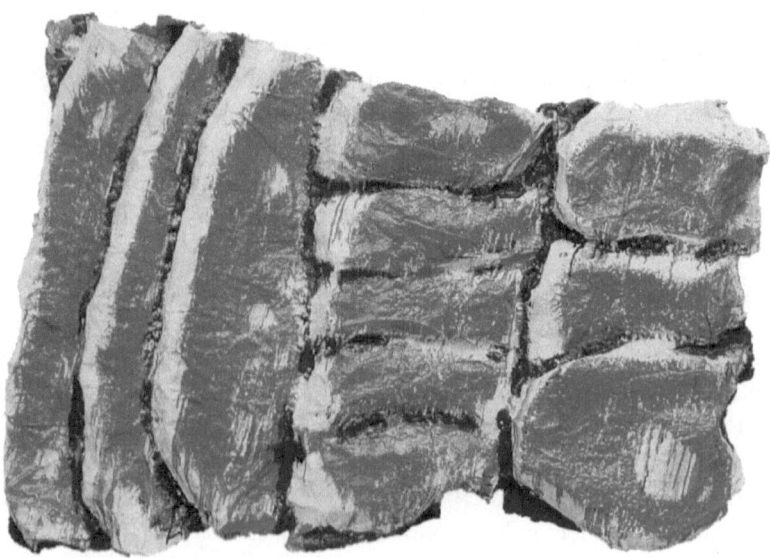

Figure 3.7   *Plate of Meat*, 1961. Plaster,
muslin, burlap, wire, painted with enamel,
38½ × 54½ × 5½ in. (97.8 × 138.4 × 14 cm).
Private collection. Photo courtesy David Zwirner.

art, a kind of shopping list for what he wanted art to look like and to do. The virtue of a sausage is that it has no requisite form. It can embody a rather broad morphological spectrum and still be understood to be a sausage. This, of course, gives the sausage-maker a great deal of freedom. Unlike other items for sale in a regular store, like clothes or accessories, the sausage has no design imperative. The emancipated formal spectrum of *The Store* objects was generated out of this absence, this reprieve. As well as the red, meaty flag—or flaggy meat?—there was the *Red Cap*, which, for a certain period, took pride of place in the *Store*'s front window. Almost too big and solid to have any use for a head, as noted above, it was more like a garage, a cave, a bunker, or a fallout shelter—one could keep going, and that is obviously the goal. It seems to perform the ideal role of the fetish, guaranteeing powerful protection to the beleaguered brain.

Other clothes items, reliefs like *Red Tights with Fragment 9*, *Blue and Pink Panties*, and *Two Girls' Dresses*, are mounted on contrasting backgrounds with which they nonetheless merge in interesting ways.[31] They speak for the encounter between desire and the projective field of the display object. The *Blue and Pink Panties* trumpet gender reversals. While the pink panties become trunks, the blue are an extreme case; large, benignly shaped and unappealing, they hardly make it into that eroticized genre of underwear design that deploys the term "panties." The *Two Girls' Dresses* construct another radical revision: they use the body to shape the dress and then amputate its extremities. What we are left with is the paradox of muscular, physically active dresses. But these are not the acéphales of surrealism; they are "products" whose texture seems to impose a brutalizing milieu of supply and demand. Like life's flypaper, their surfaces document a kind of gathering up of a materialist immunity, which constitutes their *resistance* and their enduring power as art.

While the *Tights,* the *Panties,* and the *Dresses* still enact a certain salutary buoyancy, another dress, the one on the *Mannikin with One Leg*, looks much more forlorn. For one thing, it is. What mannequin was ever put on display with just one leg? The mass of drips, whorls of sheer matter that make up the dress, pit painting against design—a kind unforming or deauraticization of the chromatic precedent of Jackson Pollock's *Full Fathom Five* (1947)—contributing to the recoding of the large looming drip technique that many of the *Store* objects enact. The crucial move by Oldenburg here is to deploy Pollockian dripping only to defy its most definitive painterly trait: horizontality (that is, no vertical runoff). With his return to the upright position, Oldenburg redefines gravity not as the action of a subject, as in Pollock, but as the effect upon an object. Just as his muslin soaked in plaster, drying on its wire, uses air and weight as a means of "sculpting"—the charged encounter between the intentional and the unintentional is also subjected to a "disenchantment."[32]

Perhaps the most unrepentantly battered and negated subject of *The Store* is the *Cash Register*, which is, of course, ironically, the vital functioning item in a real store. Far from a precision instrument, Oldenburg's *Cash Register* looks prehistoric, like the bone (foot or hoof?) of some giant extinct animal. Its bumped-around depressive curves make it appear as though it has been kicked along in the street, while its painterly surface continues the brush with "design" played out in the dress of the one-legged *Mannikin*, but with an important difference. The drips are infiltrated with longer brushstrokes, forming bumpy stripes and the suggestion of multidirectional starlike patterns, apparently giving up a Pollock obsession in favor of one with De Kooning but also, perhaps more subliminally, with Jasper Johns. This defunctionalized lump insults the reckoning of objects in terms of price. Oldenburg's attitude toward the cash register extends thematically and physically in other aspects of *The Store*. It seems to be reiterated in the transition between a sketch he made of a price tag and the reappearance of similar numbers as sculpture. In one of the drawings, the figures are so embedded into their ground that it becomes difficult to make out the exact number: Is it 13.99 or 3.99? In the sculptures, the numbers standing alone as all nines (or upside-down sixes?)—despite the miraculous hanging ball that represented the decimal point—appear like hanging pretzels, reversing the economy which would convert objects into abstract numerical values.[33]

In the sculptural transformations of *The Store*, Oldenburg thickens life for our delectation. He maims it, caresses it, tortures it, and redeems it, so that we won't refuse to recognize it. One of the weirdest objects of all is *Watch in Red Box* (fig. 3.8). Like the *Cash Register*, it is the depiction of a precision instrument subjected to a projective undoing. A watch in a case, as we would see it in life, fuses notions of precision and luxury, while evacuating the specificity of watch and case. Oldenburg's *Watch in Red Box* is a passionate attempt to reestablish an oppositional, subjective signifying chain, wherein the red box begins to share qualities with a mouth or a shell, which might contain either a tongue or marine life. He uses art, and his own imaginative associations, to unbind the erosive associations of commercial modes of representation. He thus makes

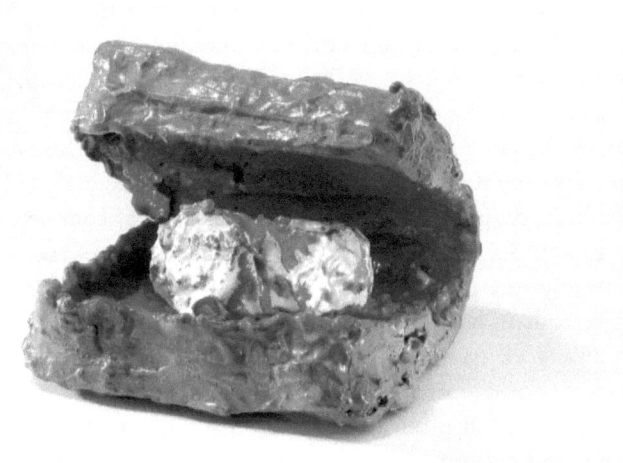

Figure 3.8 *Watch in Red Box*, 1961. Muslin soaked in plaster over wire frame, painted with enamel, 5½ × 6½ × 6¼ in. (14 × 16.5 × 15.9 cm). Collection Reinhard Onnasch, Berlin. Photo: Ellen Page Wilson, New York; courtesy the Oldenburg van Bruggen Studio.

"image-objects."[34] At the moment of *The Store* Oldenburg still believes he can contest fraudulence by manifestly opposing it, making things manifest affect—as ugly or loved. This utopia would shift as he adapted his art to the larger modes of commercial production rising up around him. But for now, the *Watch in Red Box* could express, as well as anything he touched, the all-consuming labor of *The Store* days: "to deliver like an oyster . . . a summarizing immortal form."[35]

Retooling Skill: Industrialized Compliance and Defiance

In the immediate post-*Store* period, with all its object lessons in place, the character of Oldenburg's work changed radically, as if to register actual changes in American production modes that were becoming a more and more palpable condition of daily life. The artist adapted the beaten-up object economy of the Lower East Side—and the "shopkeeper" model of critical engagement (which he shared with Céline)—toward a more ambitious attack at the level of large-scale industrial production.

A photograph of Oldenburg on the floor of the Green Gallery in the summer of 1962 shows the artist as worker. Other than a bowl and a bucket, he is the smallest *subject* in the picture. It is an image that dramatizes the condition Oldenburg was moved now to address. Here is an artist applying paint to canvas, though not in a studio; that phase seems to have been eclipsed. He is already in the space of commercial exchange: the gallery. So, while all the foundational signifiers of conventional artistic practice are present (artist, canvas, paint, gallery), all the relationships between them have changed.

His work consists of applying paint to huge, fabricated objects, like an exhibition preparator or a stage set designer. There is a large cushion form that will turn out to be a giant hamburger (the one in process), a cake in the background, and an ice cream in a cone, in the foreground, partially cropped off.[36] Though these forms reiterate the vocabulary of *The Store*, they were conceived very differently, more like obstacles (mental and physical), made for new settings—an exhibition and a performance. In their new forms and iterations they constitute a crucial transition and, *inter alia*, a significant shift in Oldenburg's mobilization of the uncanny. Like the stock characters the patient discusses with the analyst over and over, in the constant effort to develop new perspectives on them, these are not just larger versions of the earlier forms. They are depictions of new relationships—fears and ideals—that have grown in comic-grotesquery in direct proportion to the perceptions of the subject who conceived of them.

If we recall the uncanny, in its proper definition, as an effect of repression, Oldenburg's particular adaptation of it here is coupled with the gradual distancing of his own skills, submitting to another order of making. This is the uncanny that emerged from 1963 onward, starting with items most closely associated with touch as a daily ritual—the *Soft Toilet*, the *Soft Key*, the *Light Switches*, and other items associated with the home (*das Heimliche*)—projected as part of a more diversified field whose referent was industrial production. What can be tracked here is also an eclipse of the conventional media of art. In this incremental mode of transformation, Oldenburg seems to perform the losses and adjustments art has had to endure to continue all it knows, namely, just *to represent*. This loss reemerges, with almost unfathomable specificity, as the paradox of a thing *and* an in-betweenness (functioning like an ellipsis), which Oldenburg would name the "ghost version."

Not yet a ghost, the white, canvas *Soft Toilet* of 1963 was transitional, like its giant junk food forerunners, but even more so. It was a prototype for new thinking. The canvas *Toilet* enacts an incalculable violence of which its fabulously vulgar spectrum of desublimations is merely an effect, or better still, a symptom. The violence we witness is initiated in the act of evacuating painting altogether—registered in the misshapen canvas stand-in—and elaborated in the subtraction of tactility inscribed exclusively by the hand of the artist, to one that seems oddly autoenacted and never secure. The fixed expressive gestures of the artist are effectively foreclosed upon, and handed over to a future state of echo, threat, and collapse.

Of course, on Oldenburg's part, this was not merely compliance, just as Manet's idea to set his signature in the label of a bottle was not compliance. If anything, it was perception at its most acute and prognostic: "Manufactured Object: Object made by conventional industrial procedure according to plans by artist serving his purpose and not the purpose for which objects made by this procedure normally are intended."[37]

Through the mid-1960s Oldenburg charted such a course in his art. Beginning with a cardboard model, pieces like the soft and hard *Light Switches* of canvas and painted wood were developed from a kind of pattern (which took on the appearance of a blueprint). The "ghost versions," made from canvas, arrived as an important stage in the process, but they were not, as might be expected, the last stage. The "ghosts" existed in the space between plan and realization, between the original idea and its transformation into wood or (previously) non-art media such as colored vinyl.

As much as we might infer about a broader context of artistic practice in that moment through the strange link between canvas and death, the violence Oldenburg depicts is always enigmatically larger. For, whatever else "ghost" implies, in this case it is *art* that is still left with the capacity to meditate on the actual process and the stakes of massive industrial production. Meanwhile, it is the object being represented and transformed that is truly lost. The personality and plenitude of the ghost versions evoke the old object and all the old means of cerebral or somatic stimulus it might have engendered. More haunting even than the lingering presence of these "ghosts" is their status—a *version* in a process that continually goes about eclipsing its earlier stages with more ambitious media and design. In this, they stand in for an older idea of the object that has long since been mourned.

In the decade between 1960 and 1970, Oldenburg developed a conversation between fetish and foil, between art and the demise of object relations in human experience. From the extreme (not to say violent) conditions of that decade, his art has adapted to still more extreme ones since.[38] It is in those battles, and the vocabulary they have generated, that the capricious art of Claes Oldenburg has emerged, like one of his *anti-monuments*, as the mirror of our alienation and our madness; while Oldenburg himself stands (perhaps last) in a lineage of his own making, as one of the sublime form-definers of modernism.

Notes

1. These terms are Oldenburg's. See Claes Oldenburg, "Extracts from the Studio Notes (1962–1964)," *Artforum* 4, no. 5 (January 1966), pp. 32–33.

2. Charles Baudelaire, "Some Foreign Caricaturists," in *The Mirror of Art: Critical Studies*, ed. and trans. Jonathan Mayne (New York: Phaidon, 1955), pp. 337ff.

3. The concept of "still life" will be developed in this essay, read against the grain as a defining mode in Oldenburg's work and pressing upon its historical roots as a mode of protest against nineteenth-century artistic conventions. The French term, *nature morte*, in its difference from the English, seems important to preserve in light of Oldenburg's continual references to nature and death in this period.

4. Regarding Cézanne's conflation of genres, I am indebted to Carol Armstrong's luminous formulations of this idea in her Cézanne seminar at Princeton University, 2003.

5. As this idea is developed, such a grasp of form will be easily read in Oldenburg's extraordinary monuments (or anti-monuments), which are, however, beyond the scope of this essay.

6. The alienated deployment of the mannequin has a crucial precursor in the work of Giorgio de Chirico. For an important account of this function, see Hal Foster, "Convulsive Identity," in *Compulsive Beauty* (Cambridge, Mass.: MIT Press, 1993), pp. 57–98, esp. p. 68.

7. Yve-Alain Bois and Rosalind E. Krauss, *Formless: A User's Guide* (New York: Zone Books, 1997), pp. 15–16.

8. This historical connection was realized in a brief correspondence between the two artists on the occasion of Oldenburg's retrospective at the Museum of Modern Art. Dubuffet wrote: "Against my habits (of never setting foot in museums or galleries . . .) I visited the exhibition of your works at the Museum of Modern Art. . . . [Y]ou are a great creator. I was greatly touched to find the public display of a 1959 painting . . . the subject of which is my proper name associated with that of the great writer Louis Ferdinand Céline. Curiously enough I found myself at the museum, looking at this picture, accompanied by Céline's wife" (October 16, 1969). Oldenburg responded: "That you saw my show in New York delighted me. That you liked it is the highest encouragement—I have admired

your magical art for many years and it has inspired me from the beginning and continues to inspire me" (April 4, 1970). Excerpts courtesy Claes Oldenburg.

9. Louis-Ferdinand Céline, in Irving Howe, "Other Types of French," published in *Critical Essays on Louis-Ferdinand Céline*, ed. William K. Buckley (Boston: Hall and Co., 1989), p. 55.

10. Jean Dubuffet, "Céline Pilote," in *Céline and His Critics: Scandals and Paradox*, ed. Stanford L. Luce (Saratoga, Calif.: Anma Libri, 1986), p. 160.

11. Ibid.

12. Ibid.

13. See, for example, Barbara Rose, *Claes Oldenburg* (New York: Museum of Modern Art, 1970).

14. One of the most succinct definitions of "the uncanny" is to be found in Hal Foster's *Compulsive Beauty*, in regard to surrealism: "As is well known, the uncanny for Freud involves the return of a familiar phenomenon (image or object, person or event) made strange by repression. This return of the repressed renders the subject anxious and the phenomenon ambiguous, and this anxious ambiguity produces the primary effects of the uncanny: (1) an indistinction between the real and the imagined, which is the basic aim of surrealism as defined in both manifestoes of Breton; (2) a confusion between the animate and the inanimate, as exemplified in wax figures, dolls, mannequins, and automatons . . . ; (3) a usurpation of the referent by the sign or of physical reality by psychic reality, and here again the surreal is often experienced . . . as an eclipse of the referential by the symbolic, or as an enthrallment of a subject to a sign or a symptom . . . [in Freud's words]: 'The most remarkable coincidences of desire and fulfillment, the most mysterious recurrence of similar experiences in a particular place . . . the most deceptive sights.'" Foster, *Compulsive Beauty*, p. 7.

15. The first statement is from Rose, *Claes Oldenburg*, p. 67; the second is from *Claes Oldenburg: An Anthology*, ed. Germano Celant (New York: Guggenheim Museum Publications, 1995), p. 23.

16. Jacques Lacan, "The Signification of the Phallus," in *Écrits: A Selection*, trans. Alan Sheridan (New York: Norton, 1977), p. 284. Just as the ambiguity of the term "symbolic" placed Oldenburg into a position of duplicity, Lacan explains that language's articulation in the "passion of the signifier" causes words to evolve and change meaning according to the world they must characterize and the subject positions they must express. What we see in Oldenburg is something akin to what Lacan saw in Freud: the phallus puts Freud into a position of paradox.

17. Rosalind Krauss explains: "Spacing, like the doubled phonemes of *pa-pa*, is the signifier of signification, the indication of a break in the simultaneous experience of the real, a rupture." See Rosalind Krauss and Jane Livingston, *L'Amour fou: Photography and Surrealism*, catalog for the exhibition at the Corcoran Gallery of Art, Washington, D.C. (New York: Abbeville Press, 2002), p. 35.

18. Of course, by now we no longer question this as "art," a term Oldenburg wanted to escape as much as hold onto, in a manner similar to Marcel Duchamp. In that sense, the *"Papa" Ray Gun* proffers a new definition, destroying the old, conventional one, echoing Duchamp's professed desire to eschew mimesis and create something that has never existed before, something entirely new.

19. Lacan, "The Signification of the Phallus," p. 284.

20. Ibid.

21. Ibid., p. 286.

22. Ibid., p. 288.

23. Claes Oldenburg, *Store Days: Documents from The Store (1961) and Ray Gun Theater (1962)*, ed. Claes Oldenburg and Emmett Williams (New York: Something Else Press, 1967); excerpts reprinted in this volume.

24. Oldenburg, "Extracts from the Studio Notes," p. 32. This reference to the "pastry chef" evokes another great attempt (by an artist Oldenburg admired) to represent pathology in paint: Chaim Soutine's *Pastry Chef* (undated) in the Barnes Collection.

25. Foster's account of Freud's development of the concept of the uncanny (*unheimlich*)—*heimlich* for "home" and "un" as the token of departure from home, the womb, the process of psychic regression—toward a theory of the instinctual drives (in *Civilization and Its Discontents*) is crucial for our consideration of Oldenburg; see Foster, *Compulsive Beauty*, p. 7. Another important explanation, which relates to the Oldenburg of 1958–1960, is that of Rosalind Krauss in the *Formless* catalog. Speaking precisely of the multivalence issuing from the image that inspired both Freud and Oldenburg, Krauss states: "We dream in images, Freud said. When the unconscious takes over, under the cover of sleep, we *regress*; we develop backward, retracing the paths that led us up to higher orders of cognitive power in the manipulation of words and symbols, back down toward an earlier, preverbal world of image-objects. And yet the vocation of the dream is the expression of a wish, the formulation—no matter how repressed, or censored—of a desire." See Bois and Krauss, *Formless*, p. 103. She adds, "one such fantasy, the compulsively repeated erotic day-dream of one of Freud's patients: the fantasy expressed as 'a child is being beaten.'" As Krauss explains, what Freud noticed was a transfer of subject positions from: "the father beats a child (and I am watching)" to its final form "a child is being beaten"—thereby shifting from active to passive. The third shift is then: "I am being beaten by the father" (p. 104). "The unconscious," continues Krauss, "does not recognize the order, law of either/or: the idea that two opposites cannot hold true at one time. Thus the unconscious not only courts the transformation of everything into its opposite but it holds both of these things together at once." Quoting Lyotard, she adds: The unconscious "blocks together active and passive, genital and anal, sadism and masochism, and, in 'a child is being beaten,' watching and being watched" (p. 108).

26. If nonfunction as a chief trait of the work of art was asserted and instantiated in the form of Duchamp's readymade in the second decade of the twentieth century, it was recalibrated as a critical point of departure in the early 1960s through George Maciunas's repeated references to art as a "non functional commodity."

27. Oldenburg, "Extracts from the Studio Notes," p. 33.

28. Oldenburg, "Notes, New York, 1960," in Celant, *Claes Oldenburg: An Anthology*, p. 23.

29. In Oldenburg's early sketchbooks of the *Store* period there exists a compelling, if not compulsive, sequence of flag drawings as if thematizing the motor of *The Store* by building on the symbol of the flag and its trajectory, which he charts, to the birth of the brand. Sketchbooks, 1960–1961. Courtesy Claes Oldenburg.

30. Quoted in Rose, *Claes Oldenburg*, p. 31.

31. Coosje van Bruggen explains the "ripped" effect: "Adding to the confusion, the edges of the reliefs and freestanding sculptures were not always the edges of the objects or images used but the edges of torn-out advertisements containing them." See Van Bruggen, *Claes Oldenburg: Nur ein anderer Raum (Just Another Room)* (Frankfurt am Main: Museum für Moderne Kunst, 1991), p. 25.

32. In her forlornness as a freestanding object, *Mannikin with One Leg* seems like the last word in a chain of sculptures that perform the entropy of the monumental and the demise of existentialism. The enactment of that process would include the whittling away of the figure in Giacometti's postwar sculpture, such as *Standing Woman [Leoni]* (1947) and the bleak, linear instantiation of subjectivity in Barnett Newman's *Here I* (1950), mounted on a milk crate. It is in this devolutionary pathos and self-galvanization of sculpture adjusting to the world in which it is created that Oldenburg's one-legged *Mannikin* participates.

In this reading of the logic of postwar sculpture I owe an important debt to Benjamin Buchloh's essay "Sculpture, Publicity, and the Poverty of Experience" in *White Cube/Black Box*, ed. Sabine Breitwieser (Vienna: Generali Foundation, 1996).

33. The *Decimal Point*, a scrunched ball (of muslin soaked in plaster) splattered in colored enamel paint, which hung from a string between the numbers in the *Store* window, has rarely been reproduced and is difficult to discern from the mostly black-and-white photographs of *The Store*. For a recent reproduction of this piece, see my *New Realisms: 1957–62: Object Strategies between Readymade and Spectacle* (Madrid: Museo Nacional Centro de Arte Reina Sofía; Cambridge, Mass.: MIT Press, 2010), p. 191.

34. Bois and Krauss, *Formless*, p. 103.

35. Rose, *Claes Oldenburg*, p. 31.

36. These objects were made for an exhibition at the Green Gallery in September 1962, and subsequently became props for performances, such as *Sports* (October 1962).

37. From Oldenburg, "Notes, Los Angeles, 1963–1964," in Celant, *Claes Oldenburg: An Anthology*, p. 29.

38. The *Geometric Mouse* (1975) (collection Museum of Modern Art, New York)—just to name one example that hardens the soft—is prescient in the way it envisages some of the most advanced (and alienated) appeals of industrial production, such as the object vocabulary of Apple Corporation. One cannot help but think of the model of the pointing device Apple produces dubbed "Mighty Mouse." Apple's exhaustive morphological redefinition of computer hardware—making it and all the associated operating systems "friendly"—is one extreme of the prognostic object vocabulary Oldenburg had long since anticipated.

Oldenburg's Poetics: Analogues, Metamorphoses, and Sources

Ellen H. Johnson

Claes Oldenburg is sometimes called a poet, and rightly so, not simply because he has written poetry but because as a visual artist he thinks and works like a poet. Most of his poems date from 1956 to 1958; some of them are extremely metamorphic, corresponding in character to such collages as *Obsessive Shapes: Falling Forms, Elephant and Chocolate, Knees* (1957). His first one-man show in New York, at the Judson Gallery in May 1959, was a composite of drawings, sculpture, and poems. Although he no longer writes poetry as such, still his plastic art continues to betray tendencies germane to that medium. Besides using cadence and other devices common to all the arts, he builds with inference, metaphor, and analogy to convey meanings far removed from ostensible subjects. His images rhyme with each other formally as they metamorphose from one object or state of being to another (fig. 4.1). Words, which he loves for themselves as independent entities, function that way in his art; and sound, to which he is hypersensitive, is deliberately evoked through pictorial and sculptural means. His work is in accord with his statement, "I consider visual art as poetry, a form of writing, or writing a form of visual art."[1]

His 1959 *"Empire" ("Papa") Ray Gun* is what Kubler would call a "prime object," a paterfamilias as it were. Its life-filled and life-transmitting physicality and its basic form recur in an astonishing variety of guises throughout Oldenburg's work. Magnificent anywhere, it was especially effective suspended from a beam in his immense Fourteenth Street studio where, when struck by a shaft of evening sunlight, it glowed mysteriously in the cavernous darkness like a golden cult image in an ancient grotto. Some of the later ray guns are more reduced and regular

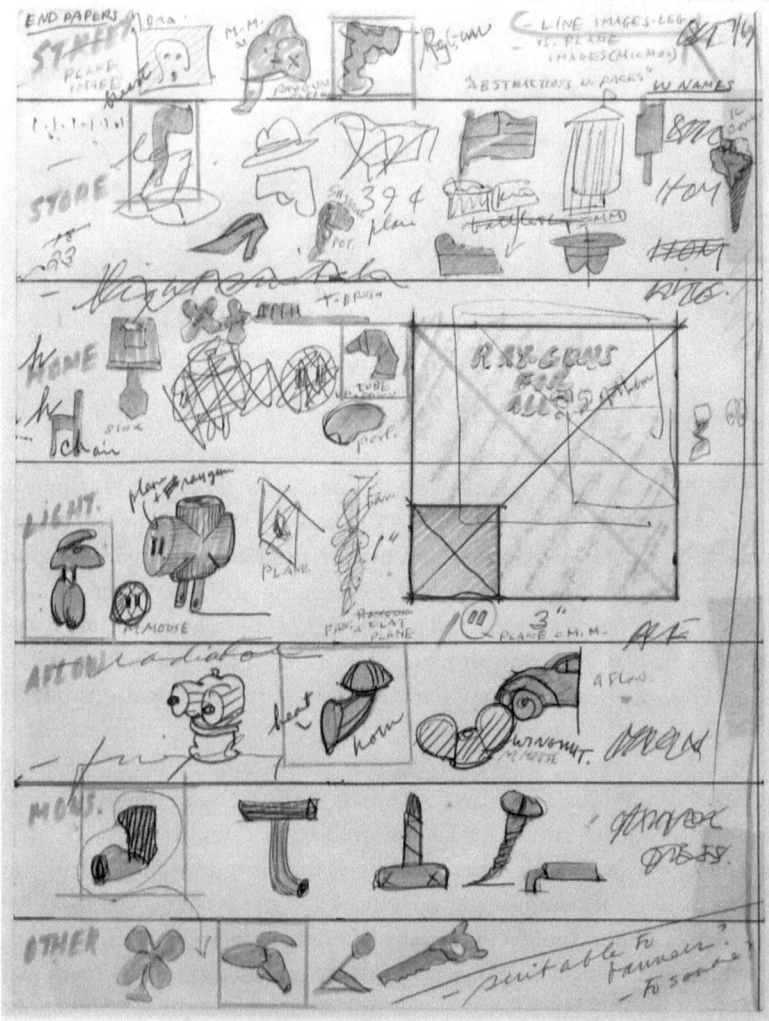

Figure 4.1 *Notebook Page: "Ray Guns for All?"*,
1969. Ballpoint pen, felt pen, colored pencil,
crayon, 11 × 8½ in. (27.9 × 21.6 cm). Collection
Claes Oldenburg and Coosje van Bruggen. Photo
courtesy the Oldenburg van Bruggen Studio.

in form and less overtly phallic, and their closeness to prehistoric mysteries is less readily apparent. Among the abundant collateral descendants of the *"Empire" ("Papa") Ray Gun* (i.e., collateral in subject but lineal in form) are an arm, a door handle, a 7-Up sign, a car, a vacuum cleaner, a Dormeyer mixer, a toilet, a shrimp, a shoe, and a map of Chicago (fig. 4.2). The fireplug, drainpipe, and lipstick monuments are double-handled, single-barreled ray guns (fig. 4.3). Reproduced is one of a series of drawings which the artist recently made to illustrate these specific analogies which I had selected from numerous reappearances of the ray gun image. One of the disguises in which he cloaks himself, it is a symbol of his manhood and his creativity and of his faith in what he calls the "ultimately unknowable."

Partly the product of his prodigious fantasy, these metamorphoses also have their origin in Oldenburg's consciously or intuitively selecting those subjects in which he recognizes his favorite formal motifs. All of his mature work is deliberately reducible to a few simple forms, primarily rectangles and circles with occasional triangles, and their spatial extension into solids. By repeating, combining, modifying, and changing the position of his formal constants, and by stressing their affinity, widely divergent things are made to "rhyme" with each other. "The countryside is afloat with doubles," Oldenburg wrote in a 1956 poem, which reads in full:

> mirrors
> polish up your annihilations
> instruct metal in ambiguity
> there is an order standing
> for revolvers panelled with invisibility
> a mouth is loose
> victims have seen themselves
> the countryside is afloat with doubles

Oldenburg's formal correspondences are largely responsible for the unity which distinguishes his exhibitions, particularly those which he himself plans; but any selection of his work is remarkable in its consistency as the consonant forms move freely back and forth cutting across major subject categories and marrying opposites. The *Floor Burger (Giant Hamburger)* can be reduced to three major and one minor circles, the *Giant Blue Shirt with Brown Tie* to a large rectangle with a "tail," *Giant*

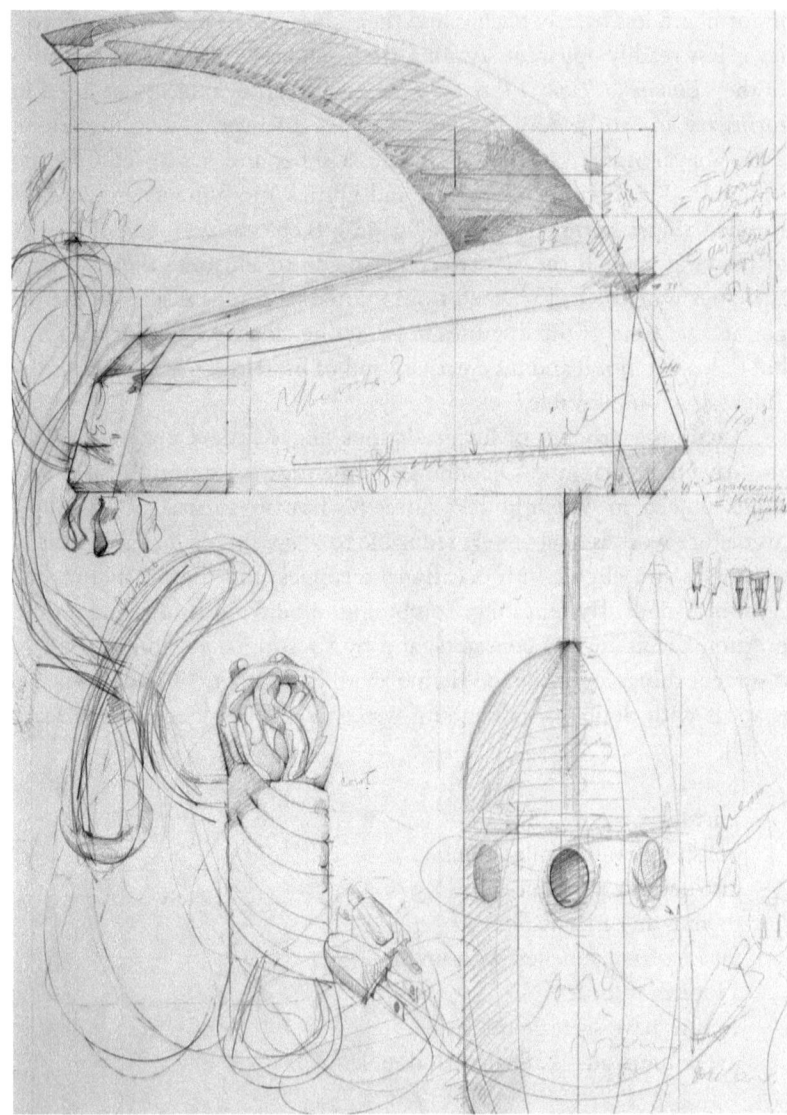

Figure 4.2   *Study of a Dormeyer Mixer*, 1965.
Pencil, 30 × 22 in. (76.2 × 55.9 cm). Collection
Mrs. Emily Pulitzer, St. Louis. Photo courtesy the
Oldenburg van Bruggen Studio.

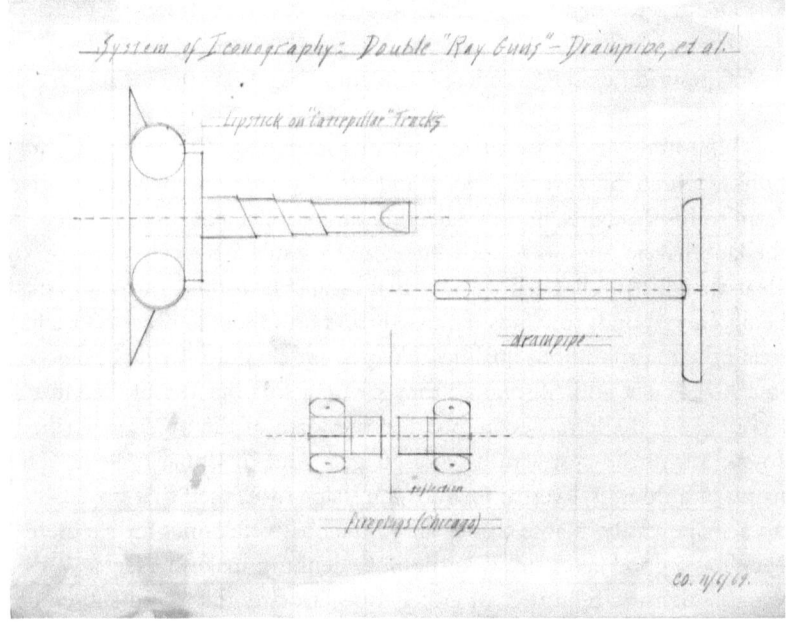

Figure 4.3   *System of Iconography: Double "Ray Guns"—Lipstick, Drainpipe, Fireplugs,* 1969. Pencil on graph paper, 11 × 8½ in. (27.9 × 21.6 cm). Collection Claes Oldenburg and Coosje van Bruggen. Photo: D. James Dee, New York; courtesy the Oldenburg van Bruggen Studio.

Soft Swedish Light Switches to four circles, and *Giant Ice Cream Cone* to a circle on a triangle (the solid form of which Oldenburg describes as "disks continued in space but seen in vanishing point perspective,"[2] i.e., a cone). The *Three-Way Plug* can be read as the crossing of two cylinders (disks multiplied), with two rectangles suspended from it; *Giant Fagends* are entirely composed of cylinders on a hexagonal prism; and the whole *Bathroom, Airflow,* and *Bedroom* ensembles are complex orchestrations of the basic motifs. Clearly, almost any art can be reduced to basic geometric forms; as Oldenburg says, "That's what gives it strength. It is the bones, the skeleton—the truth. I've just made a game of what every artist concerned with universal structure does."[3] However, Oldenburg is unique in his obsessive concern with the formal correspondences which he can find or establish between otherwise totally unlike objects, and his studio notes abound in references to such equivalents:

Drum set = bed = big "erotic" drawing = car (Airflow) Fagends
Thames ball = hat on sidewalk
Typewriter eraser = tea bag = punching bag = keyhole = sperm cell

Hundreds of similar analogs occur throughout Oldenburg's notebooks, which fill several shelves and attest to his compulsion to give
form to his thoughts, however fleeting or complex and sustained, and to
the fact that he does so as both a poet and a visual artist. They also make
clear that his intellectual activity is inescapably rooted in his physical
being; he responds to words sensuously and uses them as objects, emphasizing their autonomous qualities. "Words are, do not only do," he noted
in 1967, "Dick and Alison said they sat on a sofa but I could see it was
a couch, i.e. the letters correspond to the form of the object described.
I now attack the abstraction of language." And in January 1969, "The
name of a thing is a verbal form of the shape of it, used that way, to call
up a shape easily. Name that is an abstract as well: cone, for example."
Much as a good actor or orator does, Oldenburg makes us feel a word's
weight, density, lightness, or other aspects of its form and substance.
Sometimes he incorporates words as an intrinsic element in the work:
many of *The Street* and *The Store* drawings and three-dimensional pieces
have words or numbers painted or drawn on them. He frequently in-
scribes the name of the object on it, as in *Giant Soft Ketchup Bottle* and
on each item of *Soft Ladder, Hammer, Saw, and Bucket*. Often he writes
equivalents suggested by a work directly onto the studies for it, as on a
vacuum cleaner drawing: "= typewriter = shoe = sailboat." Occasionally a word is the sole subject of the work, as in *C-E-L-I-N-E Backwards*;
sometimes a single letter forms the work. A monument is constructed
of *T*, a tree of a compact cluster of full-bodied *B*s, and a museum of
its own letters. As has been the case for many of his contemporaries,
a major source of Oldenburg's use of words and numbers is their pre-
ponderance in the city landscape. "A city is all words—a newspaper,
an alphabet," he writes in the Gemini portfolio notes. Another source
has been maps, which he constantly consults. In 1966 he wrote, "I feel
shut in if there is no map on the wall to look at." The initials of his own
name haunt his work: a giant *C* is dropped on a building; the drainpipe is a *T*; the hamburger a series of *O*s. He notes "CTO C (see) CO
toilet cover C toilet O bathtub T sink"; and he observes that several
works are based on *A*s, such as the ladder piece, with *A* for Aquarius,

his zodiac sign. Like the runes of his Viking forebears, words and letters have magical power, and their combinations are incantations in Oldenburg's notebooks.

In incorporating words in his visual art, Oldenburg is deliberately adding the element of sound; when we see the word, we experience it aurally as well as visually. He further introduces sound not by the literal means of attaching mechanical devices but by the choice of sound-making subjects (telephone, typewriter, cash register, drum set) and, on a more subtle level, by formal allusions to the kind of sound they make (fig. 4.4). The liquid folds of *Soft Tub* fall like water slowly plopping; the *Perspective Drawing for Home Saw* whirs and buzzes around the page; the hard white circles of the *Soft Typewriter*'s keys click against the black vinyl. The *Giant Soft Drum Set* is as noisy in its extravagant variety of materials, shapes, and colors as the *Three-Way Plug* is silent in its austere oneness.

While in some respects Oldenburg has been the innovator, and in others the catalyzer of several major changes in form and attitude which sculpture has undergone during the 1960s, he retains closer ties with tradition than most advanced sculptors do; but he does so in a unique and contradictory way. His sculpture is still based on the human body but never the whole body, only parts of it, and these fragments are presented in the guise of manufactured products. The apparent subject is very different from the actual subject and the content is far greater than either. Again, unlike most of his contemporaries, Oldenburg builds multiple associations and meanings into his works and he welcomes the varying and paradoxical responses which they induce. One of the most subject-conscious of today's artists, he is also one of the most abstract in his formal constancy and concern. Because he stresses each of them to an extreme degree, Oldenburg, as much if not more than any other artist of his generation, exemplifies the truth of Picasso's contradictory statements, "There is no abstract art" and "All art is abstract."

That Oldenburg delights in such paradoxes is clear from his equivalents cited above. Contradiction is a constant preoccupation of his mind and a life-giving principle in his art. Obviously, opposition is present in all art, but he pushes the polarities so strenuously that paradox (and its resolution) must be recognized as a basic condition of his mind and sensibility. It operates throughout his work, from the fundamental tensions between subject and abstraction, nature and technology, man and the

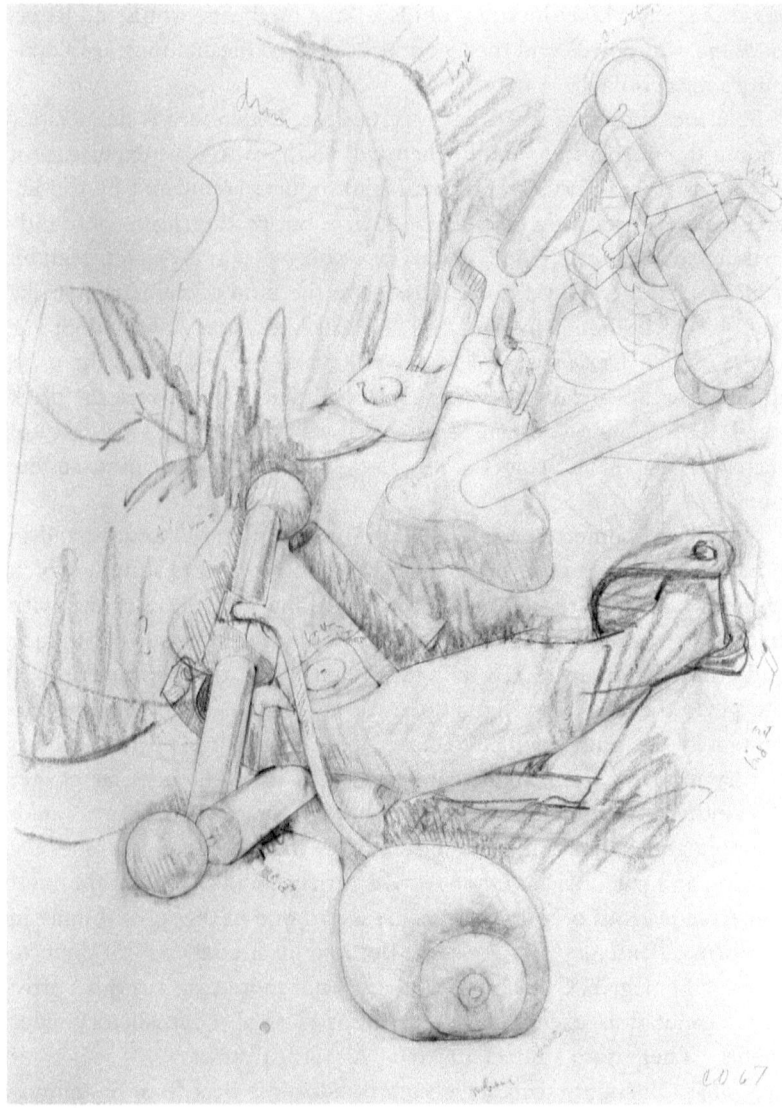

Figure 4.4   *Drum Pedal Study—Visualization
of Collapsed Version*, 1967. Pencil, 30 × 22 in.
(76.2 × 55.9 cm). Private collection. Photo
courtesy the Oldenburg van Bruggen Studio.

machine, to such specific ironies as the presenting of a rigid mechanical object in soft, yielding material.

The major thematic contradictions which engage Oldenburg are sometimes played against each other between objects in the same group, but most often within the same work. The Yale *Lipstick* monument is both phallic, life-engendering, and a bomb, the harbinger of death. Male in form, it is female in subject; a two-inch object carried in everywoman's purse stretches twenty-four feet into the sky. This amusing conceit cloaks a sober truth which Oldenburg dwells on, the interchangeability of life (Eros) and death. As he recently wrote, "The presence of death defines life."

A primary visual source for Oldenburg, as for so many artists today, is the endless barrage of advertising images in newspapers, magazines, films, television (especially the animated cartoon for Oldenburg's metamorphic ideas), billboards, marquees, and shop displays. His images are often secondhand, i.e., the sources themselves are already abstracted, isolated and enlarged. His changes in scale, from Lilliputian to Brobdingnagian,[4] owe as much to advertising and air travel as they do to the hallucinations of his fantasy. The fretted edges of his *Store* pieces reflect the very act of tearing out an ad which touched him, and they contribute greatly to the immediacy which distinguishes his art. In 1961 he referred to his fragmented images as "rips out of reality"; equating, as he did, newspaper with experience, a torn piece of it implies a "continuum of experience."[5] The original ads, many of which are preserved in Oldenburg's studio archives, and the source objects in his home (fan, juicer, typewriter eraser, three-way plug, etc.) look utterly insignificant and "puny" when compared with the powerfully existent and monumental work stimulated by them. Only a creative intensity like Oldenburg's could use these trivia as vehicles of passion and majesty.

Oldenburg never copies the clipped image; it simply starts something going in his mind, or fits in with something already in process, or reminds him of a piece which he has already completed and sent out. In many cases the actual subject of the clipping has no relevance to the finished work. An advertisement of a cup and saucer on a tray is metamorphosed into a hat lying on an empty expanse of sidewalk, his moving memorial to Adlai Stevenson. The red-tipped Con Edison towers, which rise over several sections of New York like Mont Sainte-Victoire over Aix, have taken part in the genesis of several works, particularly the Yale *Lipstick* monument.

There are several occasions in which Oldenburg has adapted and metamorphosed other works in the evolution of one of his pieces. Brancusi's *Sleeping Muse,* a little illustration of which Oldenburg pasted on a notebook page and inscribed "headlite," lies behind such works as the *Study for a Colossal Monument to Mayor Daley* and his own life mask and the *Geometric Mouse I,* which, as he has indicated, also has sources in fallen antique heads and a specific Easter Island head at the Lippincott factory in New Haven. Other Brancusi sculptures which have had special significance for Oldenburg are those which include Brancusi's own bases. Oldenburg is attracted by the contradiction between the elegantly sophisticated and highly polished marble or bronze form surmounting a rough, primitive supporting structure. Also, the piling up of one upon another contrasting shape in Brancusi's composite works is reflected in several of Oldenburg's sculptures, such as the *Soft Toilet.* Brancusi's *Torso of a Young Man* has played a decisive role in the genesis of several works, most especially the *Fireplug* group, which is as indebted to it (and, in some measure, to Duchamp's *Chocolate Grinder*) as it is to the actual fireplug which Oldenburg filmed from his window when he was a boy in Chicago. In some of the drawings and in the multiple *Fireplugs,* he softened the adamantine purity of the Brancusi into a relaxed and lumpy human configuration. Making a melted Brancusi is an inverted and playfully irreverent means of acknowledging how much that master has meant to him. In the *Fireplug* and many other Oldenburgs, forms are symmetrical, paired like the body parts for which they are metaphors: one sees a pair of shoulders, torso, and penis in the drainpipe, a pair of legs in the light plug, hips in the axle of the car and thighs and ears in its fenders, a face in an electric orange juicer, and male genitals in a Dormeyer mixer. Usually the body imagery is multiple in its references, as both breast and testicles in the soft light switches. However, as I have tried to indicate, simple identification of the subject matter and its metamorphoses does not insure recognition of Oldenburg's content, which is always more significant than it may first appear to be. In 1966 he wrote, "'Plugging in' or establishing contact is a theme, which goes beyond the merely sexual—the contact of the individual with his surroundings."[6]

The soft drainpipes are more than sexual images. As they are attached to pulleys, their differing emotive qualities can be exaggerated or decreased by varying the tautness of the cord. When cruelly bound to the crossbars from which they are hung, they not only evoke images of crucified bodies, but they do so with the violence of a Grünewald. The combination of mutilation and eroticism in the "bloody" version is more brutal than in the *Soft (Cool) Drainpipe*, whose dry texture and blue color are less carnal; but the anguish expressed in it is no less painful for that. In one of his equivalents Oldenburg wrote, "Blue drainpipe = Holy Ghost." While, according to Oldenburg, that may be a somewhat playful, and certainly not a programmatic, association, still there is no escaping the implications of his subconscious in arriving at that analog.

As is true of any serious work of art, each piece by Oldenburg springs from many levels of his being and experience, and its genesis and evolution cannot be charted with strict exactitude. Its content is never exclusive or single; were it so, it would violate life's mobility, change, and contradiction which are expressed so poignantly in every aspect of Oldenburg's art, whether it be drawing, painting, sculpture, poem, or performance.

Anyone who has experienced an Oldenburg theater piece will clearly realize that music must be as important to him as poetry is; not because he sometimes uses music in his performances, but because, like a musician, he shapes time. Through his spacing of silence and sound, and of stillness and motion, and by changes in lighting, often plunging audience and players into darkness, he makes us feel time as a physical force, almost a tangible substance. Time is not measured—so many seconds in a minute, so many minutes in an hour. It is not a concept, but a felt reality, expanded, contracted, or suspended. To stand, as one often did at the Ray Gun Theater, in total darkness in a very narrow space, is to feel time so mysteriously drawn out or even stopped that one can hardly breathe and the sweat breaks out on one's body. Even reading the script for Oldenburg's "very last happening," *The Typewriter*,[7] can evoke a physical sensation of time in duration. Like contemporary composers, he discards the linear treatment of time, preferring, in his words, to focus on the "expansion or unfolding of a moment." Oldenburg's happenings have been a rich source for his other art. The materials and the objects, which he discovered or himself constructed for use in the performances, often engendered specific works and stimulated or furthered his plastic innovations. The idea for his large *Ironing Board with Shirt and Iron* of 1964 came from the actual appliance on which soft obelisks were ironed in his *Stars*, presented in Washington in 1963. The gigantic ties used in that performance are related to many of his flexible hanging pieces. In fact, Oldenburg's invention of soft sculpture, which has been of such decisive importance in contemporary art, is sometimes said to have actually originated in the props which he made of stuffed and painted cloth, such as *Freighter and Sailboat* for *Store Days II*. The truth is, of course, that he had made a considerable amount of soft sculpture before that time, as for example, the well-known *Street Heads* from 1960, made of burlap stuffed with newspaper. However, this fact does not invalidate the assumption that the materials which he worked with in his performances were provocative to him in his other art. Nothing that he makes is wasted; he builds constantly on what has gone before in his production. In fact, one might almost say that his mature work was prefigured in his childhood invention of a whole imaginary country, "Neubern." Among his studio documents is a file of that material, most of it done when he was eight and nine years old; by the time he was twelve, he had completely put aside Neubern. There are exact-scale maps of the country and each of its thirty-six states and their principal cities, its industries, topography, national parks, temperature ranges, works of communications with plans and elevations for several types of trains, planes, and ships (both naval and commercial), all named and assigned handsome insignia. The red and white symbol of Neubern's air force is an early example of the right-angled ray gun form, which was to become identified with the mature artist and his work. There are striking pages of coats-of-arms of the states and cities, plans and drawings of their airports, terminals, stadiums, and skylines; historical charts of Neubern's territorial changes and its rulers from John Boule in 1436 to Claes Oldenburg in 1935; numerous magazines, newspapers (some in Swedish, some in English, some typed, some lettered by hand), comics, posters for film and stage productions, some of which were actually presented under the direction of the young Oldenburg. Among other prophetic childhood activities, he built models, carved planes, constructed a miniature drum set, and made plans for nonfunctional giant objects. It is all an extraordinary foretaste of the colossal scale of Oldenburg's conception and the precision of his execution. Then, as now, he did not just live in his imaginary world; he brought that world to life through form.

Notes

1. Except where otherwise noted, all quotations from Oldenburg come from his notebooks, and are published here by courtesy of the Oldenburg van Bruggen Studio.

2. From Oldenburg's original typescript, in English, for his "Eftertankar," *Konstrevy* 42, no. 5–6 (1966).

3. Conversation with the author, September 1969.

4. It is difficult to avoid alluding to *Gulliver's Travels* in discussing Oldenburg's fantastic treatment of scale, even if one does not happen to know that he deeply admires Swift.

5. Conversation with the author, June 1969.

6. Typescript cited in note 2.

7. Published in *Esquire* 71, no. 5 (May 1969).

Selected Writings on *The Store* and the Ray Gun Theater

Claes Oldenburg

The Store

this country is all bourgeois down to the last deathtail and most
of the criticism is an exhortation to observe art and justice and good
sense and humanity, which are also bourgeois values, so there is no escaping bourgeois values in America. The enemy is bourgeois culture
nevertheless.

CITY AX or TAXI
Torrent
tame
torrential
hat song
hot seng
bed

If I could only forget the notion of art entirely. I really don't think
you can win. Duchamp is ultimately labeled art too. The bourgeois
scheme is that they wish to be disturbed from time to time, they like
that, but then they envelop you, and that little bit is over, and they are
ready for the next. There even exists within the b. values a code of possibilities for disturbance, certain "crimes" which it requires some courage
to do but which will eventually be rewarded within the b. scheme. B.
values are human weakness, a civilization built on human weakness, non-
resistance. They are disgusting. There are many difficult things to do
within the b. values, but I would like to find some way to take a totally

outside position. Bohemia is bourgeois. The beat is bourgeois—their values are pure sentimentality—the country, the good heart, the fallen man, the honest man, the gold-hearted whore etc. They would never think f.ex. of making the city a value of good.

Possibly art is doomed to be bourgeois. Two possible escapes from the bourgeois are 1. aristocracy and 2. intellect, where art never thrives too well. There again I am talking as if I want to create art outside b. values. Perhaps this can't be done, but why should I even want to create "art"—that's the notion I've got to get rid of. Assuming that I wanted to create some thing what would that thing be? Just a thing, an object. Art would not enter into it. I make a charged object ("living"). An "artistic" appearance or content is derived from the object's reference, not from the object itself or me. These things are displayed in galleries, but that is not the place for them. A store would be better (Store—place full of objects). Museum in b. concept equals store in mine.

I don't consider myself in struggle w nature but in harmony w her. Neither arrogance nor humility but harmony and identification. Nothing is not nature (natural?) and nothing not suitable for the living organizational capacity which is "art."

That which everyman does when walking down street artist does as an act in itself and therefore as a model to others.
Taking on as many problems as he can.
"Beauty" is word of praise for his successful effort.
The multitude of natural possibilities prevents its having any single definition.
An artist is a specialist in synthesis of physical practical world.
He analyzes or breaks up only to rearrange and ultimately to resynthesize.

Fig/non fig is moronic distinction. The challenge to abstract art must go much deeper.

Lately I have begun to understand action painting that old thing in a new vital and peculiar sense—as corny as the scratches on a NY wall and by parodying its corn I have (miracle) come back to its authenticity! I feel as if Pollock is sitting on my shoulder, or rather crouching in my pants!

What is a big object well that is a room. I have no desire to do environments but I will do a room, I am turned on by the thick plaster and green paint of a kitchen in my neighborhood. The accumulation and mystery. The heaped up table with a radio in it. Something frying on the stove. The other stuff ought well be saved for later.

The store windows I see now serve as models for clusters—eye-clusters—formal model for a kind of visual experience: fragmentation, simultaneousness, superimposition, which I wish to recreate in the clusters.

The Store Described & Budget for the Store

The Store, or My Store, or the Ray-Gun Mfg. Co., located at 107 E. 2nd St., N.Y.C., is eighty feet long and varies about 10 ft wide. In the front half, it is my intention to create the environment of a store, by painting and placing (hanging, projecting, lying) objects after the spirit and in the form of popular objects of merchandise, such as may be seen in stores and storewindows of the city, especially in the area where the store is (Clinton St., f.ex., Delancey St., 14th St.).

This store will be constantly supplied with new objects which I will create out of plaster and other materials in the rear half of the place [fig. 5.1]. The objects will be for sale in the store.

The store will be open every day at hours I will post. F.ex. AM 10–2, PM 5–7, or the hours when I will be able to be in the store, which is also of course my studio.

The store may be thought of as a season-long exhibit, with changing & new material. It will be the center of my activities during the season.

The rent of the store is $60.00 per month, including steam heat and hot and cold water. Additional money will be needed to paint and plaster the front half and to make objects. Rent for 10 mos.—$600. Additional money to equip store—$150. Money to make objects—$250. ($24 per month). Total $1000.

13 Incidents at the Store

A customer enters
Something is bought
Something is returned
It costs too much
A bargain!
Someone is hired. (someone is fired.)

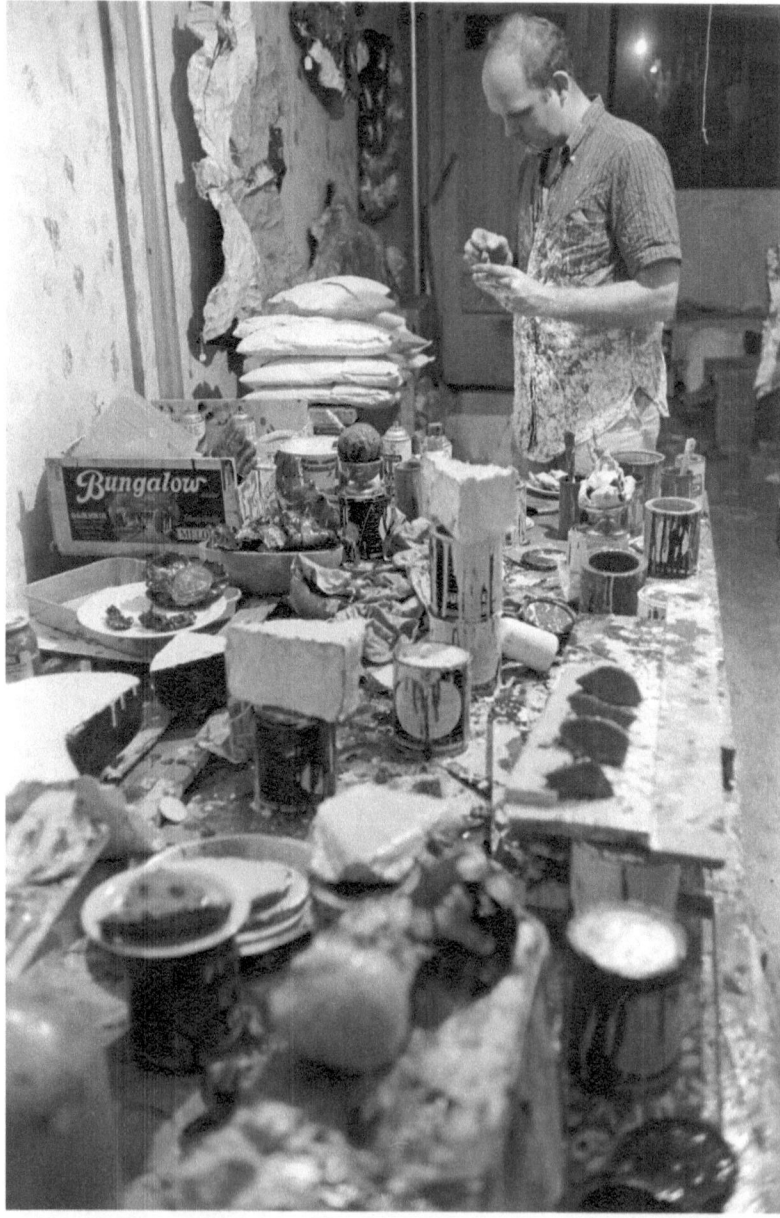

Figure 5.1   Claes Oldenburg painting plaster
sculptures in his studio, 107 East Second Street,
August 1962. Photo © Robert McElroy/Licensed
by VAGA, New York, NY; courtesy the Oldenburg
van Bruggen Studio.

The founders. How they struggled.
Inventory
Fire sale
Store closed on acct of death in family
The Night Before Christmas
Modeling clothes
A lecture to the Salesmen

1. *A Customer Enters*
The room is dark. A man sits at the table. Two female bodies on the floor. A hand hangs down from the "attic." The light is very dim. In the slowest possible gesture, the man lifts the telephone to his ear. The bodies move a little.
The hand returns to the attic. Sound of the Mickey Mouse banjo.

2. *Something Purchased*
The lights come on again, dimly. The man is still at the table talking into the phone (not saying anything). Another man enters very briskly, takes off a heavy winter coat and hangs it on a hook, then freezes. Both the man with the phone and the other man are frozen.
The hand descends to drop a glassful of water.

3. *A bargain!*
Sound of the man upstairs reading a paper (i.e., turning the pages). Everyone as they were. A red paint begins to run down around the walls from the attic. Coughing upstairs.

The goods in the stores: clothing, objects of every sort, and the boxes and wrappers, signs and billboards—for all these radiant commercial articles in my immediate surroundings I have developed a great affection, which has made me want to imitate them. And so I have made these things: a wrist-watch, a piece of pie, hats, caps, pants, skirts, flags, 7up, shoe-shine etc. etc., all violent and simple in form and color, just as they are. In showing them together, I have wanted to imitate my act of perceiving them, which is why they are shown as fragments (of the field of seeing), in different scale to one another, in a form surrounding me (and the spectator), and in accumulation rather than in some imposed design. And the effect is: I have made my own Store.

My life is a history of rooms in which I am self-locked in. My life is also a history of frantic "escapes" which come to nothing, back to a room. So, accepted.

This limits my expression to "my reality," that is, to an "artists" reality. I know my separation.

I have had something like affairs with rooms. Goodbyes f.ex. Union only with impersonal nature.

This room, enclosure is my natural attraction to environments which I conceive as interiors or even if open: high ceilings or enclosed outside (the street)

My work is thoroughly and honestly self-projective, narcissistic. This "weakness" constitutes its power. My desire for an audience is the desire to confess, a desire to reach, or be reached, be saved from enclosure. Which never happens.

Noone reaches me. I reach noone, except thru disguises and thru others (players)

Store—Eros

The Store is like the Street an environmental (as well as a thematic) form. In a way they are the same thing because some streets or squares (like TSq) are just large open stores (windows, signs etc.). In The Store the concentration upon objects is more intense, and harsh colors rather than greys and browns dominate.

I use naive imitation. This is not because I have no imagination or because I wish to say something about the everyday world. I imitate 1. objects and 2. created objects, f.ex. signs. Objects made without the intention of making "art" and which naively contain a functional contemporary magic. I try to carry these even further through my own naivete, which is not artificial. Further, i.e., charge them more intensely, elaborate their reference. I do not try to make "art" out of them. This must be understood. I imitate these because I want people to get accustomed to recognizing the power of objects, a didactic aim. If I alter, which I do usually, I do not alter for "art" and I do not alter to express *myself*, I alter to unfold the object, and to add to it other object-qualities, forces. The object remains an object, only expanded and less specific.

There is first the ice-cream cone as it is. This would be one imitation. Then begins a series of parallel representations which are not the ice-cream cone but nevertheless realistic or objective: f. ex. the ice-cream cone in a newspaper ad. The ice-cream cone or any other popular shape as a fetish object. The ice-cream cone in altered scale (giant). The ice-cream cone as a symbol etc. Only the created object—my parallel cone—will include and/or concentrate several of these.

The fact that the store represents American popular art is only an accident, an accident of my surroundings, my landscape, of the objects which in my daily coming and going my consciousness attaches itself to. An art of ideas is a bore and a sentimentality, whether witty or serious or what. I may have things to say about US and many other matters, but in my art I am concerned with perception of reality and composition. Which is the only way that art can really be useful—by setting an example of how to use the senses.

The Store
may be better understood if it is considered not itself a psychological statement but a collection of psychological statements which exist concretely in the form of signs and advertisements. Placement and relation unfixed, free. An imitation not of nature or nature in the city but nature altered toward psychology, which is to say: the true "landscape" of the city.

It is important to me that a work of art be constantly elusive, mean many different things to many different people. My work is always on its way between one point and another. What I care most about is its living possibilities.

one's own body the form of change
keep form even after making, in a situation of change
not only mechanical but psychological
moving sculptures are often all fixed
mine are not
the law of my work is time
                    change

The store tries to overcome the sense of guilt connected with money and sales which the artist has—either inherited or to rationalize his lack of ability to make money. It is to say money is life (like

Bossman) it is plenty . . . it is psychological . . . articles are child or substitute . . .

Commerce is organic and psychological

Thus again, unity—no separation between commerce and art

The store expresses a kind of contempt or disinterest in color, or it expresses the expansion of color into form in space, that is the super texture supercollage. My theme is here as often the expansion of ptg into actual space, toward sculpture, and the puns about illusion, which is actual and actuality which is illusion. The relation of painting and sculpture from the vantage pt of sculpture, whereas jim's vantage point is painting and he expresses contempt for sculpture. That is his jokes are about building without architecture.

food = love

metrecal = death of love

My idea of an environmental piece is that quite a large area (the larger the better) ought to be controlled—and any thing and all who enter this space—by certain radiating pieces or clusters of form and color. This conception for me involves both the power of pure form and color and also my belief in magic. A great deal of trial and error and thought and care goes into making certain that these centers do their work.

my art is a resolution of opposites:

strives for a simultaneous presentation of contraries and opposites

in subj the ordinary and the extraordinary

in form the aesthetic and the unaesthetic

solidity and bodylessness

pathos and indifference

mystery and commonplace

etc.

This elevation of sensibility above bourgeois values, which is also a simplicity of return to truth and first principles, will (hopefully) destroy the notion of art and give the object back its power. Then the magic inherent in the universe will be restored and people will live in sympathetic religious exchange with the materials and objects surrounding them. They will not feel so different from these objects, and the animate/inanimate schism mended. What is now called an art object is a debased understanding of a magic object. When our vision is clouded by bourgeois values and by removal from an actual functional situation (through museum-civilization) the power of the object wch was a functioning object becomes suspended and only its artificiality, that is its craft and design (which are the lowest and easiest of creations), are noted. This is "art." Think how many children a day are being perverted into art and their natural recognition of the magic in objects stamped out!

The erotic or the sexual is the root of "art," its first impulse. Today sexuality is more directed, or here where I am in Am. at this time, toward substitutes f.ex. clothing rather than the person, fetichistic stuff, and this gives the object an intensity and this is what I try to project.

Why do I not just present the real thing instead of imitating it? Because my desire to imitate extends to the event or activity of making the thing I imitate. In one instance that is to be for a moment a sign-painter, in another, for a moment a baker of cakes, in another the cutter of suits, etc. etc. In some cases especially, but really in all, it is necessary to be for a moment nature herself, if this is possible. In handling plaster and enamel I was behaving like the painter who was at the same time painting my stairway. When I carry my plaster and paints up the stairs, the neighbors assume I am improving my home.

In The Store I am naively reconstructing an act of vision, a kind of literal-scientific approach. (Here again the analogy of the lightning trapped in sand applies).

My singleminded aim is to give existence to (my) fantasy. This means the creation of a parallel reality according to the rules of (my) fantasy.
I am compelled to do this to a greater degree than most painters.
This world cannot ever hope to really exist and so it exists entirely through illusion, but illusion is employed as subversively, as convincingly as possible.
The critical moment is my act of seeing. The rest is the patient reconstruction of this hallucination and successive hallucinations which arise in the course of making.
The contribution of subject matter is almost a side effect since what I see is not the thing itself but—myself—in its form.

Experience, that is to say, is material—for an act of recognition, and having recognized something, the job one could argue is done, the rest being the act of giving evidence.

Experience is the primary material & then plaster and paint. In the case of theater, experience is both the first and the second material.

The content is always the human imagination. This I regard both as historically constant and as universal among individuals. To present the geography of the human imagination is my aim, with real mountains and cities.

Budget for [the Ray Gun] Theater

My theater activity in the coming season I would like to be in two manners. The first is a repertory type of theater, to give short performances at regular intervals, f.ex. every two weeks, on Saturdays 10 PM. These would be held in My Store, or The Ray-Gun Mfg Co., 107 E. 2nd St., N.Y.C. inside the store or in the courtyard behind the store, which is quite large [fig. 5.2]. Since these performances would be comparatively brief, a small amount would be charged for admission, f.ex. 50¢, and the audience would have to be rather small. These performances would occur one time only and be improvised out of available material and available performers, with no great expense. There would not need to be any advertising, I think. In fact, advertising might bring too many people. It is better to be word of mouth. This repertory would be like a workshop of ideas and possibilities surrounding my concept of personal theater, and not so much directed at the general public as at other artists and connoisseurs interested in developments along this line. On the basis of one performance every two wks. and starting in October, there would be about 14 performances. Assuming about 35 spectators can be accommodated, there would be an income of $17.50 per performance. A supplementary budget of $25 would be needed for each performance, or for 14 perfs—$350.

The store an efflorescence additive principle clusters agglomerations magnetic attractions extension flaming chairs and tables outrushing pictures on the wall moveables all moving earthquake Torn-birth flesh fragments. I think of space as material as I think of the stage as a solid cube or a box to be broken. That air and the things in it are one, are HARD, and that you can RIP a piece of air and the thing out of it,

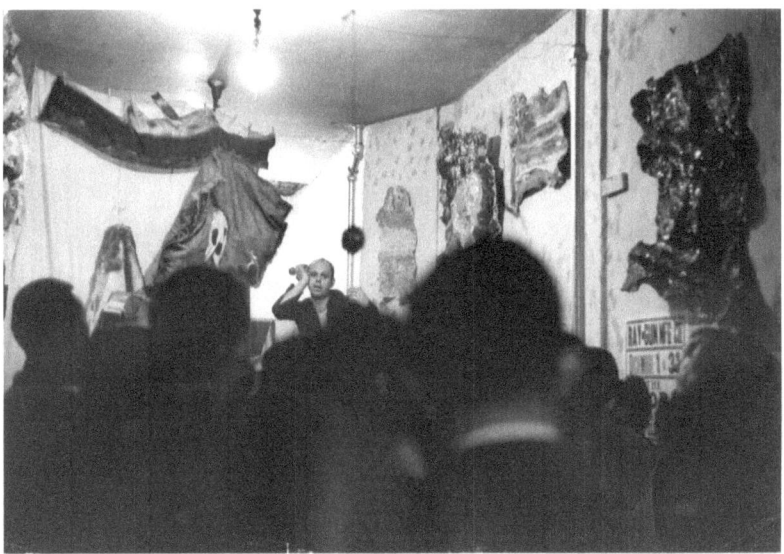

Figure 5.2 Claes Oldenburg speaking before the
start of the performance *Injun I*, Ray Gun Theater
at *The Store*, April 20, 1962. Installation view: soft
prop *Freighter* from *The Street*; *U.S.A. Flag* from the
first *Store*. Photo © Robert McElroy/Licensed by
VAGA, New York, NY; courtesy the Oldenburg van
Bruggen Studio.

so that a piece of object and a whole object and just air, comes as one
piece.
This is accompanied by a RIPPING SOUND

The starting point of the realist is to be the scientist. Nature *means*
nothing by itself. Man supplies the meaning of things. My theater may
be called the theater of the real or the theater of the object, is a meeting
place of realistic and subjective nature whose sentimental representation
is juxtaposed with non-sentimental.

A theater of action or of things (people too regarded as things).

but above all, am i worth coming to see? it is a poor man's theater and
the lead is a beggar.

A series of plays dealing with the US consciousness, really noncon-
crete in content though expressed concretely. The content is the US
mind or the US "Store." This is not understood. Despite what I say, the
pieces are called happenings. I might have done happenings or may do
in the future but these are not my idea of them. RG is something else,
closely related to my Store pieces. It seeks to present in events what the
store presents in objects. It is a theater of real events (a newsreel) . . .
Have shorts?

Giving hair and muscles and skin to thoughts

Nothing is communicated or represented except through its attachment to an object (even though the object will mean different things at
the same moment to different people) . . . It is the play of consciousness
in reaction to certain objects . . . a play which involves the consciousness of myself my actors and my audience . . . This differs from conventional theater in that the communication is less fixed . . . more in
doubt . . . there is a sequence but not plot or given relation of the events
and objects as they occur . . . the sequence is purely a practical device . . .
plot to me is sentimentality, predetermination, an arrogance on the part
of an author, a harmful fabrication which creates a residue of sentimental
patterns that keep men from perceiving experience . . . this theater aims
to make man compose experience as it changes a constant pleasure and
an instrument of survival . . .

Who is the bum the Rag Man of my dreams

The theater differs from the store in that the objects of the store are
reproductions, reconstructions or alterations of the actual object. This is
also an anti neorealist expression. I have tried to represent my consciousness in relation to the actual object at the moment of my perception of
it. This is complicated by the facts of construction . . . and there is only
one way to handle this: to treat the materials as a complicating factor of
the object, themselves objects of consciousness. On top of this I have
complicated the object by introducing conventions of popular representation and artistic practise (a sort of travesty). The object is a record of
passage through these complications . . . and must be seen as itself and
not in relation to any theory. The aim of putting the store in an actual
neighborhood is to *contrast* it to the actual object . . . not as might be

thought in neorealist terms to point up similarities . . . The store title is in fact a play on words . . . the store means for me: my consciousness. . . .

In the store then, the work is as if done for the spectator whereas in RG theater, using actual objects (though affected by situation) . . . the spectator has more latitude in perception . . . actually there is always this latitude even in relation to the prepared object . . .

my characters are the city-bird-child (chick) and the beggar. innocence and experience. that is my theme: innocence vs. experience (or evil).

good vs. evil. comic innocence. pat.

Farce for Objects, in a bright light . . .

A black and white (upholstered) white convertible
Gold shoes
Water (in the gutter)
An iron . . . in the sun

I am very grateful to the audience for coming each weekend. I cannot deny it is good to have an audience, though the nature of this theater is such that it would go on without an audience as a painter might go on painting with noone to watch him . . . This space has great limitations, I am aware of this . . . partly I enjoy the pressure these limitations put on me . . . I mean the time, the expense and the space . . . I hope you are not too miserable . . . my aim is to develop under these concentrated circumstances a sort of kernel of infinite expansion so that at the end of this season I shall have ten extremely powerful seeds It is becoming obvious I guess that these pieces are not unrelated . . . the "happening" which was in the beginning a very limited form is bearing fruit as a new physical theater, bringing to the dry puritan forms of the US stage the possibilities of a tremendous enveloping force . . .

Theater is the most powerful art form there is because it is the most involving . . . but it is forever becoming lost in trivialities . . . loss of power is a chronic disease of the form . . . realism . . . distance . . . commercial pressures . . . poor theater I no longer see the distinction between theater and visual arts very clearly distinctions I suppose are a civilized disease . . . I see primarily the need to reflect life . . . to give back, which is the only activity that gives man dignity . . . I am especially concerned with physicality, which is evident . . . only painting and sculpture have the power to give man back his physicality (which is not primitivism) when he loses it . . . painting and sculpture have the unique privilege of affecting the other arts in this respect . . .

Documents of the Ray Gun Theater

Ray Gun Theater was a theater among friends. First, through all the theater, there was Pat Oldenburg and Lucas Samaras, and a lot of the style of the theater comes from how they did it. Then there were Gloria Graves, Carolee Schneemann, Lette Eisenhauer, Billy Klüver, Henry Geldzahler—and that is the beginning of a very long list which reaches from the Lower East Side of New York to Los Angeles. Much later, there were many people, volunteers who became friends. All these people worked very hard and without pay. The result was Ray Gun Theater—a wordless, non-narrative theater which consisted of what I could invent with the aid of these friends in time for the performance. It was not doctrinaire. The method was to use fragments, a collage of living parts, in series or in series juxtaposed or superimposed.

At first the ideas came from my notebooks, from clippings and brief descriptions, from the present or past. When these ran out in 1962, incidents for the Theater were developed out of meetings between the performers and from the details of the site where the performances took place.

The documents tonight[1] recall visual details but may leave you guessing as to their connection. It is important to remember that the images were related visually more than thematically, and unities of time and place were often ignored to favor visual unity—Ray Gun Theater was an artist's theater.

The events were also related in time. Duration was an important subject and there was careful, analytical attention to movement, and the relation of movements. This is not evident in the slides of course, and imperfectly evident in the film records which have their own time scheme.

The movements were slow and repetitive, usually. I found that Hawaiian music made the best accompaniment. The Theater was lyrical, but the situation under which it was presented and the audiences often disturbed the mood I was trying to establish.

Ray Gun Theater was a theater of mood, of light, of time, and often approached a sense of the mystery of things—which is always more apparent when words are not used and narrative avoided. Many of the incidents developed into a ritual shape.

Like my group of sculptures shown in the museum below, Ray Gun Theater was a panorama of responses to life and a world to itself. It has recurrent themes which are better recalled by writing about them. There are also many anecdotes which record the problems of presenting personal theater in a puritan society but this too can be written about. This presentation is limited to showing the texture and details of the Ray Gun Theater—what it looked like.

When the notebook sources and the Lower East Side site of the theater seemed exhausted, after the series of performances held in The Store, I took the Theater "on the road," using found sites as fresh stimulation and staging the performances in these sites. These sites included an uptown gallery—to offset the notion that Ray Gun Theater could only be done in funky surroundings; a parking lot in the middle of Los Angeles [in *Autobodys*]; [in *Injun*] a farm-house in Dallas, Texas; and a swimming pool in Al Roon's Health Club on the West Side [in *Washes*]. In this phase, the Theater became more difficult and also more sprawling. The casts grew larger because I could not resist volunteers. Audiences were less prepared. The satisfaction of these pieces was often measured by how they left the community changed by the contact.

After 1966 the original performers had gone their separate ways, into their own fantasy, and I became too engaged by sculpture to do any more but an occasional impromptu composition. The last ambitious performance was [*Massage*] in Stockholm in 1966. I will probably not do any more (but I might). They were a relief from the introspection and loneliness of studio work. By engaging life and other people and their fantasies—the performances fed my work in sculpture.

Out of the Ray Gun Theater came the soft sculptures and many other possibilities for subject matter and materials were discovered and tested in the performances [see *Freighter* in fig. 5.2, *Floor* series in fig. 5.3]. It was really a workshop in natural effects. I tried to restage whatever captured my interest in life around me. The theater was indispensible to developing an art such as mine which grows out of contact with reality.

Note

1. This text was written for a talk at the Museum of Modern Art, New York, in 1969.

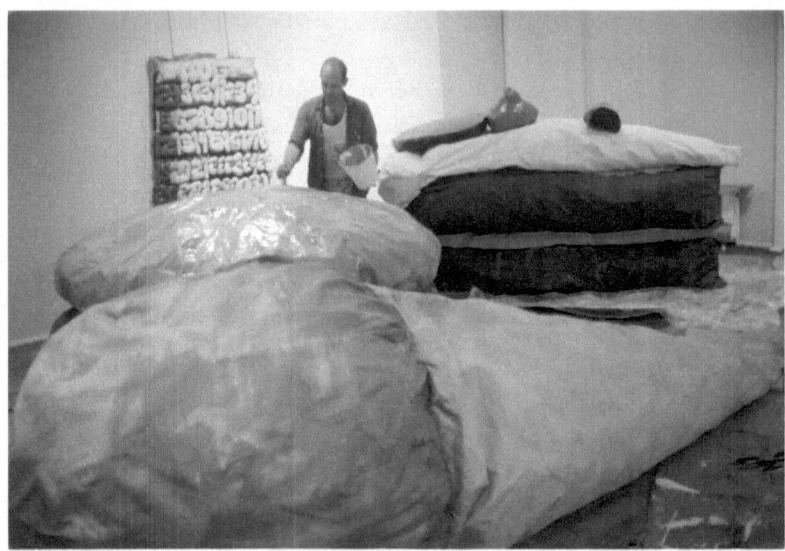

Figure 5.3   Claes Oldenburg working on the
Floor series at the Green Gallery, 15 West Fifty-
seventh Street, New York, August 1962. Photo ©
Robert McElroy/Licensed by VAGA, New York, NY;
courtesy the Oldenburg van Bruggen Studio.

In Conversation with Claes Oldenburg

Benjamin H. D. Buchloh

BENJAMIN BUCHLOH: Did you know Duchamp? Did you have any exchange with him at all?

CLAES OLDENBURG: I had some interesting encounters with him, but not long talks or anything. In Pasadena, in 1963, was really the first time I saw the work, I mean really saw the work, except for rumors, and it was a very exciting show. Then he made himself available after the show to talk to people and sign things and so on. And he used to come, before that, to performances.

BB: Yes, he does actually mention this, that he sometimes went to happenings.

CO: He came to at least three performances that I had done. I remember one performance [*Moveyhouse*] in 1965 which took place in a movie theater where the performance was in the seats and the audience had to stand. Duchamp asked if he could sit down because he was too tired to stand, so he became the only person in the audience sitting in the performance. Another performance, in 1962 in *The Store*, ended with performers in burlap bags, crawling out of the bags, expiring at the feet of the audience.

BB: That was one of your performances?

CO: Yes. I found that I was expiring at his feet. So there were contacts, but never anything more than a cordial hello if I met him at a party, and so forth. I never played chess with him.

BB: Also, if, as you say, in the early 1960s the major points of departure in your own work were already clearly defined . . .

CO: Yes, he was a historical figure.

BB: What about iconography? That is obviously an art-historical problem; you are, as I see it, the first sculptor after Duchamp who uses a kind of iconography that is completely alien to all preceding sculpture, which is the industrially produced, ready-made object.

CO: Well, I saw some of Duchamp's work at Yale when I was an undergraduate there in the late 1940s. I did see that wonderful painting, that long painting [*Tu m'*, 1918] which has the brush sticking out of it. So I saw his work and was aware of it also through art history courses and such. And certain works had certainly stuck in my mind, like the dust-gathering pieces, and the *Three Standard Stoppages*.

BB: Some of them were also in the Museum of Modern Art collection. I don't know if they were on display in the 1950s, but the *Stoppages*, for example, have been in the collection for quite a while. But your iconography, you would say, comes from a variety of sources, primarily from American art of the late 1950s?

CO: I would say so.

BB: Happenings, Rauschenberg, Johns—if anything, they parallel, rather than being a direct reference to Dada, or to Duchamp in particular. Your selection of materials, your iconography, your procedures or production, were all denying every single prevailing sculptural convention. If one compares what the literature at the time presented as sculpture . . .

CO: Yes, that is true. I don't think I took the word *sculpture* very seriously, because I don't think the issue was whether or not it was sculpture or painting. It was just construction of some kind, and I think that's the important thing because that gave you a sense of freedom.

BB: Did you want your work to have stability and permanence, or did you consider it to be props that could be discarded?

CO: Well, that was an issue. Everybody was wondering whether things should be permanent. You had someone like [Allan] Kaprow who maintained that nothing should be permanent, and yet he did manage to have a few pieces survive.

BB: Luckily. Now we are glad that we can see them.

CO: In 1959 I worked a lot in papier-mâché, using newspaper and cardboard, which is all acid content, and yet some pieces have survived, at least up to this point. I wasn't trying to make perishable art; I was just trying to make an art out of perishable materials, or materials which under normal conditions were perishable. What I did to them made them less perishable.

BB: Did your materials or your choice of materials have political connotations?

CO: Definitely, yes.

BB: Like denying high art conventions and materials?

CO: Right. Art can be made out of rags. Eventually I put this all into a kind of programmatic statement.

BB: The long statement in *Store Days*?

CO: Yes. That was directed against anybody's claim about sculpture. If someone had started an argument about sculpture, I would have maintained that I had a right to do this as sculpture. But that wasn't really the main issue. The issue was to make art, or to make something which reflected my presence in a certain context.

BB: But the issue that is even more important than the question of permanence is that of the "public-ness" of your sculpture. Since your works *The Street* and *The Store*, we have encountered a radically new definition of what public sculpture can be in the present. After all, *The Store* was meant to function potentially like a store. People from the street were allowed to come in, weren't they?

CO: Yes, they were. But realistically speaking, it was stacked against that because people in that neighborhood just aren't going to come in when they see something as strange as this. If people came in from the street, it was kids, or just curious people. I would see them at the window— they'd look in, but nobody would come in.

BB: So it was more conceived as a private studio that could be open on certain occasions to art world people and friends.

CO: It was open—anybody could come in at any time—and I worked there more or less in view of the people who looked in. Even at night I would be visible.

BB: But wasn't there an inherent assault on esoteric qualities of high art, in every aspect of *The Store*?

CO: Yes, but I think it was a matter of two things. One thing was to admit the commercial nature of art production by comparing it to ordinary production, and of course that was carried further because people came down and bought things at absurd prices. They bought a loaf of bread for ninety-nine dollars [fig. 6.1, on top of the stove].

BB: A loaf of bread *piece*, work.

CO: Yes. Instead of paying a normal price for a loaf of bread, they would pay ninety-nine dollars for it. Then, on the other hand, it was an anti-museum situation, an antipedestal situation, with all kinds of jokes on pedestals, museum presentations, and so on. But it never was—and I think it would have been naive in a way to have made it—a real store. I think that would have meant *not* recognizing the realities of artistic existence. And I didn't want to be a hypocrite about that; I wanted to air all of the issues.

BB: Yes, I remember you referring in one statement to *The Store*, or any store—at the time you were looking at the Lower East Side—assuming the role or the function of the museum, so that you make an explicit equation between the museum and the store. So that means the commodity status of the work did become an issue; the fetishization of the singularized object, as it happens in the museum context, was an issue for you at the time. And I think probably very much in the way that it had become an issue in Duchamp's work. Possibly you weren't even linking it up to the full ramifications of the readymade in the late 1950s.

CO: No, I think that's very true. And it wasn't so much against sculpture as against methods of dealing with the presentation of art, the definition of art.

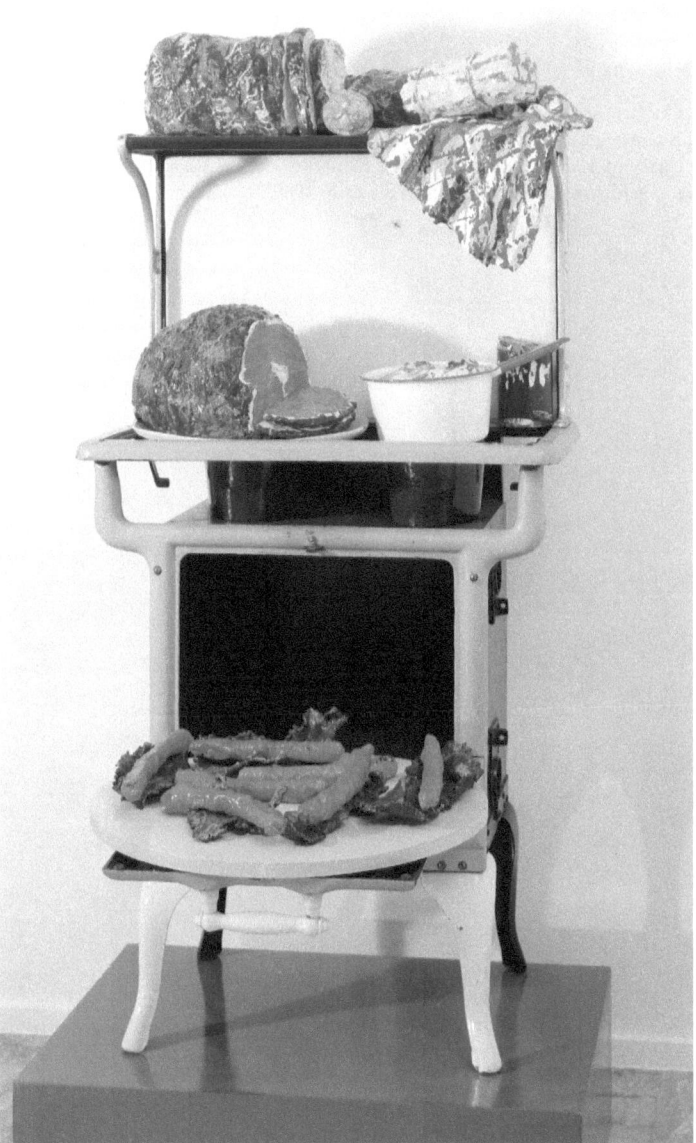

Figure 6.1 *Assorted Food on a Stove*, 1962. Muslin and burlap soaked in plaster, painted with enamel, with utensils and stove, 58 × 28 × 27½ in. (147.3 × 71.1 × 69.9 cm). Ludwig Collection, on permanent loan to Kunstmuseum Basel, Switzerland. Photo courtesy the Oldenburg van Bruggen Studio.

Note

This is an excerpt from interviews that were conducted for the purposes of research in 1985. This conversation centered on the reception of the historical avant-gardes, specifically the legacy of Marcel Duchamp and the rediscovery of the work of the Russian and Soviet avant-gardes by American artists in the early 1960s.

Oldenburg's *Store*

Cécile Whiting

"The truth is, the art galleries are being invaded by the pinheaded and contemptible style of gum chewers, bobby soxers, and worse, delinquents," complained Max Kozloff in March of 1962.[1] Dorothy Seckler added: "Gallery walls formerly devoted to dribbles now display mammoth spaghetti. A niche once reserved for crushed tin and picturesque castoffs now bristles with bright and shining tinned merchandise. The invaders have cornered galleries known for their cachet of sophistication."[2] Sounding an alarm, a number of critics in the early 1960s warned of aliens mounting an assault on the hallowed halls of the art gallery. Critical outrage targeted the artists, a number of whom had backgrounds in commercial art, and the visual rhetoric of pop art, which was largely indebted to the mass media. But critics also bristled at the new audience for pop art and its novel ways of looking at images.

Displays of pop art disrupted expectations fostered by gallery shows of abstract expressionism about how works of art should be viewed. In exhibitions of abstract expressionist painting, best exemplified by presentations of color field art during the 1940s and 1950s, images hanging side by side dominated the walls of stark, carefully lit, intimate spaces.[3] Such displays implicitly promised the critic and connoisseur a quasi-religious refuge from the clamor of the marketplace in which to focus exclusively on the work of art. The distribution of pop art in the gallery marked a breach in the protocols of display observed by shows of abstract expressionism: for instance, in 1962 Claes Oldenburg's sculptures of food and clothes spilled across the floor of the Green Gallery in New York in an apparently haphazard manner, while at the Ferus Gallery in Los Angeles

Andy Warhol's paintings of Campbell soup cans aligned themselves on a ledge around the wall like so many cans on the shelf of a supermarket. Though diverse in kind, exhibitions of pop art repudiated the conventions of auratic display and the concomitant hushed modes of viewing promoted by galleries specializing in abstract expressionism.[4]

Displays of pop art did more than disturb the ambience of the gallery; they also welcomed in the practices of consumerism. Critics, while perhaps justified in their fear of a rejection of the established conventions of abstract expressionist exhibition practices, were mistaken to imagine a general cultural leveling when consumer artifacts met artworks face to face in these spaces. For, while pop exhibitions did presume a certain group of visitors incapable of distinguishing works of art from commodities, they also anticipated a privileged set of spectators able to assay, with nuance, the difference between the two. Over and again, we shall see that the most significant cultural work performed by these exhibitions lay in the manner in which they juxtaposed these two groups of viewers and their ways of evaluating objects.

On East Second Street, far from the grand emporia ensconced on Fifth Avenue, a plain shop of one modest room opened its door to the public in December of 1961. For a period of two months, Claes Oldenburg converted his small studio on the Lower East Side of Manhattan into a discount store. During its short-lived existence, *The Store* displayed for sale over one hundred sculptures emulating a wide range of inexpensive goods (fig. 7.1). *The Store*, with its diverse merchandise covering every available surface of the interior, did not immediately leap out from the other neighborhood shops. At first glance, Oldenburg's transformed studio seemed to join the surrounding delis and variety shops in welcoming the shopper to snoop for tempting bargains.

The sculptures in *The Store*, viewed in the literal terms of what they portrayed, duplicated the sort of cheap merchandise available in many of the small shops located in the surrounding Lower East Side. Oldenburg's slices of pie evoked the sweets produced by local bakeries; his sandwiches corresponded to those found in delis on Houston Street; his wedding mannequin and bouquet mimicked the type displayed along "bride's row" on Grand Street; and his girdle, dresses, and jacket echoed the inexpensive clothes in the open air shops along Orchard Street. One did not go to *The Store*, or for that matter to any of the shops on the Lower East Side, to purchase the newest, mass-produced appliances and packaged foods for sale in the chains of department stores, supermarkets,

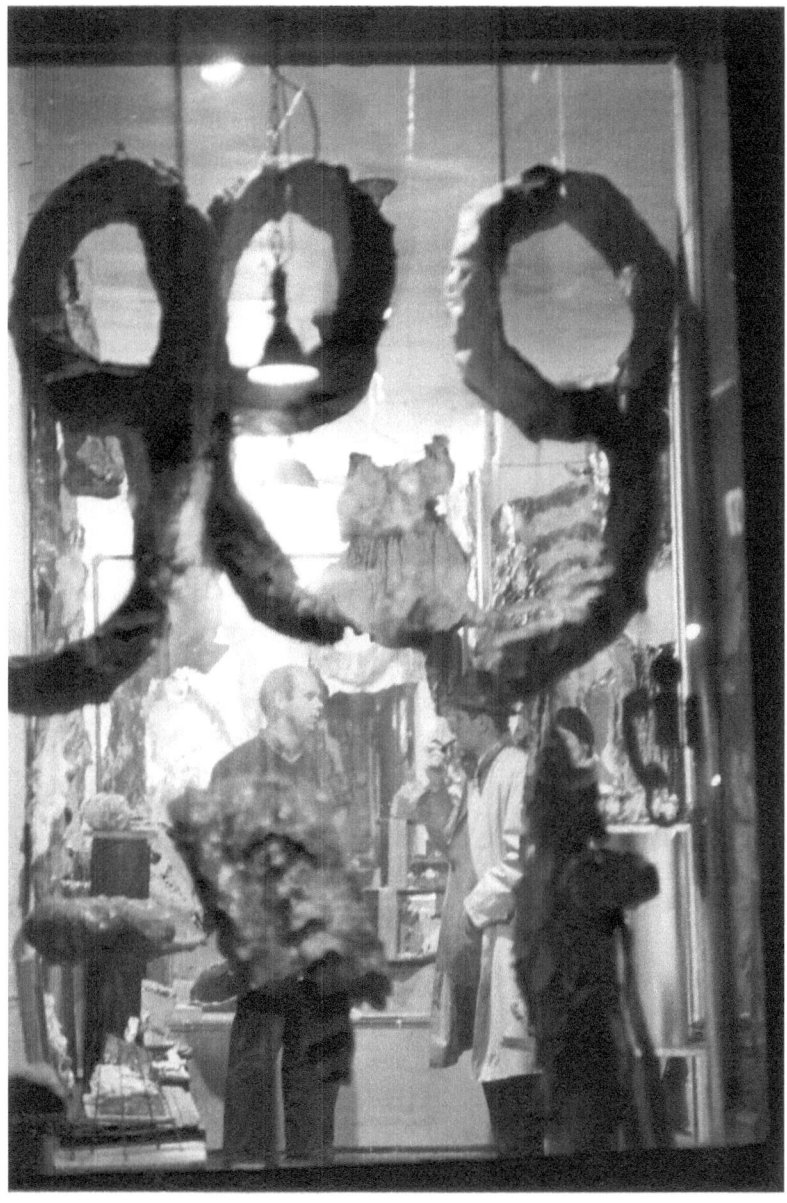

Figure 7.1 *The Store*, December 1, 1961–January
31, 1962. 107 East Second Street, New York
(view through the front window). Photo © Robert
McElroy/Licensed by VAGA, New York, NY;
courtesy the Oldenburg van Bruggen Studio.

and fast food restaurants that proliferated across the country after World War II.

Oldenburg, moreover, borrowed the display techniques of the small discount shops of the area. "After seeing Oldenburg's *Store*, or a performance of his theatre," critic Ellen H. Johnson confessed, "one feels compelled to walk and linger through the Lower East Side, suddenly aware of the curious, tawdry beauty of store-windows full of stale hors d'oeuvres, hamburgers on Rheingold ads, stockinged legs."[5] "Full," Johnson said, and the term applied equally well to both *The Store* and its neighboring shops. Oldenburg's clothing, food, and assorted wares crowded the storefront window, hung from the ceiling and walls, rested on chairs and tables, or lay in glass cases.[6] Similarly, the closely packed shops in the neighborhood, whether specializing in one type of merchandise such as hardware or offering a variety of goods for sale, placed all of their stock on view. Merchandise even spilled onto the streets: clothes at one apparel shop, for instance, hung on racks standing on the sidewalk and swung from the signs above the door. The display techniques at *The Store* and the surrounding shops invariably stressed abundance and diversity of cheaply manufactured goods.

With their teeming, disorderly array of goods, both *The Store* and the neighborhood shops exhibited precisely those principles of merchandising that window-dressing "how-to" manuals criticized as outdated and ineffectual. "Another lost cause in display is 'mass' merchandise," Emily Mauger carped. "Some store owners feel compelled to stack, pile and place as much merchandise in their windows as possible. . . . Focused attention on one item is much more powerful than on a dozen."[7] As early as the turn of the twentieth century, certain stores selected a handful of articles, rather than flaunting a cornucopia of varied goods, as a strategy to sell precious items.[8] By the 1950s, selectivity contributed to the "art" of display in most expensive stores. As Robert Kretschmer commented in 1952: "The modern high-class store shows a few carefully chosen articles in a single unit of a display to give an atmosphere of quality and exclusiveness of style."[9] Based on the criterion of selectivity, *The Store* failed to demonstrate modern display techniques and to espouse the standard of good taste expected on Fifth Avenue; it adopted instead the practices of shops targeting a broader and more popular audience.

Nothing about the type of goods, mode of display, or scale of operation of *The Store* summoned forth the practices of modern-day consumerism. The thematic selection of Oldenburg's artworks certainly associated them with a bygone age. Writing in 1963, Johnson recalled her assessment of *The Store*: "On first impression the cash register and other 'machines' in the Store looked surprisingly nostalgic and old-fashioned."[10] Sidney Tillim similarly concluded about *The Store*, "it was all so hopelessly nostalgic."[11] Tillim's reaction conformed to the retrospective tone characteristic of many descriptions of the neighborhood in general. Although only a few guidebooks to New York City mentioned the area, even in passing, they filled their pages, then as now, with black-and-white documentary photographs from the turn of the century, and reminisced about the immigrants from Eastern Europe who had flooded into the Lower East Side at that time.[12] All touristic descriptions of the Lower East Side, whether they expressed sentiments of fascination or repulsion, associated this neighborhood with the historical past.[13]

Divorced from midtown by both display practices and time, the Lower East Side shops—and seemingly Oldenburg's *Store* as well—addressed a different type of shopper than did Bonwit Teller. Guidebooks from the 1960s revealed expectations about who shopped in each neighborhood in New York, and how they purchased goods. In photographs of the Lower East Side, modestly dressed women scrutinized products hanging on racks or piled on tables, and picked up individual items one by one.[14] They selected goods through the sensory mode of touch rather than relying on vision; and certainly the practice of displaying like items in open abundance catered to this shopper's habit of tactile selection. Careful scrutiny of merchandise and modest attire suggested a consumer ethic of common sense and thrift. *The Store*, with its apparently inexpensive, slightly outmoded merchandise arrayed on easily accessible tables and walls, would seem to have conformed to the conventions of display and consumption operative in the neighborhood.

And yet *The Store* obviously did not actually sell cheap merchandise even as it emulated that mode of commerce. It offered for sale pop sculptures instead. The handcrafted appearance of Oldenburg's objects—their rippling edges, irregular shapes, odd sizes, and richly encrusted surfaces—repudiated the external uniformity of the machine-made products available in neighboring shops. Oldenburg's objects, moreover, disdained the imperative of the bargain store whereby all objects had to have a functional use. The brightly painted strawberry shortcake could not be eaten; the dress seemingly blowing in the wind could never, in its rocklike stiffness, be worn. And, of course, the prices on the tags, which reflected the actual expense of the artworks in dollars rather than the cost of cheap consumer goods, far surpassed the pocketbook of the hunter of real bargain wares.

Even as its parodies represented the activities of the bargain shopper, *The Store* actually welcomed a different class of viewer to the Lower East Side: the art connoisseur well versed in recent trends in contemporary art, exercising distanced, aesthetic evaluation of the sculptures. No need for such viewers to manipulate the objects of display to assess their worth; no need to choose by the sense of touch to determine value among a collection of like items. Rather, artistic vision claimed this space as its rightful domain: to appreciate the thick, lavish drips of enamel paint covering the surfaces of Oldenburg's food and clothing depended on a familiarity with the abstract expressionist brushstroke. Critic Jill Johnston articulated the point most bluntly: "Oldenburg has refined an Action-like technique, many objects being pleasurable in pure color and sponta-neous design."[15] Among Johnston and her like, the trained eye, not the instinctive hand, ferreted out quality in the works of art.

Yet knowledge of contemporary art also allowed for a humorous response to the formal aspects of the sculptures. Detecting an ironic turn, a crossing of cultural if not class lines, between the spontaneous surface brushstroke and the sausage or hamburger that it bedecked offered ob-vious comic relief to the high seriousness of abstract expressionism. A number of critics reveled in the humor. Sonya Rudikoff, writing about Oldenburg's objects when they were later exhibited at the Green Gallery uptown, asserted: "My first reaction was one of enormous amusement and pleasure. . . . The paint is applied with equal disdain, is high in col-our, weird: who ever saw such hideously green salad, such orange-y and brown-y bread?"[16]

As Rudikoff's question suggests, recognition of the formal and pa-rodic qualities of Oldenburg's sculptures secured the difference of these objects from their commonplace sources. Indeed, the extent and meaning of the distinctions between Oldenburg's sculptures and actual consumer goods developed among commentators into a topic of analysis and de-bate built upon the distinction between real items and artistic representa-tions of them. All critics writing about *The Store* and its contents shared the presupposition that the world of lower-class commerce evoked by Oldenburg's installation really existed out there in the tiny stores of the Lower East Side, distinctly beyond the realm of artistic representation. And these same critics, even when they argued over whether *The Store* nostalgically recalled the real world or parodied it mercilessly,[17] regarded the work not as a true example of such commerce but as a representation of it. The difference between the surfaces of Oldenburg's sculptures and the hefted weight of functional objects in the bargain store thus not only marked out the distance between vision and touch, refined sensibility and consumer acquisition; it also defined the distinction between representation and the real.

The two corresponding manners of viewing objects on display, however, lacked symmetry: where shoppers apparently lived only in the world of the real, the critic and connoisseur could see both and assay the relation between the reality of commerce and the representations of art. Even more, the critic and connoisseur, unlike the lower-class shopper, could apply the skills of aesthetic evaluation to both realms. "He is the Cecil Beaton of the regressive Skid Row of our lost and slightly smelly innocence,"[18] pronounced Jack Kroll about Oldenburg in *Art News*. To compare Oldenburg to Beaton, the famous postwar photographer of haute couture, and to see the Lower East Side through Beaton's lens repudiated the claim to objective reportage implicitly asserted by documentary photographs and historical reminiscenses of the neighborhood. Many critics hinted that they had discovered an aesthetic in the mundane objects that they had previously taken for granted;[19] they viewed this world of commerce as if it were a work of art. Where bargain shoppers appeared engaged directly in the real as they handled and bought artifacts, critics established their distance from the neighborhood—and lower-class commerce—by treating it as aesthetic spectacle.

Evaluating the objects in Oldenburg's *Store* based on their formal qualities, assessing their differences from the real, and subsequently treating the real as an object of aesthetic contemplation were the critical pleasures made possible by Oldenburg's *Store*. In savoring the aesthetic dimensions of the sculptures and goods in surrounding stores, art critics such as Tillim and Johnston distinguished themselves from the bargain shopper and her practices of judging real objects in the neighboring shops. Like the sophisticated shopper viewing display director Gene Moore's Andy Warhol window on Fifth Avenue, the critic and connoisseur deployed the skills of aesthetic visual analysis in order to differentiate themselves from those viewers—mere shoppers, lacking aesthetic sensibility—who seemingly failed to maintain a proper analytic distance from the objects on display.

From the perspective of the department store owner, the sophisticated shopper in front of a Bonwit Teller window ultimately lost that distance as she entered the store to buy the dresses sharing space with the paintings. From the perspective of Oldenburg in his role as the proprietor of a temporary storefront gallery, connoisseurs could potentially follow that same path as they purchased real works of art. Critics, not themselves making purchases of either the bargain or artistic variety, might seem to avoid this collapse of analytic distance, this slide from aesthetic contemplation to commercial engagement. In practice, however, even the critics appeared to succumb to commercial allure. After trotting out his predictable set of formalist pronouncements on Oldenburg's painted surfaces, for instance, Tillim felt the tug of a consumer's urge generated by the subject matter of the works: "It was a pleasure, and then it became disturbing, and I fell into the critic's habit—or was it the consumer's—of examining individual items. I began, in other words, to draw away from the experience via the aesthetic outlet that had been so carefully provided. I found the candy sticks too unformed, mere varied blobs of plaster and color."[20] Jill Johnston, like Tillim, switched from analytical observer to yearning shopper with striking ease: "Oldenburg's painted plaster food, clothing and other living accessories are as personal as any sculpture has ever been. Yet most of his objects simulate the original product to the point of arousing the same desire associated with the original."[21] The confusion of roles in these texts discloses a type of aesthetic judgment that did not necessarily keep consumer desire safely at bay. Aesthetic taste, which had served to differentiate the sophisticated shopper from her unrefined compatriot on Fifth Avenue before collapsing into the good taste of the high-class shopper, here devolves further into taste of a purely alimentary sort: the critic's mouth waters at the prospect of cake and candy stick.

The critics, of course, hardly succumbed wantonly to the tugs of such basic desires.[22] Indeed, the critics' prose could toy with the conceit of equating art to food precisely because their aesthetic pose held sufficient self-assurance to play it all as a joke: not consuming the cakes actually but rather parodying the consumption of this parody food. Their comments, however, may reveal more than the conceit intended. For if the critics could control their appetites for food, the parody could collapse on itself to disclose a hunger for art that ultimately underwrote the critical enterprise. What purpose, ultimately, for this scribbling around painted surfaces and such if art was not something to be desired? It was the pretense of the art market, after all, that the aesthetically inclined needed art in a manner akin to the needs for basic survival of less sensitive souls. In the end, the temptation for art set up by the practice of criticism for one class of viewers paralleled the temptation for consumer goods set up for another by the displays of abundance on the Lower East Side. Just as the Warhol window at Bonwit Teller could draw its various female consumers together at the moment of the tasteful purchase, Oldenburg's *Store* could unite its class-stratified audience under the sign of desire.

Notes

1. Max Kozloff, "'Pop Culture,' Metaphysical Disgust, and the New Vulgarians," *Art International* 7 (March 1962), p. 36.

2. Dorothy Gees Seckler, "Folklore of the Banal," *Art in America* 50 (Winter 1962), p. 57.

3. Generally, art galleries during the twentieth century, as Brian O'Doherty has demonstrated, increasingly dispensed with decorative ornamentation, which might distract from artworks; they painted their walls white, sealed their windows, and flooded their rooms with even light. Brian O'Doherty, *Inside the White Cube* (Santa Monica: Lapis Press, 1986). My understanding of displays of color field painting is based on Joanna R. Roche, "The Rhetoric of Exhibition: Regarding Rothko," M.A. thesis, University of California, Los Angeles, 1991. The quasi-religious aura created by the art gallery exhibiting color field painting finds its literal realization in the Rothko Chapel in Houston.

4. Happenings in the late 1950s also formed an alternative tradition of display to abstract expressionism by introducing crowds, noise, and debris into the space of the art gallery.

5. Ellen H. Johnson, "The Living Object," *Art International* 7 (January 1963), p. 43.

6. Claes Oldenburg's inventory of *The Store* from December 1961 lists 107 items and their prices. Claes Oldenburg, *Store Days: Documents from The Store (1961) and Ray Gun Theater (1962)*, ed. Claes Oldenburg and Emmett Williams (New York: Something Else Press, 1967).

7. Emily M. Mauger, *Modern Display Techniques* (New York: Fairchild, 1969), p. 73. See also Lester Gaba, *The Art of Window Display* (New York: Studio Publications and Thomas Y. Crowell Company, 1952).

8. Leonard S. Marcus, *The American Store Window* (New York: Whitney Library of Design, Watson-Guptill, 1978), pp. 18–19. L. Frank Baum promoted "the simple artistic arrangement of a few attractive goods," in *The Art of Decorating Dry Goods Windows and Interiors* (Chicago: Merchants Record, 1924), p. 14.

9. Robert Kretschmer, *Window and Interior Display: Principles of Visual Merchandising* (Scranton: Laurel Publishers, 1952), p. 6.

10. Johnson, "The Living Object," p. 44.

11. Sidney Tillim, "Month in Review," *Arts* 36 (February 1962), p. 36.

12. Oliver E. Allen, *New York, New York: A History of the World's Most Exhilarating and Challenging City* (New York: Atheneum/Macmillan Publishing, 1990); Fred W. McDarrah, *New York, N.Y.* (New York: Corinth Books, 1964); Andreas Feininger, *New York in the Forties* (New York: Dover Publishing, 1978); Victor Laredo, *New York City: A Photographic History* (New York: Dover Publications, 1973); *New York City Guide and Almanac*

1957–58 (New York: New York University Press, 1957); *Portal to America: The Lower East Side 1870–1925*, ed. Allon Schoener (New York: Holt, Rinehart and Winston, 1967); and Norval White, *New York: A Physical History* (New York: Atheneum, 1987).

13. Compare, for instance, the celebratory commemoration of the Lower East Side in Schoener, *Portal to America*, to the obvious disgust expressed in *New York: A Guide to the Empire State* (New York: Oxford University Press, 1940; no author).

14. See also Feininger, *New York in the Forties*, p. 133.

15. Jill Johnston, "Claes Oldenburg," *Art News* 61 (November 1962), p. 13. While Johnston is commenting on the Oldenburg exhibit at the Green Gallery, she is specifically discussing the plaster objects that were seen at *The Store*.

16. Sonya Rudikoff, "New York Letter," *Art International* 6 (November 1962), p. 62.

17. Examples of this debate culled from reviews of exhibitions of Oldenburg's sculpture, including his work shown at the "New Realists" exhibit in 1962 at the Sidney Janis Gallery, include: Dore Ashton, "High Tide for Assemblage," *Studio* 165 (January 1963), p. 25; Thomas Hess, "New Realists," *Art News* 61 (December 1962), pp. 12–13; Johnson, "The Living Object"; Hilton Kramer, "Art," *The Nation* 195 (November 17, 1962), p. 334; "Pop Art: Cult of the Commonplace," *Time* 81 (May 3, 1963), pp. 69–72; Pierre Restany, "The New Realism," *Art in America* 51 (February 1963), pp. 102–104; Barbara Rose, "Dada Then and Now," *Art International* 7 (January 1963), p. 25; Sonya Rudikoff, "New Realists in New York," *Art International* 7 (January 1963), pp. 39–40; and Irving Sandler, "In the Art Galleries," *New York Post*, November 18, 1962, section 2, p. 12.

18. Jack Kroll, "Situations and Environments," *Art News* 60 (September 1961), p. 16. This quotation actually refers to Oldenburg's exhibition in the fall at the Martha Jackson Gallery. The critic refers to the sculpture in that exhibit as "giantesque rummage sale, huge papier-mâché bargains in little girls' dresses, mink coats, prosthetic limbs, abandoned flags and suicides' bathing suits." Many of these same items reappeared a few months later in *The Store*.

19. See, for example, Johnson, "The Living Object," p. 43; Hess, "New Realists," p. 13; Restany, "The New Realism," pp. 102–104; and Sandler, "In the Art Galleries," p. 12.

20. Tillim, "Month in Review," p. 36.

21. Jill Johnston, "The Artist in a Coca-Cola World," *Village Voice*, January 31, 1963, p. 24.

22. Barbara Rose writes that while *The Store* was a "rousing public success . . . only a small part of its 'inventory' was sold, and it closed with a net loss of $285." Barbara Rose, *Claes Oldenburg* (New York: Museum of Modern Art, 1970), p. 70.

The Transformation of Daddy Warbucks: An Interview with Claes Oldenburg

Robert Pincus-Witten

It is fitting that the thirty-four-year-old pop artist Claes Oldenburg should look somewhat like Skeezix in *Gasoline Alley*. Pop art draws on comic strips, as well as on the brutal realism of billboards, movie stills, and the mass-produced objects (for instance, beer cans and car parts) that are an inescapable part of urban, everyday living. The familiar pop image is transformed, like stock newsreel footage in a Truffaut movie.

Seemingly incongruous events and objects flash upon the pop canvas, again like other movies—Alain Resnais's—and the random placing of the incongruous suddenly changes the expected continuity and environment of a pop painting. It is the way the city obtrudes on us, and Claes Oldenburg is a city artist.

He was born in Stockholm, spent twenty years in Chicago (his father was the Swedish consul here), and moved on to New York anonymity and now acclaim. He is largely responsible for a kind of dramatization of pop painting, called a happening. The Oldenburg happening, billed as the Ray Gun Theater, is mounted in New York at The Store, an old emporium that is both studio and salon for his objects—sculptures of pie wedges, ice cream sundaes, heterogeneous garments, and the like.

Oldenburg recently returned to Chicago and brought controversy with him. His objects were exhibited at the Richard Feigen Gallery and in the Art Institute's 66th Annual American Exhibition. In February [1963], he staged three performances of his happening [*Gayety*] in Lexington Hall at the University of Chicago. The following interview by Robert Pincus-Witten, art lecturer and critic, took place at that time.

ROBERT PINCUS-WITTEN: Claes, what is a happening?

CLAES OLDENBURG: A happening is a breaking down of the barriers between the arts, and something close to an actual experience. It should be a very free form, a very ambiguous and suggestive form. I think it's filled with unexplored and primitive possibilities. I like it to be that way—like it to be as unpredictable as possible.

RPW: How does it look?

CO: Well, for example, at one point during the performances at Lexington Hall, I was watching my wife, Pat, dancing in the middle of the room with a couple of red oil-cloth hearts about five and a half feet in diameter. There was smoke in the air from talcum powder that had been raised . . . dust. It looked like a night club, and yet it wasn't a night club; there were other things going on in the space. So it had this double view, a dislocated aspect. It looked real and yet wasn't real.

RPW: How would you describe the symbolic content of a happening? Apparently, in the Lexington Hall happenings, you created a miniature version of Chicago [fig. 8.1]. I can be quite specific about the layout of the thing and the sources of certain situations in that happening.

CO: For example, the space was a large space in contrast to the congested small space which I use in New York, which seems more suitable in New York. The space in Chicago is very wide open and high, and gives you a sense of nostalgia. There happened to be some sinks in the space, and those represented the lake to me. In the back of the room, in a direction which might be south if you took the sinks to be east, there was Harry Bouras's studio. He is a welder and when he welds, he throws up a lot of light—which reminded me of Gary and the South Chicago steel works. In the center of this space—not really in the center, it was placed in about the location and relationship that the Loop has to the rest of the map of Chicago—was a square stage . . . and that came to represent the Loop to me. Then I had the North Side, the West Side, and you see, starting with this layout I could make some identifications which were sort of frivolous; George Kokines, the artist, throwing mud across from east to west hitting the west wall could somehow be identified with the rising sun, the sun going across the landscape and down.

RPW: Would a spectator immediately realize the symbolic import of these experiences?

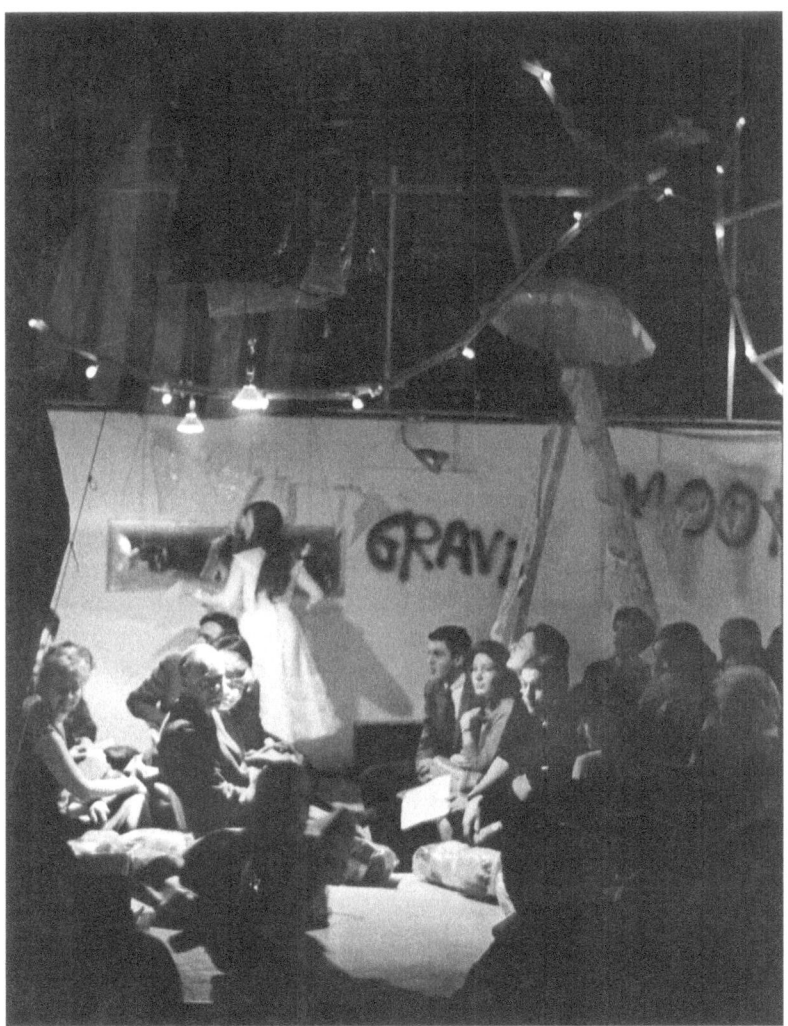

Figure 8.1   *Gayety*, February 8–10, 1963.
Lexington Hall, University of Chicago. Photo
courtesy the Oldenburg van Bruggen Studio.

CO: On the program I put "A Map of Chicago" and, if somebody read that and thought about it, it might occur to them [fig. 8.2]. I'm not sure that it's terribly important that they realize it, however. It's just a way that made it possible for me to get a number of ideas—a number of formal situations. If you get one good idea like that, then one thing leads to another. I like to work with very simple ideas.

RPW: Do you consider the happening a work of art, or is it only the experience of this unraveling, this deciphering of the scene as it unrolls or unfolds?

CO: Well, I think the happening is a potential work of art. I talk of it all the time as a composition or a work of art. But maybe that's not so important. Maybe it's more important that it's a certain kind of experience: simply sitting and watching in an isolated way something that's very familiar. I'd like to get away from the notion of a work of art as something outside of experience, something that is located in museums, something that is terribly precious. I'd like to think of a normal, natural experience in terms of a work of art. I don't think the notion of the detached work of art—this aristocratic work of art—is a very useful notion anymore. People don't want that. They suffer with that notion and they would prefer to have a redefinition of art in something closer to themselves.

RPW: Is the audience's pleasure derived from an intellectual recognition of this formal content, or does it take pleasure in the passions evoked by the sudden and unexpected coming together of the formal experiences that you've arranged?

CO: Well, if your audience had been Japanese, there would have been no problem; they simply would have watched it, and then, at the end of the performance, they would have left and asked no questions about it. But a Western audience has to have explanations. They really can't watch anything for its own sake. They have to have an explanation first or a reason for watching it. They really don't watch a thing. They follow an idea as it unravels, and everything represents the unraveling of an idea. The happening, as I practice it, creates a lot of discomfort for the audience. It's an attempt to rattle them out of the notion that they're going to watch a play or an idea unfold. I try to make them uncomfortable to a certain degree, to make them bored to a certain degree, and to make them receptive to a new way of looking at things. For example, and this

RAY   THEATER   GUN

Our Want and Need List

1. Soap and tooth paste.
2. Boys' basketball shoes, sizes 6-10.
3. Sheets and sheeting—twin beds.
4. Army blankets for twin size beds.
5. Bed spreads for twin beds—any color; or material to make them.
6. Toilet paper and paper hand towels, $10 and $4.50 per case respectively.
7. Loose leaf paper, scratch pads, composition books and pencil tablets.
8. Little girls' coats and jackets.
9. Girls' white socks, sizes 6-10.
10. Boys' briefs or shorts, sizes 6-12.
11. Boys' jeans and shirts, all sizes.
12. Boys' socks, sizes 7-12.
13. Little boys' shoes, sizes 13, 1, 2, 3, 4.
14. 4H and 6H drawing pencils.
15. Mechanic and carpenter hand tools.
16. Tools, hammers, saws, paint brushes.
17. Material for dresses and skirts.
18. Sewing machine needles — No. 15x1, size 16.
19. Table cloths, either white or colored 60''x120'', or material to make them.
20. Adhesive tape, all widths.
21. Nash's and Butter-Nut coffee strips.
22. Betty Crocker coupons, Hi-lex coupons, Rawleigh's coupons.
23. Gold Bond coupons.
24. Rakes.
25. T-shirts for grade and high school boys.
26. Basketballs.
27. Shoe Polish—Black, Brown & White.
28. Portable electric tools (Drills, Sanders, etc.)
29. Unbleached muslin for sheets.
30. Toboggan and skis.

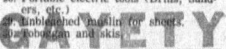

OVERTURE
6 - COMBINATIONS - 6
FINALE
By

CLAES OLDENBURG

February 8, 9, 10
1963
8:30 P. M.

In Lexington Hall, 5835 South University Avenue. $1.50 Per Person. Reservations necessary. Please call WH 4-6638 9 AM to 6 PM weekdays and BU 8-9682 after 6 PM and Sundays.

Figure 8.2 Program for *Gayety*, February 8–10, 1963. Lexington Hall, University of Chicago. The text "Wopeedah" was found by the artist on a bus in Chicago, and served as a starting point for materials used in the performance. Photo courtesy the Oldenburg van Bruggen Studio.

is characteristic of all my happenings, the audience is made to wait a long time for the thing to begin, and under very difficult conditions. When they came into Lexington Hall, I threw a lot of chairs in front of them so that they had a hard time walking, and then they were seated in a peculiar way so that they couldn't see all of the action at the same time; they could only see fragments.

People say that I'm against the audience, but that's not true at all. I don't know much about Zen teaching . . . but I understand the preliminary is some sort of punishment or some sort of dislocation of ordinary notions through enigmas. Sometimes the teacher beats the student over the head, and so on. As I say, I don't know enough about this, but it sounds somewhat like the sort of thing I want to do. Say we have the kind of person I would like to have at my happening. That would be a person who would come not once but each of the three evenings, since, of course, it changes from one evening to another. Each time he came, he would sit in a different place and see a different relationship and different fragments. This person would not only come to the three performances that I had here, but would reserve his judgment until he had seen a few more happenings. I wish to lead the audience into a special way of looking at things so that one happening should be followed by another happening and each happening should be seen several times.

RPW: How would you distinguish your happenings from the happenings created by other artists, say George Brecht or Jim Dine?

CO: Well, they're all different, they're all quite individual. Jimmy Dine's happenings—he hasn't done any for a long time now—always revolved around himself and really were the drama of himself. As against that, my happenings involve a large cast and the development of these people by themselves. After it's been put together, I step out of it and the people find themselves in the situations that I have set up for them.

RPW: What kind of situations, for example?

CO: They're very simple. I take a person and I try to know him very quickly. I provide him with certain objects that will interest him and also limit him and then he's forced to find himself within this limitation. For example, I had one man who is a teacher and very verbal—he's always talking. I gave him some fins for his feet and some very large gloves, asbestos gloves, that made it very hard for him to gesture with his fingers, and then I gave him a book made out of pieces of wood, which was hard to handle. I put a helmet on his head, and then I told him that he should move his mouth, but not really speak. This was his set of limitations.

After a couple of nights, all this stuff became quite natural to him. He began to find himself in terms of his role. I told him to start off by saying street names of Chicago, but he didn't like that, so in the end he was mouthing Shakespeare sonnets. It wasn't evident to anybody, but this is what he liked, what he thought he could do, and you had to see him develop.

RPW: But in terms of the visual experience, what was happening?

CO: Well, formally you had an interplay of flipper forms. We counted five flipper forms: one was the flippers of the feet, another was the flipper of the book covers. Then there was the flipper of a trash can that was on stage, the kind that you push and it flops up and down. Then there was the flipping up and down of his lips. All these flipping things were working at once, and so you got a continuous formal relationship between all these flippings.

RPW: How many of these formal relationships were premeditated, or were they realized after the fact?

CO: In this case of the flippers, I didn't realize what I was doing. This, of course, is the only good way. When you paint, for example, you go to school, and you learn all the ways to design a painting—how to make a pyramid or a circle and so on. But it's much better if you find these things out by yourself. Design is much better when it's an instinctive thing. You start in one way; it's natural that you find echoes and repetitions and variations. This is the structure of art.

RPW: Your work is associated with a movement called pop art, or new realism, or neo-Dada, in which the autonomy of the object is once more emphasized. Where do you place yourself in this movement? Or don't you consider yourself an artist related to this movement?

CO: Well, of course, my motives are very complex. Often they're contradictory, and so my approach to the object or to anything is bound to be a complicated one. For example, you have people that approach the object trying to isolate it from human sentiments, such as George Brecht. He also does happenings in which there is no personal interference. George simply announces that the sun will rise, and it does.

Then you have another group of artists who are interested in the object as a receptacle of human sentiments. I would say that I'm interested in both. In my work the altered object is always in juxtaposition with the unaltered object. I'm interested in the play between the two—just as I have the event or situation, the unaltered event or situation, in relation to an artificial one. My idea is that I want to present a complete picture of perception, which I think is a mixture of things as they are and things as they are imagined to be.

RPW: What sources led you to a presentation of "the complete picture" in this way?

CO: Well, almost any kind of panoramic view, such as exists in literature; in Joyce, for example, in *Ulysses*; and Proust, and Dos Passos in the American novels, and Dante—anything that shows the complete picture, its ins and outs. That's the way the happening tends to be. The happening tends to be panoramic.

RPW: In terms of your objects, where does your inspiration lie?

CO: I believe that art, or at least the creation of things, should be very closely related to my daily experience, and this is what has gotten me into the pop art classification. I work with very simple things that I come across while walking to work. Usually, they are things I see in the Lower East Side of New York, such as a certain kind of pastry, a certain kind of clothing, or certain kinds of displays or presentations and advertisements that I naturally come across as part of the urban landscape. I'm not really so much a pop artist as I am an urban artist—a completely urban artist. I never go out in the country and draw trees and things like that. I draw things that I come across in the city. Even there I don't draw an orange, imitate an orange as it is, but I imitate the picture of the orange as I know it in the city because the orange is always being represented to me by somebody.

RPW: In advertising, magazine illustrations?

CO: Yes. And the fact is, of course, that more and more the actual objects begin to look like the representation of them. Oranges become bigger and more orange. There's more color added and they lose their seeds. They get to be monstrous. That's part of the culture, I guess. I'm also fascinated by the amount of obsessive imagination that flourishes in representation of objects in magazines, etc. That seems to me very close to a thing called art.

RPW: Pop art draws heavily on the style derived from comic book illustration, an extremely gross visual or graphic style—are you much attracted by it?

CO: Yes, but I'm not sure it's gross. It's just that it has its own peculiar conventions, and these conventions are perhaps gross in relation to what we expect art to be, but, in fact, they're very sophisticated. Take comic strip drawing; it's been flourishing for years. People are so good at it. I can see a good comic strip artist with his pen, you know, doing sszzwt, sszzwt, sszzwt, like this, you know, and he can draw a face in an instant. It isn't that it's gross. It's more that it's a mechanical or industrial type of art, such as industrial printing. It's an anonymous kind of art.

RPW: Claes, I was wondering about the influence of certain graphic styles, such as the conventional graphic style of the comic book or contemporary art. Do you see any relation between them—that strong style—and your art?

CO: Well, I like it and, of course, anything you like, you are naturally influenced by. But I've never imitated it, really. I've appreciated it and enjoyed it and bought it and studied it, and so on. It's part of the urban environment. I came to Chicago for Christmas in 1960, and I bought an *Orphan Annie*—an old *Orphan Annie* comic book for what seemed like a ridiculous price. It was ten dollars—a hard-covered thing. It was all about Daddy Warbucks and the Depression and so forth, and it was a very beautiful book. It had very wonderful economical blacks and the drawing was very voluminar. It had very simple realizations of situations. Of course, the comic book is like a film in that it introduces movement into graphic art—real movement. Having studied this *Orphan Annie* book in particular, I used the succession of rectangles with action in it as the model for a happening [*Circus: Ironworks/Fotodeath*] I did in February 1961, when I went back to New York. It had, let us say, one square of action, followed by another square of action, followed by another square of action, not necessarily developing. It's similar, also, to Muybridge's books—you know, animals in action—in which you see the action move from one square to another—see it develop. I used it as kind of a model. Of course, the action in my pieces doesn't really develop; it's simple action that repeats itself in relation to another simple action that, in turn, repeats itself.

RPW: Do you think the sense of the absurd in the comic strips comes out in the creation of your own objects, or is it transferred into the somewhat dramatic form of the happening? Or don't you see a close inspirational relationship?

CO: Well, I love the ridiculous, and I love the absurd, and I love certain types of heroes. I love the pathetic city-waif-type heroes. That's very common in comics, like Little Orphan Annie or Kayo. I think that I certainly use all these stereotypes. We're all victimized by stereotypes in the films and in the comics, and the artist is forced to deal with stereotypes. His attitude can be that he tries to rescue the stereotypes. He can use the clichés or he can make fun of the clichés. But whatever he does, he has to deal with them if he deals with urban life, because urban life is just a set of clichés. If you're a sensitive person, and you live in the city, and you want to face the city and not escape from it, you just have to come to grips with all these clichés; just as you have to come to grips with the landscape of the city, with the dirt of the city, and the accidental possibilities of the city, and so on. So you have to come to grips with the clichés, and my attitude has been to meet them head on, and, as a sensitive person, to use them. I don't want to escape them but to make something out of them, something as good as anything else in the history of art. So I deliberately choose clichéd or ugly objects that are thought to be outside the realm of art—such as cream pies and hamburgers and hot dogs—things that live large in our consciousness just because we come in contact with them all the time. I have never taken a witty attitude toward clichés. I try to extract something valuable out of them.

We're living in the movie age in which all our expectations and relationships with people and things are determined to a great degree by what we saw in the films when we were kids and what we still see in the films. And this is also true of comics. So, of course, you have to deal with these things. My drawing has been influenced by comics just as my happenings have been influenced by the films, particularly silent films; but that doesn't mean that I have tried to imitate them absolutely, as some artists do. I mean that they have passed through my imagination.

RPW: Who at the moment are artists and writers who interest you?

CO: I tend to be very self-centered and I look at my childhood, say, more than at other artists' work. The writer who inspired me a great deal is dead now. That was Céline. It was in reading Céline that I sort of developed an attitude and a physical relationship to the city that started me on the theme of the city, a theme which I've pursued for about a year now. That was preceded by the theme of the store. Currently, I'm trying to read Gertrude Stein who has a lot of talk about happenings. I spoke of Dos Passos as interesting. He has a kind of panoramic city view in *Manhattan Transfer*. Of course, he never gets really very deep into it, but I kind of like the detachment he has. And then everybody reads, and I do too, Robbe-Grillet, or parts of him. His attitude toward the object is very interesting.

RPW: Among painters and sculptors, who interests you?

CO: I'm very interested by young painters and sculptors—my age—who are doing something similar, like Bob Whitman, and Jim Dine, and Allan Kaprow, Roy Lichtenstein, and Andy Warhol. Then, of course, I'm very interested by what Jasper Johns draws, does, and Rauschenberg.

RPW: On the spur of the moment, what would be the most comic situation you could imagine?

CO: On the spur of the moment—I go back to this thing I saw last night, where Buster Keaton is shaking his girlfriend out of a big bag in the freight car. I don't have to think of Buster Keaton in connection with this. I can just imagine that it would be very nice, to have a girl in a bag and to have the bag lifted up and have her shaken out. I think I will probably use that in my next happening.

RPW: On the spur of the moment, what would be the most tragic situation that you could imagine?

CO: That Marina Towers would fall down . . . I mean, I can't imagine tragic situations. I don't like to imagine them. There was a tragic situation in the film last night. A locomotive went over a bridge, and the bridge collapsed and fell down. I've been reading a lot of Mark Twain lately because he's fascinated by violence and disaster. He wrote about the sinking of a steamboat, where the steam escapes. In the instant before the explosion, you have to know that you have to keep your nose and your mouth covered because if you inhale the steam, you'll be all burned out inside. I guess my tragic situations have to do with accidents or something. I'm not sure I know what a tragic situation is.

RPW: Pop art or new realism or neo-Dada, or now your "Urban Renewal," is described as a movement set against the influences of abstract expressionism. Do you feel that this is a fair view?

CO: I usually deny this because I don't feel any antagonism toward the individuals in the abstract expressionist movement. I respect them a great deal. But I would be dishonest if I said that this wasn't true. When I came to New York, I felt very weary of abstract expressionist painting, though they had always used the city and de Kooning had even used Marilyn Monroe and references to the landscape. But it had always been quite artified. I think that now there's a tremendous reaction which takes the form of wanting both to make a real object and to relax the personal involvement to some degree, to forget about yourself a little bit. I was in a three-man show at Oberlin College with Joan Mitchell and Robert Rauschenberg and the thing the students found most fascinating was my necessity to represent clothing and pies and food and stuff like that—real things that are not in my world alone but are in other people's worlds too. That interested them.

RPW: Pierre Restany, who is the official spokesman of new realism in Europe, claims that American pop art, while being a reaction to abstract expressionism, is, at the same time, a very logical continuation of it.

CO: That's also true. Certainly I don't reject abstract expressionism, particularly Pollock and de Kooning. They mean a great deal to me, both in terms of how to use paint and in their engagement with their surroundings. Sometimes I feel that what I'm doing with living material, with people and objects and situations, is something like what they did with paint. I just have substituted material. There is a lot of what you might call "action painting" in the course of a happening. It's a sort of tradition that we all inherited. A critic like Harold Rosenberg, also, just naturally refers to a happening as the next logical step after action painting. And maybe it is. But it's both a protest and a continuation of the tradition.

The Theater of Action

Barbara Rose

As a people the Americans are said to have had no childhood, and the circumstance has been shown to contain pathos as well as loss. . . . The mask was a portable heirloom handed down by the pioneer. In a primitive world crowded with pitfalls the unchanging, unaverted countenance had been a safeguard, preventing revelations of surprise, anger, or dismay. The mask had otherwise become habitual among the older Puritans as their more expressive or risible feelings were sunk beneath the surface. Governor Bradford had encouraged its use on a considerable scale, urging certain gay spirits to enjoy themselves in secret, if they must be convivial.

—*Constance Rourke,* American Humor

It was a rather eccentric-looking person who spoke; somewhat ursine in aspect; sporting a shaggy spencer of the cloth called bearskin; a high-peaked cap of raccoon-skin, the long bushy tail switching over behind; raw-hide leggings; grim stubble chin and to end, a double-barrelled gun in hand—a Missouri bachelor, a Hoosier gentleman . . .

—*Herman Melville,* The Confidence-Man

A happening is a breaking down of the barriers between the arts, and something close to an actual experience. It should be a very free form, a very ambiguous and suggestive form . . . filled with unexplored and primitive possibilities. I like it that way—like it to be as unpredictable as possible.

—Claes Oldenburg, from "The Transformation of Daddy Warbucks: An Interview with Robert Pincus-Witten"

Because happenings have had their denouement in the multimedia discotheques, it is hard to remember that they were originally semiprivate, semiritual performances attended by a handful of initiates. The performances of the Ray Gun Theater, for example, which were given in Oldenburg's studio at 107 East Second Street in the spring of 1962, after *The Store* had closed there, were attended by groups limited to thirty-five people at a time, because the narrow space could accommodate no more. The members of the audience were jammed together, physically touching one another and occasionally brushing against the limbs of the actors in front of them, below them, or above their heads. This intimacy was part of the direct involvement demanded by the original happenings, and the involvement in turn accounted for much of the impact of the events. Oldenburg's emphasis on structure, insured through repetition of action and planned movement, his control of his means, his attention to detail, and the originality of his images, all distinguish his happenings from those of others. But he was by no means the inventor of happenings and was in fact a relative latecomer to the genre. By the time that Oldenburg's first happening, *Snapshots from the City*, took place in late winter 1960, Allan Kaprow had already produced his *18 Happenings in 6 Parts* at the Reuben Gallery in the fall of 1959, and Red Grooms's prototype tableau, *The Burning Building,* had been performed throughout that December in his Delancey Street Museum.

At the time, the first happenings appeared to be a weird composite of painting and theater. It is now clear, however, that they were a direct extension into the theater of the "action" or gestural element of abstract expressionism. The connection was made consciously by Kaprow, whose "environments" of the late 1950s were the bridge between the paintings of Pollock, de Kooning, and others and their later outcome— "happenings." Oldenburg himself was quite conscious of the relationship: "Sometimes I feel that what I'm doing with living material, with people and objects and situations is something like what they (de K and P) did with paint. I just have substituted material," he wrote.[1] In keeping with the literalizing tendency of the art of the 1960s, happenings make literal the concept of action by representing real gestures and actions as opposed to their pictorial metaphors. For Oldenburg, the replacement of action in painting by actual movement in live performance carried still further the process of the literalization of pictorial qualities in his reliefs. Moreover, linked sequences of action not only added the element of time that was unavailable in painting, but also allowed an enrichment of content, while simultaneous or superimposed actions could express interlocking levels of psychological associations.

Oldenburg had been interested in the theater long before he came to New York, and his close association with Dick Tyler from 1957 on intensified this interest. During 1959 and 1960, he was also in contact with, and directly or indirectly influenced by, Kaprow, Grooms, and Dine. In January 1960, he took part in Kaprow's *The Big Laugh*, one of the second group of happenings presented at the Reuben Gallery. As one might expect, however, Oldenburg's happenings differed from those of others, just as their emphasis on intelligible even though alogical content differentiated them from the theater of the absurd, to which their bizarre imagery bore some relationship. What distinguishes Oldenburg's happenings is that they were more conceptual than others, and had virtually no narrative but were conceived as "pictures"; in addition, they had a consistent content that linked them to the iconography of his sculpture. What counted was not so much the individual parts of each performance, however, as the allover mood that was conveyed. Oldenburg's early happenings presented a panoramic, generalized experience; the "plot" was associational rather than logical. In other words, Oldenburg's primary concern in the happenings was not drama, and certainly never narrative; it was psychological content, physical movement, vivid imagery, and above all, spatial relationships.

Oldenburg's concern with the body in space, related to other objects of a constructed environment, links his happenings to the new form of choreography that has followed the work of Merce Cunningham and Paul Taylor. He himself has defined his intentions in using this medium: "The 'Happening' is one or another method of using *objects in motion*, and this I take to include people, both in themselves and as agents of object motion. . . . I present in a 'Happening' anywhere from thirty to seventy-five events or Happenings (and many more objects), over a period of time from one-half to one and a half hours, in simple spatial relationships—juxtaposed, superimposed. . . . The event is made simple and clear, and is set up either to repeat itself or to proceed very slowly, so that the tendency is always to a static object."[2]

The term "happenings" is in itself something of a misnomer, for these performances have no plot, and nothing in the sense of narrative actually "happens." Happenings are not meant to be interpreted, but to be experienced directly. Oldenburg's are particularly static and often have the quality of vignettes passing before the spectator. As a result they, like his sculpture, ultimately invoke a synthetic image, a general feeling or mood about what has transpired, with the intention of leading people "away from the notion of a work of art as something outside of experience, something that is terribly precious," so that they may eventually "think of a normal, natural experience in terms of a work of art."[3] For, in spite of stylized, nonnaturalistic qualities that relate them to such theatrical forms as Grand Guignol and Japanese Noh plays, Oldenburg's happenings use ordinary situations, gestures, and movements—walking, sitting, smoking, eating, swimming.

"The Happening," Oldenburg has declared, "is for me a personal composition out of elements at hand. It is not a question of chance or random effects. . . . The relation of the incidents is fortuitous as is the case in real life. Imagine a map where all that goes on in the city can be seen from above at once, such as the fire charts of the fire department or the multiplicity [and] simultaneity of the taxi or police radios. A city is overlay upon overlay of incident." He described happenings as "a certain kind of experience: simply sitting and watching in an isolated way something that's *very familiar.*" As with his sculpture, Oldenburg's use of familiar, even banal, subject matter was meant to be a way of giving his audience something in his art that they could readily grasp. At the same time, he was disheartened by their unwillingness to go beyond the obvious. "A Western audience has to have explanations," he complained. "They really can't watch anything for its own sake. They have to have an explanation first or a reason for watching it. They really don't watch a thing. They follow an idea as it unravels, and everything represents the unraveling of an idea."[4] He was nevertheless determined to try to change this.

Oldenburg's original conception was that the audience for his happenings would be small, and that the repertory would be like a "workshop of ideas and possibilities surrounding my concept of personal theater, and not so much directed at the general public as at other artists and connoisseurs." He thought of happenings as "a theater of action or

of things . . . a poor man's theater and the lead is a beggar." The happenings were also a theater of license and permissiveness that in many
ways paralleled the permissiveness of the homosexual drag world of Jack
Smith's film *Flaming Creatures* [1963] as much as they prefigured the permissiveness of hippie costume drag. Oldenburg's permissiveness consisted
of setting up situations with given limitations, including the use of speci-
fied props, and then stepping out of the situation, allowing the participants a certain amount of leeway. His instructions to performers were
nevertheless quite specific, and the line between audience and performer
was well defined.

Like much of pop art, Oldenburg's happenings deal with stereotypes.
Happenings in general are an eclectic form, and his are especially so.
He has borrowed freely from newsreels, silent movies, horror films, slap-
stick comedy, school pageants, vaudeville, burlesque, and other popular
performing traditions, and has mixed these borrowings with elements
of dance, mime, psychodrama, *commedia dell'arte*, baroque festivals, and
drama. His characters, familiar from all these sources but especially from
the movies, include the Chaplinesque tramp, the *Tobacco Road* drifters,
and the W. C. Fields buffoon. Certain roles of the early happenings were
standardized in terms of the people who assumed them, their repertory
cast featuring Oldenburg himself, Pat Oldenburg, Gloria Graves, and Lucas Samaras in the principal roles (fig. 9.1). The characters were drawn
from the picaresque, raffish outcasts of society—the crook, the drunk, the
simpleton, the transvestite, and the beggar. Pat Oldenburg incarnated the
female principle. She played the Street Chick, the City Waif, the Bride,
the "City Venus," the Tart, the Muse, and the doll or *poupée* (Oldenburg's
nickname for Pat was "Poopy").

Oldenburg himself, on the other hand, always assumed in the happenings a Pirandelloesque part that combined his real relationship to the
action as director with aspects of two main types of theatrical stereotypes—the magician–hypnotist–spellbinder, and the fool or the clown.
He took for himself the role of Ray Gun, the hero of many masks, the
metamorphic "hero into loonie." Like Melville's confidence man—the
eternal nomadic stranger, the innocent sophisticate—Oldenburg skirted
the action, changing his role at will, from circus barker to medicine man
to bum.

These roles reveal his conception of the role of the artist in society.
To Pat's "City-Bird-Child," he often played the predatory monster, the
voyeur who peeks around openings, the grossly violating "Rag Man."

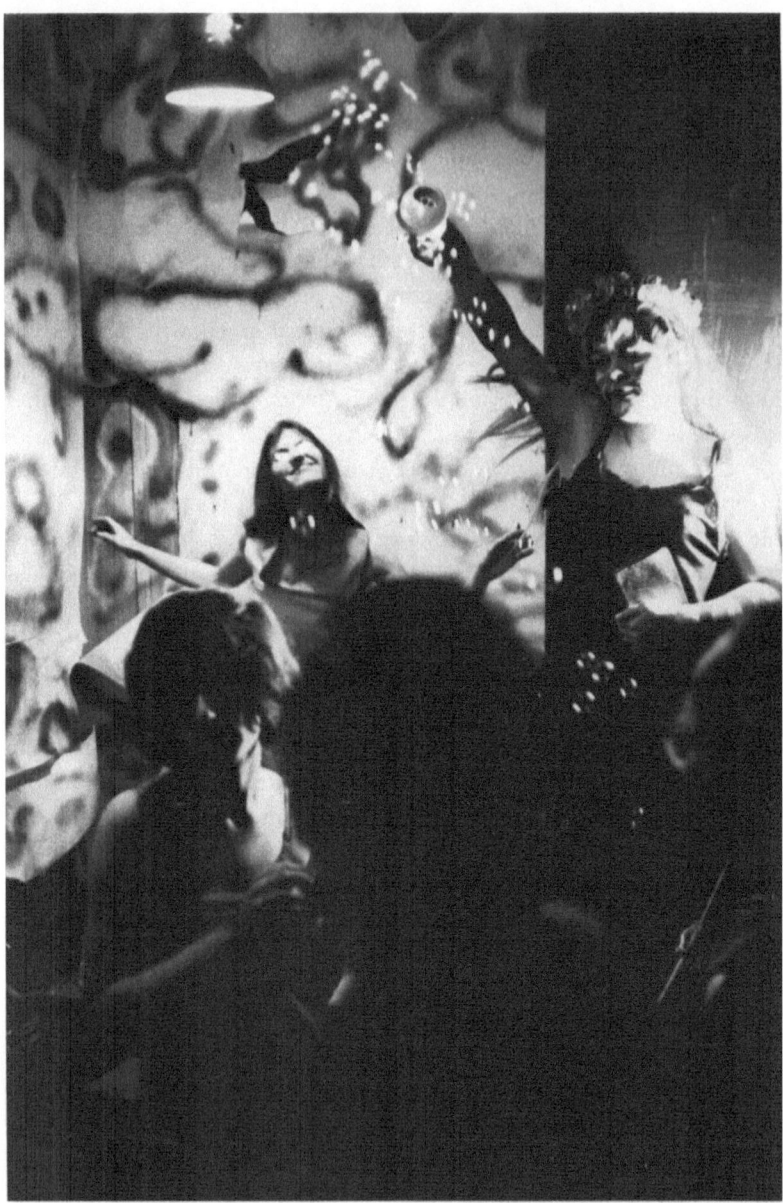

Figure 9.1 *Store Days II*, Ray Gun Theater, March
2–3, 1962. 107 East Second Street, New York.
Pictured: Patty Mucha dancing with fifty-cent
pieces on her eyes; Gloria Graves as the Statue of
Liberty, bubbles blowing from her torch. Photo ©
Robert McElroy/Licensed by VAGA, New York, NY;
courtesy the Oldenburg van Bruggen Studio.

He identified, in short, with the fringe elements of society, seeing the artist in his adventures as close to the criminal. Or else he impersonated Prospero, "a curious sorcerer because he is like the rational man, the kind man, the leader, a very worldly figure, who makes magic easily and surrounds it with no mumbo-jumbo." As Prospero, he could manipulate the pure spirit embodied by Pat's Ariel or Puck. In this guise, Oldenburg conceived the artist as sorcerer, a magician who transforms the world through his own vision. He was both the "voyeur" who observes and the "seer" who prophesies. It was the latter role that Oldenburg usually assumed in his early happenings, which combined elements of primitive ritual, *rites de passage*, and ancient dramaturgy with popular farce and melodrama.

Oldenburg's earliest happening was *Snapshots from the City*, a series of posed, frozen tableaux that he and Pat performed at the Judson Gallery during the showing there of *The Street*. "The performances were intended to add the ultimate note of actuality to *The Street* with the artist's actual presence in his creation," he explained. His second effort, which he regarded as showing less the influence of Red Grooms and more that of Robert Whitman and Kaprow's use of objects, was *Blackouts*. Presented at the newly relocated Reuben Gallery at 33 East Third Street in December 1960, it was a half-hour performance divided into four parts, "Chimneyfires," "Erasers," "The Vitamin Man," and "Butter and Jam." Oldenburg has described it as being a pendant to *Snapshots from the City*, but more lyrical, sparse, and objective in its effect. A much longer piece was his third happening, *Circus* (so-called because its presentation of events in five superimposed rows under weak electric bulbs was inspired by circus light and space); this was put on at the Reuben Gallery in February 1961. Each of its two parts, called respectively "Ironworks" and "Fotodeath," lasted about forty-five minutes, with a quarter-hour intermission during which "Pickpocket," a sequence of photos from magazines, was projected in the form of slides. In contrast to the strobe effect of the earlier works, in which a quickly paced succession of scenes was illuminated between blackouts, *Circus: Ironworks/Fotodeath* was well lit and gave the spectators an impression of "attenuated time and repetition."

During the following year, Oldenburg worked to refine his aesthetic of the theater. The result was the Ray Gun Theater, the series of ten happenings presented at what he dubbed the Ray Gun Manufacturing Company, 107 East Second Street, from February to May 1962 following the closing of *The Store*. Of this cycle, *Injun* was the most literary,

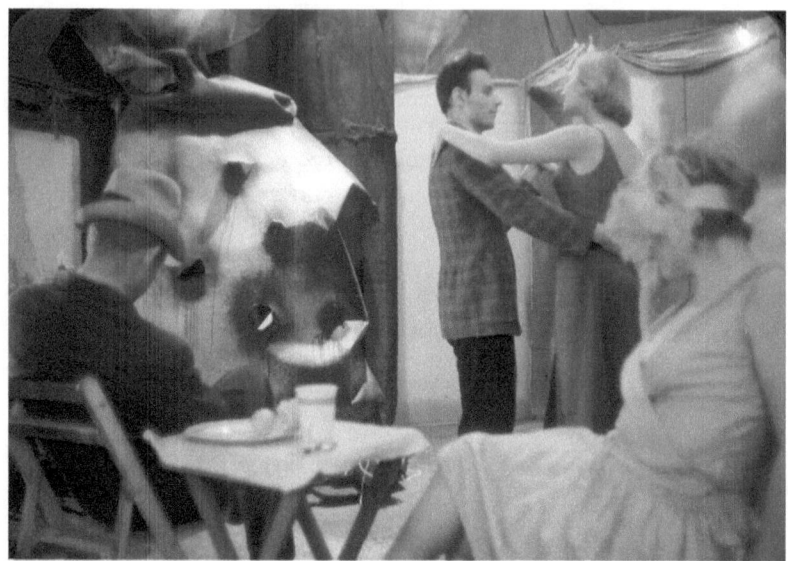

Figure 9.2 *Circus: Ironworks/Fotodeath*, February
21–26, 1961. Reuben Gallery, 61 Fourth Avenue,
New York. Left to right: Claes Oldenburg, Lucas
Samaras, Claire Selley, Gloria Graves. Photo ©
Robert McElroy/Licensed by VAGA, New York, NY;
courtesy the Oldenburg van Bruggen Studio.

incorporating much material from American history. Oldenburg's preparatory notes indicate that he conceived of *Injun* as "strong in setting,
more setting than anything else, wild and not cool, and fantastic, not realistic." Its conception dates back to the summer of 1960 in Provincetown,
when Oldenburg found himself critically evaluating the previous winter's
Snapshots from the City. In the Provincetown locale, where he focused
more specifically upon American history, he began to formulate a central
character who would combine traits of Crusoe, Noah, and Adam—a sort
of first-man explorer or frontiersman. The first mention of this figure
is as "Indian" or "the American Crusoe"; but whereas Crusoe was associated with the sea, the Indian stood for the "inland American forest."
Eventually, he was to become the central character of the Ray Gun Theater, which Oldenburg developed in order to add the dimension of time
to the Ray Gun enterprises. (His earliest conception of *The Store*, in fact,
had been as a work which "will look like a merchandising street and the
stores and the plays will pursue history.")

The title *Injun* was taken from the corruption of the word "Indian" by Mark Twain, who had been fascinated with themes of American violence and who was much on Oldenburg's mind at this time (fig. 9.3).[5] Oldenburg's early happenings were satires on American foibles, comparable to Twain's sardonic, mock folk epics. They had a seedy Depression mood, very much in keeping with the cracker barrel atmosphere of *The Store* in whose locale they were presented. The macabre character of the action, however, was modified by the multiple focuses of the action and by humorous interludes.

The apocalyptic quality of the early happenings in New York, with their intimations of massacre, rape, catastrophe, and primitive forces rising from the lower depths, reached their crescendo in the second version of *Injun*, presented in 1962 on the property of the Dallas Museum for Contemporary Arts, which had commissioned the piece in conjunction with its showing of objects from *The Store*. This version was influenced by a Wallace Beery movie that Oldenburg had seen as a child, in which Beery played a Civil War veteran returning to a farmhouse where his family had been slaughtered by an axe murderer. In Dallas, the spectators were forced to bear witness to the violence of the American past, shortly to have a bloody sequel in that very city.

In structuring *Injun* in terms of movement, Oldenburg visualized the hidden movements of Indians in the forest; its use of spectators as performers makes this Oldenburg's most total happening. The Dallas presentation was subtitled "Country-piece for a house, a yard, a shed and a lean-to" and took place in an abandoned complex of buildings on the museum's grounds. Spectators were conducted one by one out of the museum into the darkness and were led by masked figures into the house, where they were locked in. The house was littered with bodies and filled with people performing obscurely scatalogical actions, like slinging mud and squirting paint. Some rooms were lined with chicken wire and paper in order to simulate caves (a typical setting for early happenings). At one point, cars were maneuvered so that their headlights illuminated the scene—a device later used in Los Angeles for *Autobodys* (fig. 9.4). During the first performance, the police who invaded the premises in response to a riot call and began questioning the performers were themselves incorporated into the action—an illustration of Oldenburg's dictum that disorder and the unexpected must also be accepted as part of existence.

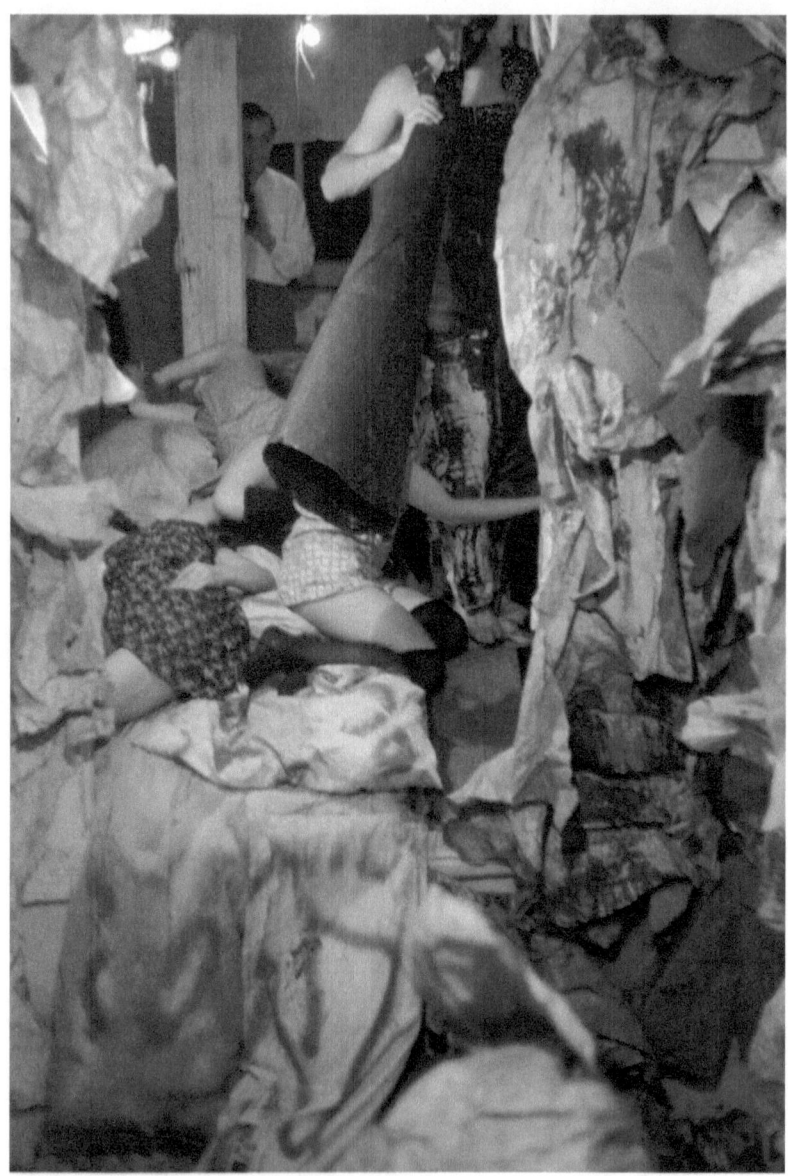

Figure 9.3 *Injun I*, Ray Gun Theater, April 20–21,
1962. 107 East Second Street, New York. Pictured:
Terry Brook, Lette Eisenhauer, Patty Mucha, Lucas
Samaras. Photo © Robert McElroy/Licensed by
VAGA, New York, NY; courtesy the Oldenburg van
Bruggen Studio.

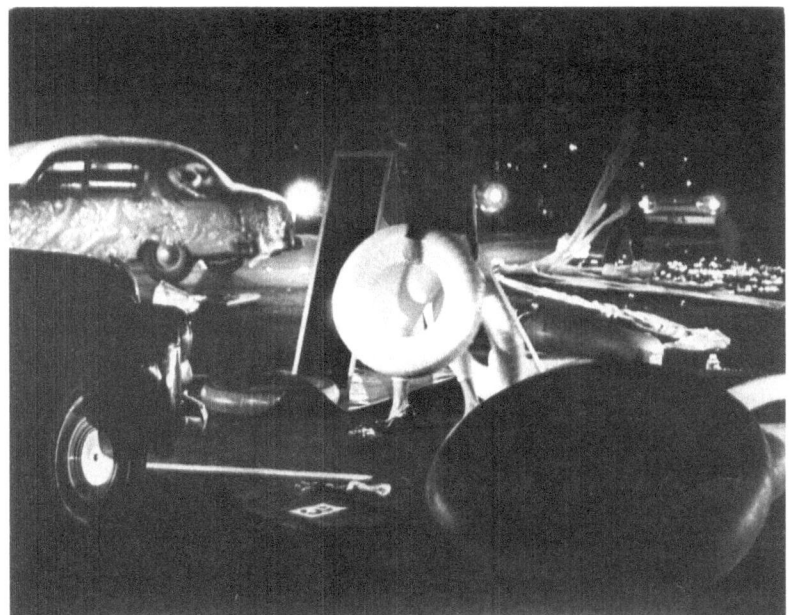

Figure 9.4 *Autobodys*, December 9–10,
1963. American Institute of Aeronautics and
Astronautics, Los Angeles. Pictured: Patty Mucha.
Photo: Julian Wasser, Beverly Hills, CA; courtesy
the Oldenburg van Bruggen Studio.

This version of *Injun* presaged the changing character of Oldenburg's happenings after the Ray Gun Theater closed in May 1962. Thereafter, audiences were larger, contact was not so intimate, and settings were not constructed but taken from found ambiences. The three happenings that Oldenburg produced in 1963 after leaving New York for the West Coast were originally conceived as a transcontinental trilogy: they included *Gayety*, *Stars*, and *Autobodys*, produced in Chicago, Washington, and Los Angeles, respectively. *Gayety* was presented in February in Lexington Hall, a little-used building on the University of Chicago's South Side campus—an area thoroughly familiar to Oldenburg. "In *Gayety*," he wrote, "I want to create a civic report on the community of Chicago, in the way I see it. After the overture there are six 'combinations' of events, persons, articles, sounds—all the elements of experience in representative situation, either plain or enigmatic, demonstrating such categories as weather, climate, geography, education, culture, poetry, homelife, crime,

products, food, traffic, heroes, art, entertainment, and so on. This is like
the civic projects one did in sixth grade."[6] Again, one is reminded of
the comprehensiveness of Neubern, the imaginary country Oldenburg
created as a child, with its mixture of reality and fantasy. *Stars: A Farce for
Objects*, on the other hand, which was presented during a pop art festival
at the Washington Gallery of Modern Art, emphasized public spectacle,
pretty girls, nudes, and glamorous costumes. *Autobodys* had a two-night
run in a Los Angeles parking lot, where spectators sat in their cars with
their headlights illuminating the action. Originally, its theme was the
automobile, ubiquitous in California, and the sterility of freeway culture.
In this sense, *Autobodys* was a theatrical forerunner of the Airflow theme.
While this happening was taking shape, the emphasis on death and violence became accentuated when, late in November, President Kennedy
was assassinated while riding in a motorcade, and endless images of the
black cars in his funeral procession filled television screens throughout
the country.

Oldenburg's happenings of 1965 were, by contrast, far more re-
laxed and less intense in their imagery than his earlier ones. *Washes*, a
complex work in many parts, which took place in May in Al Roon's
Health Club on West Seventy-third Street as part of the First New York
Theater Rally, dealt humorously with sex and leisure.[7] In December,
Oldenburg's twenty-minute-long *Moveyhouse* preceded happenings by
Robert Rauschenberg and Robert Whitman during a festival at the
Film-Makers' Cinematheque, thus serving as a kind of prolegomena
to a "painters' cinema," a possibility that had interested Oldenburg for
some time (fig. 9.5). In fact, if one seeks a connecting theme for the
happenings from *Snapshots from the City* through *Moveyhouse*, one might
say that it is the invention of the movies, or their development from the
original still photograph through the multiple-image motion picture.
From this point of view, *Snapshots* represents the primitive stage of the
still photograph; its clear, isolated images of actions stopped in medias
res parallel the frozen moments caught by a photographer. "There is a
practical problem in 'mounting' the images which periods of darkness
helped," Oldenburg wrote in his notes on *Snapshots*. "Time is slowed
down in order to really dwell on action and images. The point was 'a
feast for the eyes . . . a poem for the eyes.'" In *Fotodeath*, the theme
of the camera that captures life is clearly related to Oldenburg's understanding of the relation between art and life. The photographer

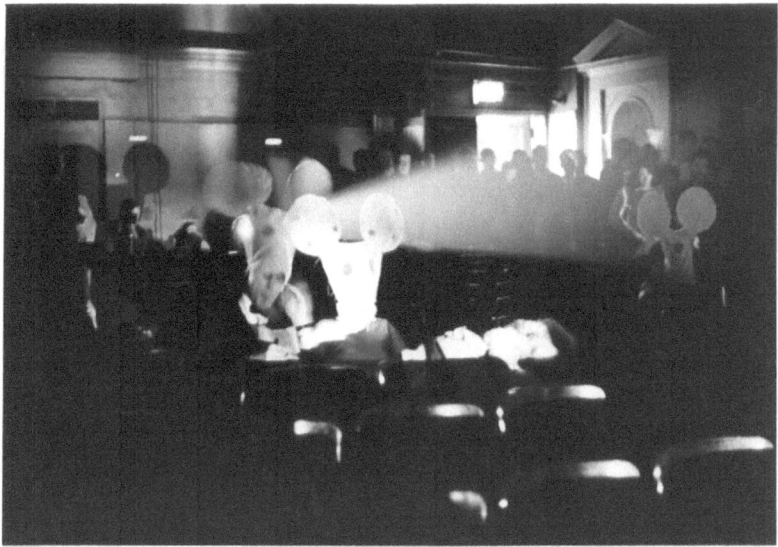

Figure 9.5 *Moveyhouse*, December 1–3 and 16–17, 1965. Forty-first Street Theater (now destroyed), New York. Photo © Robert McElroy/ Licensed by VAGA, New York, NY.

"shoots" the people posed before him, and they fall over as if dead. But art is not life; art does not kill, and they are soon revived. ("When Ray Gun shoots, no one dies.") In *Fotodeath*, which Oldenburg envisioned as "a cosmos a whole reconstruction of NY," the series of isolated events of *Snapshots* is extended to form a continuous action with overlapping movements—like Muybridge's motion photographs, which represented an intermediate phase between still photographs and the movies.

Oldenburg's happenings, in spite of his emphasis on role-playing, are essentially visual theater, "painters' theater," with the emphasis on images. Since they have no plots, and the characters are stereotypes rather than being developed, it is the costumes, props, and lighting that become the centers of attention and often determine the action. With habitual responsiveness to his environment, Oldenburg usually selects his setting first or uses a location assigned to him as a given limitation. The happenings in Dallas, Washington, and Los Angeles each contained material generated by his associations and experiences in those places. Oldenburg

has described the procedure he followed with *Washes* as being characteristic of the method he used in previous pieces:

> 1. A period of . . . priming myself with possibilities—practical and
> impractical . . . recording these in a book, and writing a number of
> script drafts. 2. Familiarizing myself with the particular place. . . .
> 3. Recruiting the cast from volunteers, some new and some fa-
> miliar from past performances. . . . 4. Purchase of objects and cos-
> tumes. . . . 5. First . . . rehearsals, combining prepared ideas, actual
> place, individuals in cast, and objects and costumes. Confusion and
> numerous trials and errors. 6. Final rehearsal: simplification of results
> of first rehearsals to strongest incidents, discarding of the rest. Im-
> position of simple time scheme of cues. 7. . . . performances before
> audience . . . with changes continuing to final performance.[8]

Props and costumes are usually collected from what is readily available in hardware stores and thrift shops, because happenings are above all
"homemade," amateur productions—the very opposite of the slick commercial theater. Preliminary notes derived from the motivating conception lead to a "script" without dialog, which Oldenburg has never used,
although sound may be incorporated in the form of random grunts,
groans, and noises resulting from the manipulation of props.[9] Scripts exist for a few of Oldenburg's happenings, and several of his early pieces,
notably *Injun*, had several revised texts; but most of the action is improvised. Only the bare bones are contained in the script, which structures
action into overlapping compartments and designates which participants
are on stage at a given moment, and what they are doing. Entrances and
exits are carefully timed to create suspense. Such characterization as exists
is the semiautomatic result of Oldenburg's selection of the participants,
whose actual personalities or physical appearance correspond to the images or stereotypes he desires to use as his living material. Predictably,
disguises and masquerades are frequent, and images of concealment and
exposure are analogous to the relationship between obvious subject matter and disguised content in his sculpture.

Michael Kirby has called happenings "non-matrixed" theater, by
which he means that they differ from conventional realistic drama in
lacking any focus of time, place, or character; there is no climax. This
lack of focus, of defining context, gives to the action an allover quality
that tends to overlap and interweave within the frame of the performing

area. Obviously, this is derived from Pollock's allover painting style, which, translated into theatrical terms, allows the artist to treat the very stuff of life itself as his plastic material.

Although Oldenburg's happenings are not theater in the round, his use of space is different from that of the conventional theater. He often presents odd or fragmentary views; for example, in the early, more static happenings, views through openings were used to suggest an aura of mystery. Partial or obstructed views also pique the curiosity of the audience, which experiences an unfamiliar sensation when watching something familiar isolated from its normal context. In some of the happenings, the action took place around the audience, as in *Injun* and *Moveyhouse*, in which the audience was literally in the midst of things and participated actively in the performance. In *Washes*, the audience was involved through the humid atmosphere while standing around the edges of a swimming pool; the action took place beneath them in the pool. The spectators were asked to wear bathing suits, although a proposed mass swim had to be called off because of the management's objections. Such random focus and unwillingness to observe the conventions of wall, floor, and ceiling of the boxlike proscenium stage, or even the relative freedom of an arena, is again traceable to the impact of Pollock's allover compositions, which present images without focal points or mandatory orientation. Although Oldenburg was first drawn to the theater because it permitted him the use of live materials, in his theater, as in his sculpture, the boundary between life and art is nevertheless quite clear. His stylized theater of live action is at the opposite pole to the naturalistic theater with its imitation of life, which for the duration of the action demands that the spectator believe art and life to be identical. Oldenburg's happenings have large casts, who are given a certain degree of freedom, so that there is significant variation from performance to performance. "After it's been put together, I step out of it and the people find themselves in the situations that I have set up for them," he explains. In spite of his encouragement of improvisation, however, he carefully fixes its limits, just as in his sculpture he permits automatism to go only so far. He constantly molds, manipulates, and changes his material to structure it, for his main preoccupation is the overall structure of the work, which remains unchanged. Throughout the making of a happening, he exerts total critical control, rejecting material that for one reason or another does not work out. The structure of the happenings always includes a finale. Frequently, the finale is conceived as "an apotheosis in the form of a destruction . . . in which the forces of the community are released functionlessly in relieving chaos." *Washes*, for instance, ends with a moment of stillness in which the entire cast floats like dead bodies after an apocalypse, only to be revived at the last moment. "In surveying experience," Oldenburg wrote, "I find I must assign death a large role. I like Céline's constant sense of death." Thus, the two forbidden themes—sex and death, Eros and Thanatos—play the largest role in Oldenburg's Freudian iconography.

Among the advantages of happenings as a form, Oldenburg has cited totality, living quality, intelligence guiding yet free, unreproducible spontaneity, and demands on the spectator to become directly involved by reconstructing, in terms of his own experience, the fragments of experience offered. "The Happening, as I practice it," Oldenburg has written, "creates a lot of discomfort for the audience. It's an attempt to rattle them out of the notion that they're going to watch a play or an idea unfold. I try to make them uncomfortable to a certain degree, to make them receptive to a new way of looking at things." Obviously, Oldenburg's intention is to remove a good deal of the passive entertainment of conventional Western theater and instead transform the performance into a heuristic experience something like a Zen lesson. His attitude conforms to Morse Peckham's redefinition (in *Man's Rage for Chaos* [1967]) of the function of art in contemporary society. According to Peckham, in an advanced stage of a technological society such as our own, there is already too much order. If this be the case, then the proper aim of art is to disrupt conventional patterns of behavior and force new types of psychological adaptation. Such a definition of the purpose of art is well in keeping with Oldenburg's views.

The importance of happenings in terms of infusing new life into the theater cannot be overemphasized. Much of the fresh material that stimulated the development of a more physical, intimate, direct, and participatory theater was first synthesized in the happenings, which, at least in Oldenburg's case, had extraordinary vitality, originality, and impact. The happenings also provide a way of looking at the world that counters the "American disease of wishing to be efficient in solving problems," as Oldenburg puts it. They present images of disorder and unresolved frustration that are in many ways painful to follow but are also part of common experience. Aimless eating and walking and such basic activities as play, work, and conflict are the contents of an ordinary day. In this sense, the happenings were the first art manifestation to articulate a highly problematic, as well as a highly pervasive, contemporary feeling that life *is* theater, and that the relationship of the viewer to historical events witnessed on television is that of the audience to theater. That such a view presents genuine political dangers need scarcely be pointed out further.

As we have noted, several of Oldenburg's happenings—notably *Foto-death* (originally called *Cinema*) and *Moveyhouse*—deal with the movies. He had been thinking about the possibilities of film as a distinct medium since 1960, when he wrote notes for a program of "Seven Films of Close Inspection." In their emphasis on static images and slowed-down time, these fragmentary notes on a cinema of contemplation are prophetic of some of Andy Warhol's films. Oldenburg suggests filming "the same action, a very simple action . . . seen from many different viewpoints, in space and in time, over and over, slowly and rapidly," so that "all that can be gotten from it physically and metaphysically is extracted, from this very simple thing." In this context, he advises the use of scale changes, alternating distant and close focus, and shots from above and below. All the films that Oldenburg has made himself up to now [1970] have been only fragments, although in 1961 he claimed, "I am reinventing the movies." They consist mainly of close examinations of objects from many angles, just as his happenings are not narratives but rather the presentation of "events" to be examined from several angles of vision. A number of Oldenburg's happenings have been recorded on film by Stan Vanderbeek, Raymond Saroff, and others; but in these films he himself has had little control of the camera, so that they cannot be regarded as reflecting his own efforts as director. For *Birth of the Flag*, however, made by Vanderbeek as a filmed version of *Washes* (1965), Oldenburg completely reformulated the contents of the original action and transferred the locale from an indoor swimming pool to the open countryside. The main similarity between the two versions is that water remains a dominant motif in both. With its stress on nature, the film is a far more lyrical piece than the original happening. Its many outdoor scenes, such as the night scene of nudes on the river holding torches, are reminiscent of some of the films by Ingmar Bergman. Once again, we are reminded of Oldenburg's Scandinavian heritage.

The single dramatic film that Oldenburg has worked on is *Pat's Birthday*, made in 1962 in collaboration with Robert Breer. This portrayal of lumpen-middle-class mores utilized the repertory cast of the Ray Gun Theater, and in fact Oldenburg himself appears in this film more as actor than as director. *Pat's Birthday* is a reflection of Breer's concentration on editing and therefore hardly realizes Oldenburg's preference for a careful examination of prepared images. Objects chosen by Oldenburg for their loaded conceptual meaning appear instead as ordinary phenomena, thereby more or less subverting his intention.[10]

Oldenburg understands the camera as a subjective eye, a painter's eye, which interprets and organizes what it sees. Perhaps his recent fragmentary films with their close-up examination of single images are the beginnings of a significant facet of his career. His approach to film is like his approach to all other mediums: an investigation of its basic premises, an attempt to define its essence, and ultimately a "reinvention" of the medium—as movies are metaphorically reinvented in the progression from the still photograph to the moving image in his happenings.

Notes

1. Except where otherwise noted, all quotations from Oldenburg come from his notebooks, and are published here by courtesy of the Oldenburg van Bruggen Studio.

2. Claes Oldenburg, "A Statement," in Michael Kirby, *Happenings: An Illustrated Anthology* (New York: E. P. Dutton, 1965), pp. 200–201. This book includes an introduction that is a useful summary of the early history of happenings and the influences upon them, and it contains statements and scripts of happenings by Kaprow, Grooms, Robert Whitman, Dine, and Oldenburg.

3. Quoted in Robert Pincus-Witten, "The Transformation of Daddy Warbucks: An Interview with Claes Oldenburg," reprinted in this volume.

4. Ibid.

5. Oldenburg's "Two Scenarios from an Incomplete Pageant of America," including "Injun" and "Crusoe" (published in *Injun and Other Histories* [New York: Something Else Press, A Great Bear Pamphlet, 1966]), were humorous travesties much in the style of Twain's short works, which Oldenburg admired. Popular American stereotypes like Major Hoople, an old colored slave (Walt Whitman), and Teddy Roosevelt appear in them. There is a typical Oldenburg metamorphosis, in which "Friday changes into a bear and climbs the chimney," and there are liberal doses of murder, mayhem, and sheer madness. Another playlet, "Faustina," presents a mixture of Orphan Annie woe-is-me and the perverse comic sexuality of *The Naked Lunch*, which Oldenburg was reading at the time. (At one point in his notes, Pat Oldenburg, who is also called "Faustina," is referred to as "my orphic Annie"—to whom Oldenburg himself is presumably Daddy Warbucks.) "Faustina," a pornographic mock epic, prefigures the action in *Fotodeath*, emphasizing Oldenburg's favorite themes of transformation and metamorphosis. "Ah, the passage of things!" he writes in "Faustina." "The bridges are joined to the houses and the water is joined to the bridges, and even the clouds are metal, moving against one another like Coney Dodgems, clanking & dropping nuts. . . . AwMaMaGeddon! One night the bombras come, splitting and plopping. . . . The Great Ghost G.W., Grand Obelisk, The Polar Beast, the great ravenous Ice, slides down in the night. Making the old walls scream with pleasure as

they crumble, deflowering the bridges, wrapping them around his phallus-head, casting the shouting ships in the air like a bull. . . . All's mud and silence. A new map. Faustina, neither human nor recognizable, without pencil or paper to draw a map, tromps on, but the old photo resembles nothing at all anymore." Ibid., p. 11. A kind of intense lyric poetry written in shorthand, "Faustina" is also a threatening, unsettling vision of a pornographic apocalypse.

6. Oldenburg, "Gayety: The Script," in Kirby, *Happenings: An Illustrated Anthology*, pp. 234–235.

7. One of the events in the First Theater Rally (1965) was Oldenburg's curtain raiser, [*Piece for*] *Telephone*. The action consisted in having a telephone placed in the middle of an empty stage. On signal, Oldenburg—who was not in the theater—made a call to this telephone; if no one in the audience answered, he hung up, and the instrument was removed.

8. Oldenburg, "Washes," *Tulane Drama Review* 10, no. 2 (Winter 1965), p. 108.

9. Because Oldenburg writes constantly, one might logically assume that his verbal sense is highly developed; yet in his writings, as in his happenings, he tends to express himself in "eidetic imagery," in terms of completely visualized pictures rather than verbal details.

10. Some of the conflict between Oldenburg's intentions for this film and Breer's ideas of filmmaking are amusingly recorded by the latter in an article entitled "What Happened," *Film Culture* 26 (Fall 1962), p. 58: "Let's shoot some equivalents Claes would say. By equivalents he means that a biplane equals hot dog or battleship equals pie equals hat equals ice cream equals sailboat equals pants on hanger and Christ on cross and hamburger equals pussy equals hat again and so on. That's his way of looking at things. So I go along with him knowing I can change it all later if I want. . . . Why things happen after each other in this film is because there isn't room for everything at once. But it's really a still picture and time is not supposed to move in one direction anymore than it does in the other. I'm sorry it takes half an hour."

"In the Galleries," *Arts Magazine* 38, no. 10 (September 1964)

Most of the work in this show ["Exhibition of Recent Works by Claes Oldenburg," Sidney Janis Gallery, April 7–May 2, 1964] is different from Oldenburg's other work and is even better. It is some of the best being done. The show is fairly various: there are several soft objects, a switch, toaster, typewriter, tube of toothpaste, telephone; and some other vinyl things, French fries and string beans; also canvas "ghost" models for the soft objects (fig. 10.1); a double wall plug and a double wall switch are hard objects. A ping-pong table and the paddles are parallelogrammatic, like the furniture in Oldenburg's bedroom suite, which wasn't praised as it merited. A vacuum cleaner and an ironing board are like those of the 1930s. There is a blue cloth shirt with a brown corduroy tie on and the size of a mobile "clothing rack." A piece of pie and some small pieces are plaster painted with enamel, probably earlier work. Some of the drawings for the new work are good, and some, most of those on black paper, are comparatively glib, possibly too near a shot at the quality of the swank modern furniture Oldenburg's interested in. The vinyl switch (fig. 10.2) is a softened vermilion, maybe flamingo colored. It sags from its upper corners; it's a swag. The rectangle of the switch is partially stuffed with kapok, and the two switches, set side by side, not above and below, are filled. The switches fit in pockets in the rectangle and can be switched on and off. I think Oldenburg's work is profound. I think it's very hard to explain how. The swag of flamingo vinyl seems to be a switch. It is grossly enlarged and soft, flaccid, changed and changeable. It seems to be like

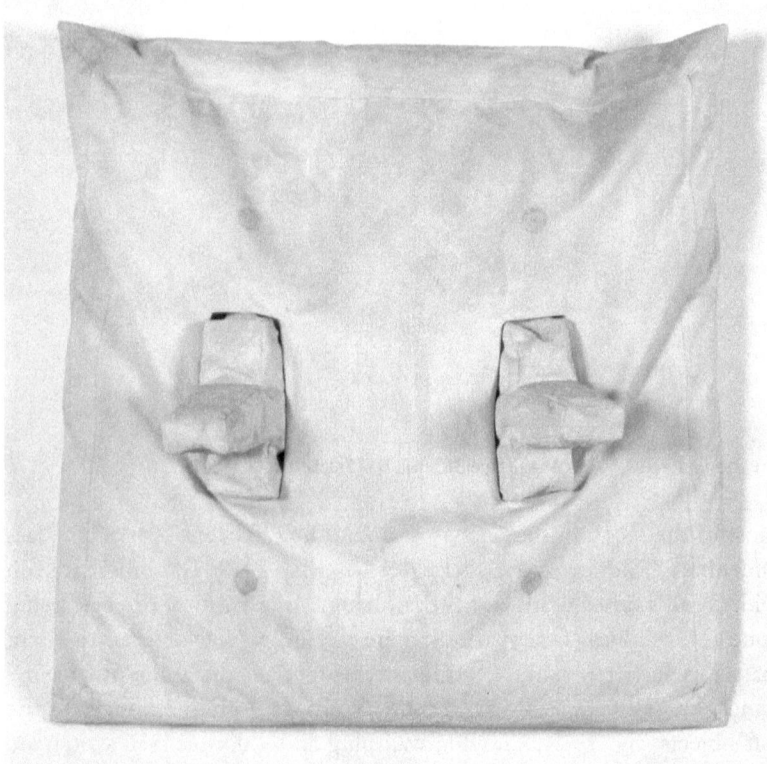

Figure 10.1 *Soft Light Switches—"Ghost Version"*
II, 1964–1971. Canvas filled with kapok, gesso,
pencil, 47 × 47 × 12 in. (119.4 × 119.4 × 30.5
cm). Collection Claes Oldenburg and Coosje
van Bruggen. Photo courtesy the Oldenburg van
Bruggen Studio.

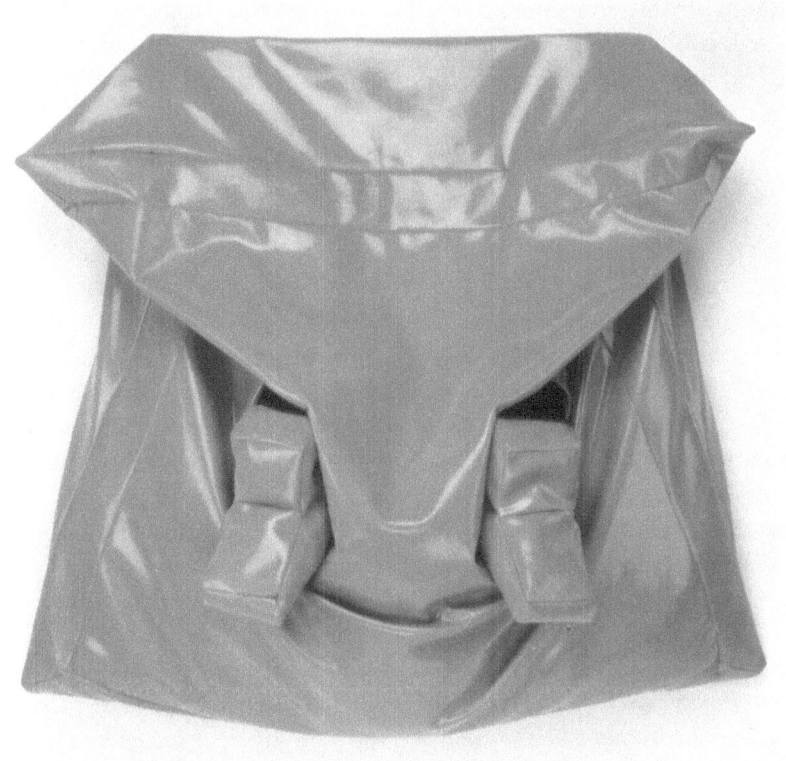

Figure 10.2 *Soft Light Switches 1/2*, 1964. Vinyl filled with Dacron and canvas, 47 × 47 × 3⅝ in. (119.4 × 119.4 × 9.1 cm). Collection The Nelson-Atkins Museum of Art, Kansas City. Gift of Claes Oldenburg and Coosje van Bruggen. Photo courtesy the Oldenburg van Bruggen Studio.

breasts but doesn't resemble them, isn't descriptive, even abstractly. There aren't two breasts, just two nipples. The two switches are too distinct to be breasts. As nipples though, they are too large for the chest. Also they can be directed up or down, on and off. The whole form of the mammarian switch is a basic emotive one, a biopsychological one, an archetypal sense of breasts. Their size is felt as enormous and the nipples seem most important. The switch doesn't suggest this single, profound form, as do the breasts of Lachaise's women, but is it, or nearly it. This sort of basic form occurs in most of Oldenburg's work. The form is single, as it is felt, is single in form, is without discrete parts. It's enough. The emotive form is equated to a manmade object. This show, incidentally, is of things from the home; before that the things were from the store and before from the street. Ordinarily the figures and objects depicted in a painting or sculpture have a shape or contain shapes that are emotive. Oldenburg makes one of those subordinate shapes the whole form. Real anthropomorphism is subverted by the grossly anthropomorphic shapes, manmade, not shapes of natural things or people. The preferences of a person or millions are unavoidably incorporated in the things made, either through choice or acquiescence. Nothing made is completely objective, purely practical or merely present. And of course everything after it's made is variously felt. Part of the switch's anthropomorphism is that it's changing—as if melting and sliding in time. The hard objects are as grossly hard and geometric as these are soft. There are few artists as good as Oldenburg.

From "Specific Objects," *Arts Yearbook* **8 (1965)**

Little was done until lately [in sculpture] with the wide range of industrial products. Almost nothing has been done with industrial techniques and, because of the cost, probably won't be for some time. Art could be mass-produced, and possibilities otherwise unavailable, such as stamping, could be used. Dan Flavin, who uses fluorescent lights, has appropriated the results of industrial production. Materials vary greatly and are simply materials—Formica, aluminum, cold-rolled steel, Plexiglas, red and common brass, and so forth. They are specific. If they are used directly, they are more specific. Also, they are usually aggressive. There is an objectivity to the obdurate identity of a material. Also, of course, the qualities of materials—hard mass, soft mass, thickness of $\frac{1}{32}$, $\frac{1}{16}$, $\frac{1}{8}$ inch, pliability, slickness, translucency, dullness—have unobjective uses. The vinyl of Oldenburg's soft objects looks the same as ever, slick, flaccid, and a little disagreeable, and is objective, but it is pliable and can be sewn and stuffed with air and kapok and hung or set down, sagging or collapsing. Most of the new materials are not as accessible as oil on canvas and are hard to relate to one another. They aren't obviously art. The form of a work and its materials are closely related. In earlier work the structure and the imagery were executed in some neutral and homogeneous material. Since not many things are lumps, there are problems in combining the different surfaces and colors and in relating the parts so as not to weaken the unity.

Three-dimensional work usually doesn't involve ordinary anthropomorphic imagery. If there is a reference, it is single and explicit. In any case the chief interests are obvious. Each of [Lee] Bontecou's reliefs is an image. The image, all of the parts and the whole shape are coextensive. The parts are either part of the hole or part of the mound which forms the hole. The hole and the mound are only two things, which, after all, are the same thing. The parts and divisions are either radial or concentric in regard to the hole, leading in and out and enclosing. The radial and concentric parts meet more or less at right angles and in detail are structure in the old sense, but collectively are subordinate to the single form. Most of the new work has no structure in the usual sense, especially the work of Oldenburg and Stella. [John] Chamberlain's work does involve composition. The nature of Bontecou's single image is not so different from that of images which occurred in a small way in semiabstract painting. The image is primarily a single emotive one, which alone wouldn't resemble the old imagery so much, but to which internal and external references, such as violence and war, have been added. The additions are somewhat pictorial, but the image is essentially new and surprising; an image has never before been the whole work, been so large, been so explicit and aggressive. The abatised orifice is like a strange and dangerous object. The quality is intense and narrow and obsessive. The boat and the furniture that [Yayoi] Kusama covered with white protuberances have a related intensity and obsessiveness and are also strange objects. Kusama is interested in obsessive repetition, which is a single interest. Yves Klein's blue paintings are also narrow and intense.

The trees, figures, food, or furniture in a painting have a shape or contain shapes that are emotive. Oldenburg has taken this anthropomorphism to an extreme and made the emotive form, with him basic and biopsychological, the same as the shape of an object, and by blatancy subverted the idea of the natural presence of human qualities in all things. And further, Oldenburg avoids trees and people. All of Oldenburg's grossly anthropomorphized objects are manmade which right away is an empirical matter. Someone or many made these things and incorporated their preferences. As practical as an ice cream cone is, a lot of people made a choice, and more agreed, as to its appearance and existence. This interest shows more in the recent appliances and fixtures from the home and especially in the bedroom suite, where the choice is flagrant. Oldenburg exaggerates the accepted or chosen form and turns it into one of his own. Nothing made is completely objective, purely practical, or merely present. Oldenburg gets along very well without anything that would ordinarily be called structure. The ball and cone of the large ice cream cone are enough. The whole thing is a profound form, such as sometimes occurs in primitive art. Three fat layers with a small one on top are enough. So is a flaccid, flamingo switch draped from two points. Simple form and one or two colors are considered less by old standards. If changes in art are compared backward, there always seems to be a reduction, since only old attributes are counted and these are always fewer. But obviously new things are more, such as Oldenburg's techniques and materials. Oldenburg needs three dimensions in order to simulate and enlarge a real object and to equate it and an emotive form. If a hamburger were painted, it would retain something of the traditional anthropomorphism. George Brecht and Robert Morris use real objects and depend on the viewer's knowledge of these objects.

"Claes Oldenburg," text written for *Claes Oldenburg: Skulpturer och teckningar, 1963–1966,* **Moderna Museet in Stockholm (1966)**

Oldenburg's work is so extremely anthropomorphic that it isn't anthropomorphic in the real sense of the word. The real sense is one of the main aspects of old European art. Any of the remnants of this are a liability in the work they're part of. The philosophy and its formal means are backwater; anything new is mainstream.

The real or usual anthropomorphism is the appearance of human feelings in things that are inanimate or not human, usually as if those feelings are the essential nature of the thing described. Oldenburg's pieces have nothing to do with the objects they're like. You don't feel that he's saying anything about toothpaste tubes, light switches, or telephones. The pieces have only the emotion read into objects; they have no sense that it is really there. Anyone particularly interested in objects in the past, Chardin, Cézanne, or lately [Giorgio] Morandi, believed that the things themselves had a reality that could be understood and shown. This belief came from rationalistic philosophy and through that from religion.

A remnant of the anthropomorphic form is one of the main parts of most fairly good work being done now. The parts in most sculpture move and are stressed in an anthropomorphic way. The usual composition of major and minor parts is hierarchical and anthropomorphic. The shapes and lines in most abstract painting are also anthropomorphic in stress and movement and are based on natural shapes, actually abstraction, the essentials of the source shown alone. A small amount and the best abstract painting—it shouldn't be called abstract—isn't anthropomorphic in any way. It has none of the attitudes and characteristics of traditional European art. Some three-dimensional work isn't anthropomorphic or abstract. Oldenburg's work is, then, some of the little that is very good and free of unbelievable interpretation.

Oldenburg or anyone that good has made something that didn't exist before. Much in the work is new. The distance from other art is considerable. The relationships to other art are loose and irregular. But usually art is discussed as if it happens neatly. Its social situation, which seems orderly because it exists, is substituted for the actual ways it occurred and the actual relationships it has or doesn't have. Some terms and much writing imply that new forms fill in predetermined places. Very often someone's work is characterized by only one aspect, Oldenburg's by its subject matter, more superficially by pop. Oldenburg's work is less related to that of other pop artists than it is to that of several artists usually thought completely different. Frequently everything is simplified by making an aspect, a form, or a technique a necessity for first-rate work. This becomes the only direction for art to take, the mainstream. It's certainly academic to say that the next good artist is going to use means that have already been well used. Anyway the main thing for anyone now is to invent his own means. The persistent characteristics of art are very general and not always present, such as large scale, wholeness, unmodulated color, and an emphasis on materials. The best work is related through its most general aspects and never through its specific and obvious ones. The absence of anthropomorphic and other old forms is one of the general aspects common to the best art.

It's pretty obvious that Oldenburg's work involves feelings about objects; his objects are objects as they're felt, not as they are. They're usually desirable objects, sometimes interesting or necessary ones. They're exaggerated, as interest is, gross and overblown, and simplified to what's most desirable about them or to what's used most. The grossness of the scale, simplicity, and surface make it obvious that it's the interest in the object that is the main thing, not the object itself. A show at Janis a couple of years ago had a hard light switch and a soft switch [see figs. 10.1, 10.2]. The hard one is exceedingly hard. A girl said once that sometimes the corners of things would seem to be points pointing at her. The soft switch hangs on the wall like a swag of material and would be different or just flamingo-colored vinyl on the floor or in some other position. It's changeable, likely to collapse or dissolve, and unreliable. The soft objects are half stuffed and reducible; only irreducible things have been serious and permanent. In the old arguments about the nature of substance, tables and chairs were always the examples; they didn't argue about the primary and secondary qualities of their pants and shirts. Softness or hardness can be good or bad. A soft switch is fine, except as a mechanism. A soft toothpaste tube is bad; or a hard outlet.

Most of the pieces, the switches, the soft telephone and typewriter, the big shirt, and the enormous hamburger and ice cream cone shown earlier at the Green Gallery, involve only a sense of objects. At most the objects are a little dated, like the ironing board and vacuum cleaner, or very common—popular—like the hamburger and ice cream cone. A few pieces, especially the bedroom, which is a great room, involve identifiable attitudes toward things (fig. 10.3). It's American modern and a thorough corruption of all its sources. There are even little drip paintings on the walls. There's little real modern furniture and none of it recent, but there's an enormous quantity of debased modern derived from it. The geometric shapes of the furniture in the bedroom are grossly geometric and inanely simple. The cylindrical lampshades are marbled, the pillows are zebra-striped cloth, and the black vinyl bedspread imitates leather. That's pretty familiar. The sheets though are clean white plastic. The materials together are slick and dry; the colors are turquoise, black, and white.

The sense of objects occurs with forms that are near some simple, basic, profound forms you feel. These disappear when you try to make them into imaginable visual or tactile forms. The reference to objects gives them a way to occur. The reference and the basic form as one thing is Oldenburg's main idea. It's completely his idea; it's a remarkable one and it's full of possibilities. A lot of the simple forms are sexual, such as the switches, the hamburger, and the ice cream cone. These are senses of the body; some of the pieces are just that alone and aren't particularly

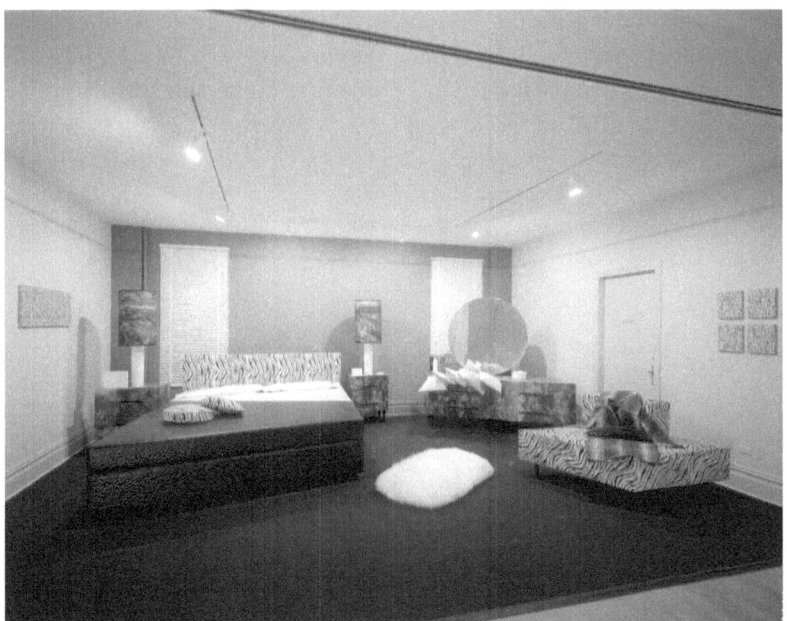

Figure 10.3 *Bedroom Ensemble 2/3*, 1963–1969.
Wood, Formica, vinyl, aluminum, paper, fake
fur, muslin, Dacron, polyurethane foam, lacquer;
overall: 10 ft. × 17 ft. × 21 ft. (303 × 512 × 648
cm). Collection Museum für Moderne Kunst,
Frankfurt am Main, Germany. Photo © Rudolf
Nagel, Frankfurt am Main; courtesy the
Oldenburg van Bruggen Studio.

sexual. Some of the pieces are shapes that have little to do with the body. They're shapes or movements of feelings. The bed in the bedroom is like this. It's oversized, it's a parallelogram, and the white plastic sheets and the black vinyl bedspread or quilt are very flat. The white plastic is turned back, pulled flat across the bedspread at an angle to the parallelogram. The slick white slides across the black vinyl, which is stamped to look like it's tooled or embossed.

The soft vermillion switch is sexual and also infantile. The two switches or knobs, set side by side rather than above and below, fit into the rectangle and can be switched on and off. The whole switch seems to be like breasts but doesn't resemble them and isn't descriptive, even abstractedly. There aren't two breasts, just two nipples. The two switches don't seem like two breasts. As nipples though, they are too large for the chest. Also, they can be turned up or down. The whole switch is big and soft and the nipples are enormous—the main things. The form is whole and simple and has no discrete parts. The two switches aren't separate from the rectangle; the three physically separable parts don't, visually, add up to the whole. They're made as a whole. They're the same material and it bulges and sags the same throughout. The three parts sag according to one position.

Claes Oldenburg's Soft Machines

Barbara Rose

Claes Oldenburg is the single pop artist to have added significantly to the history of form. In order to perceive this, however, one must look beyond the Rabelaisian absurdity of his grotesque imagery to the inventiveness of his shapes, techniques, and materials. These are sufficiently original to identify Oldenburg, not, as he has erroneously been seen, as a *chef d'école* of pop art, but as one of the most vital innovators in the field of contemporary sculpture, whose vision has affected the work of many other young artists of his generation.

Every major artist dreams of reconstructing the world in his own image, but Oldenburg has actually succeeded in translating the external environment into a series of shapes and images that physically resemble the large, mesomorphic frame of Claes Oldenburg. To accomplish his solipsistic goal, he had to invent a vocabulary of forms that would be as vulnerable, as irregular, as eccentric, unique and expressive as the human body itself. Oldenburg began to recreate the human anatomy in his own terms in the late 1950s with crude pieces like the papier-mâché leg. In 1962 he hit on a way to make forms that were entirely foreign to the traditional concept of sculpture because they were soft rather than hard, as one expects sculpture to be. But this reversal of expectations is important, not because it conflicts with our notion of the nature of solid objects—this would be trivial—but because it challenges our ideas about the nature of sculpture, which we expect to be rigid and resistant like metal or wood, not soft, yielding and pliable like the stuffed and sewn canvas and vinyl world Oldenburg has created in his soft sculpture. By the same token, if Oldenburg were merely involved in a series of ironic puns of a conceptual nature, then his work would hold little interest. Fortunately, he is involved in much more; concept in his art is relatively unimportant when compared with his concern with the sensual and the expressive.[1]

Like many important innovations, soft sculpture was arrived at accidentally. Its origin was the oversize props Oldenburg made for use in his happenings. According to Oldenburg, sewing as a technique began with the costumes and props for the Ray Gun Theater, a series of happenings produced in 1962, which called for props like an eighteen-foot airplane and a fifteen-foot man. From these colossal props to the gargantuan stuffed cloth articles of food like the hamburger, ice cream cone, and slice of cake exhibited in Oldenburg's 1962 Green Gallery exhibition was but a short step. What led to taking this step, however, tells us something important not only about Oldenburg's art, but also about the aesthetic of the new sculpture in general, in which his work surely participates.[2]

In his notes, Oldenburg mentions that he began to think of making sculpture when a collector bought a boat and a freighter from *Store Days*, staged at the store on lower Second Avenue that he filled in 1961 with misshapen replicas of objects sold in general stores. Oldenburg admits he began to think of these objects as independent sculptures because they were treated as sculpture. In other words, the work became sculpture by virtue of the way it was used. Such a view is, of course, to a degree merely an extension of Duchamp's insistence that art is art by virtue of context, but its adoption as a working premise by artists as different from Oldenburg as Morris, Flavin, Judd, and Andre demonstrates the degree to which the concept animates the thinking of a younger generation of sculptors and object-makers.[3]

Oldenburg's first three-dimensional objects were painted plaster like the reliefs that preceded them. Like the splattered and blotched surfaces of the reliefs, the surfaces of these objects recalled the painterly brushwork of abstract expressionism. In the soft cloth pieces that followed, however, Oldenburg arrived at a way of translating pictorial concerns, such as chiaroscuro modeling, color, and texture entirely into sculptural concerns. In some works, like the "ghost" models of the typewriter and telephone, or the map of the postal zones of Manhattan, light and dark passages are added directly to simulate, literally, the chiaroscuro of painting (see fig. 11.1, a giant fan). This transferal of painting problems to sculpture is typical not only of Oldenburg but of many young artists. Like the object makers in general, Oldenburg is a literalist. In this spirit

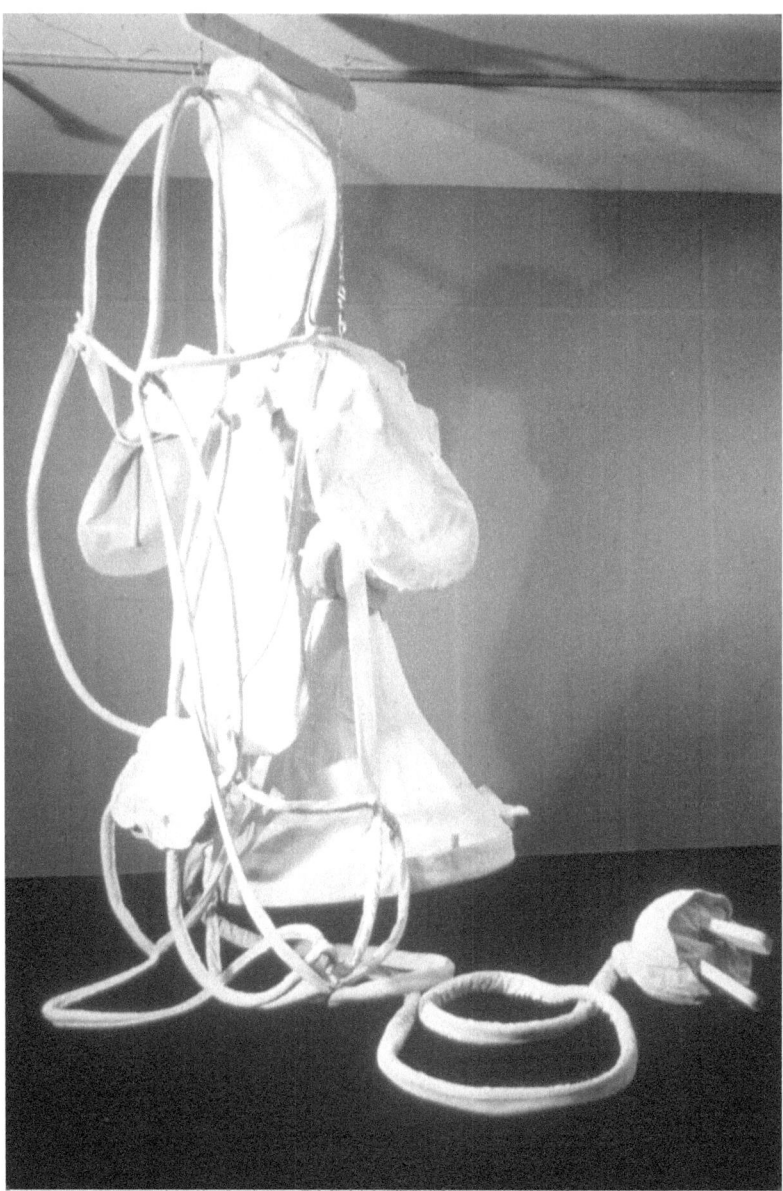

Figure 11.1 *Giant Soft Fan—Ghost Version*, 1967. Canvas filled with polyurethane foam, wood, metal, plastic; fan: 120 × 59 × 64 in. (304.8 × 149.9 × 162.6 cm); cord and plug, length: 290 in. (736.6 cm). Collection The Museum of Fine Arts, Houston. Gift of D. and J. de Menil. Photo courtesy the Oldenburg van Bruggen Studio.

he describes his softening as "not a blurring (like the effect of atmosphere on hard form) but in *fact* a softening." As artists like Bell, Judd, and Mc-Cracken make concrete and literal effects formerly used allusively or illusively in painting, so Oldenburg uses softness literally, as a quality that is both actual and specific.

In executing a work, Oldenburg proceeds as follows: first he makes a model of the object he wishes to reproduce, then he makes a pattern with stencils, which is transferred on the material to be used; the stenciled shapes are cut out and sewn together (usually by Oldenburg's wife) and finally stuffed by Oldenburg, who fixes the actual form of the work by "modeling" it from within (fig. 11.2). Technically, Oldenburg's modeling is the opposite of conventional modeling through building up clay or wax on an armature or cutting away from a solid block. Because the "modeling" is done from the inside, the outside surface is uniform and continuous, and lacks marks of touching. Oldenburg describes choosing the "kind of stuffing and how much and where it will gather—fat or

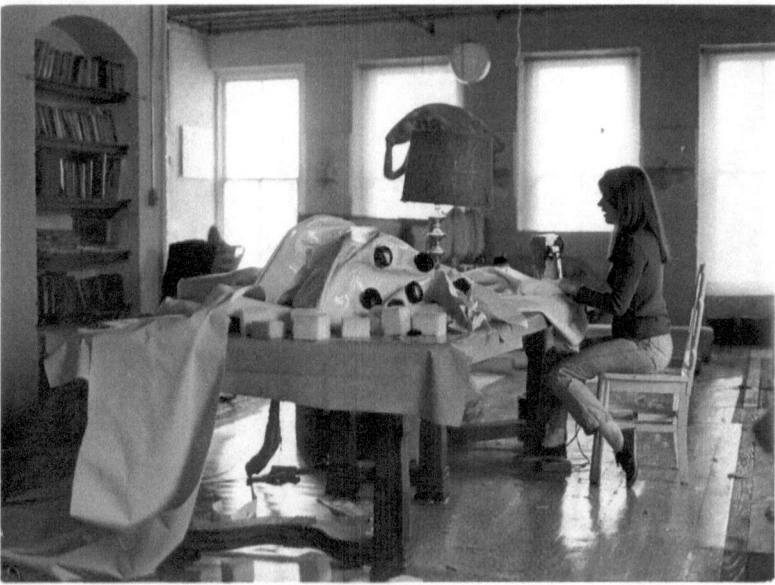

Figure 11.2 Patty Mucha sewing the *Soft Juicit* in Fourteenth Street studio, New York, 1965. Photo: Ugo Mulas; courtesy the Oldenburg van Bruggen Studio.

lean" as the crucial moment in the work. In the stiffened canvas sculpture, which tends to stay put as placed to a greater degree than vinyl or soft fabric, his degree of control is naturally greater.

Oldenburg's interest in modeling relates him formally to traditional casting and carving just as his material and technique separate him from it technically. In many ways he is closer to Rodin and Matisse than to the cubists and their heirs. For Oldenburg relies not on plane, as in cubism, nor on volume, as in primary structures, but on undulating mass, the means of expression of pre-cubist sculpture. Despite the fact that there are no finger marks to remind one of the sculptor's personal touch, Oldenburg's is both an extremely personal and an extremely tactile art. Moreover, his aim is not to reject, but to enhance this tactility, intensifying the urge to touch "devices which prevent touching, like the silver chain in the door to the *Bedroom Ensemble* . . . or the glass of the pastry cases." This interest in the tactile once again relates Oldenburg to abstract expressionism.

Like the human body, which it resembles in its lumps, bumps, folds, and crevices, soft sculpture is literally subject to the force of gravity to a degree that rigid sculpture is not. Gravity, which Oldenburg calls his "favorite form creator," determines the final form a piece will assume. Thus, one of the reasons Oldenburg prefers the large form is because "on a large scale gravity most wins out completely." Oldenburg's choice of an oversize scale, which again has its origin in a theatrical problem—the necessity for props to be large in order to attract attention—has had many repercussions for the future of sculpture. His 1962 exhibition was, to my recollection, the first one-man show of sculpture in which the pieces, meant to impede circulation and to demand a certain kind of inescapable focus, were executed on the superhuman scale that is so familiar today.

The reliance on gravity to determine the final shape of a work can be viewed as a reliance on chance. The casual manner in which a soft form settles, or even better, relaxes into place suggests that the work is self-composed, or at least relatively uncomposed. This tendency toward relinquishing total control over composition is something Oldenburg shares with a number of advanced artists. It is part of the legacy of Pollock's drip paintings, and very much part of the current attitude that assigns a lesser role to composition than that assigned to it by cubism, with its insistence on the initial relationships of discrete parts. This attitude also accounts for Oldenburg's choice of the single image as a format. Again, the preference for the single image is one that relates Oldenburg to many younger artists; it, too, is ultimately traceable back to Pollock's arrival at the single image in the drip paintings.

Like Lichtenstein, Oldenburg shares more with the abstract artists of his generation than he does with the pop artists, just as Johns and Rauschenberg, despite their pop imagery, remain essentially second-generation abstract expressionists. In its large scale, use of the single image, and lack of internal relationships, Oldenburg's sculpture has far more in common with the advanced art of Morris, Poons, Stella, Judd, et al. than it does with any pop art, which, outside of Oldenburg and Lichtenstein, is indeed as reactionary and academic as most responsible critics have claimed it is. Like many object sculptors, Oldenburg is more interested in creating new shapes and surfaces than in concentrating on the tasteful arrangement or harmonious balancing of analogous forms that has characterized composition in Western art from the Renaissance through cubism. Composition is treated casually, informally, even arbitrarily, and chance—in the form of the action of gravity—is a determining factor. Of his monuments (immense, unrealized, and possibly unrealizable projects to be erected in public squares and parks), Oldenburg writes: "The thrown versions of the monuments originated in disgust with the subject, the way one would kick over or throw a piece of sculpture that hadn't turned out well. Instead of destruction, I accepted as result a variation of form and position." Such an acceptance of chance and the arbitrary as part of the creative process is characteristic in general of post-abstract expressionist art. Whether Oldenburg has received it directly through Duchamp and Cage, or indirectly through abstract expressionism—which seems more likely, given the extent to which his early reliefs and environments grew out of abstract expressionism—is unimportant; what matters is the degree to which it has liberated not only his imagination, but that of a generation of young artists.

Because Oldenburg's work is imagistic, one must take into consideration the relationship of the soft forms to the types of images used, since part of the expressiveness of the work arises naturally out of this relationship. Oldenburg selects his range of images from the three environments that constitute his universe: The Home, The Street, and The Store. The identification of the image is crucial; it is necessary in order to establish the active relationship between viewer and object that Oldenburg desires. For this reason, he chooses food or objects of personal use, such as clothing or furniture. Normally these are objects we would pick up, handle, or consume. "The name of the thing tells you how to grab it (camera, gun) or what to do with it (ice cream, chair, jacket)." In each case, active participation is called forth. And the reaction of the viewer to these objects, even when they are recreated on a mammoth scale and eccentrically deformed, is still within the context of the intimate and the personal. In this way, both Oldenburg and the makers of abstract object-sculpture, it seems to me, are working to erode the concept of "psychic distance," the sense of estrangement that we normally bring to the aesthetic experience. By choosing to make objects or things, rather than paintings or sculptures that look immediately like "art," they force the viewer to react in terms of his normal environment, not in terms of the specialized reaction we associate only with art. This works to short-circuit perception in a sense, forcing a more direct, intimate, personal contact with the work.

"Sanding the wooden typewriter keys," Oldenburg writes, "I feel like a manicurist." At another point he speaks of "the perception of mechanical nature as body." Pursuing the concept of anthropomorphizing to its logical extreme, Oldenburg has invested inanimate objects with the breath and pulse of life, and cast them in the irregular, sagging, lumpy forms of the human body (fig. 11.3). Interestingly enough, this tendency to anthropomorphize the inanimate can be seen in earlier American artists, such as Dove and Charles Burchfield. In some ways Dove's bug-eyed ferryboats and dancing trees and Burchfield's houses in which windows become eyes and doors become mouths are the ancestors of Oldenburg's lewd grinning typewriters and sad-sack telephones.

Because they provide analogies with the human physiognomy and anatomy, one can see Oldenburg's soft machines as a kind of reformulated figurative sculpture. In their humanization, the soft machines are the opposite of the dehumanized, mechanical figures of cubist sculpture. And indeed they represent an attitude diametrically opposed to that of the earlier twentieth century, which viewed industrialism and its concomitant alienation as a cataclysmic threat. Oldenburg makes analogies between the body and the machine, much as cybernetics sees analogies between the brain and the computer. As the distance between man and machine narrows, man does not become more like the machine, as Ortega prophesied, but the machine, which now appears not menacingly strange but reassuringly familiar, becomes more like man—singular, changeable, and, above all, vulnerable.

Softness implies vulnerability. Duchamp was perhaps the first to invest objects with feelings in his "unhappy ready-mades." Oldenburg is pleased with the Airflow as a theme because "the implication of a bent

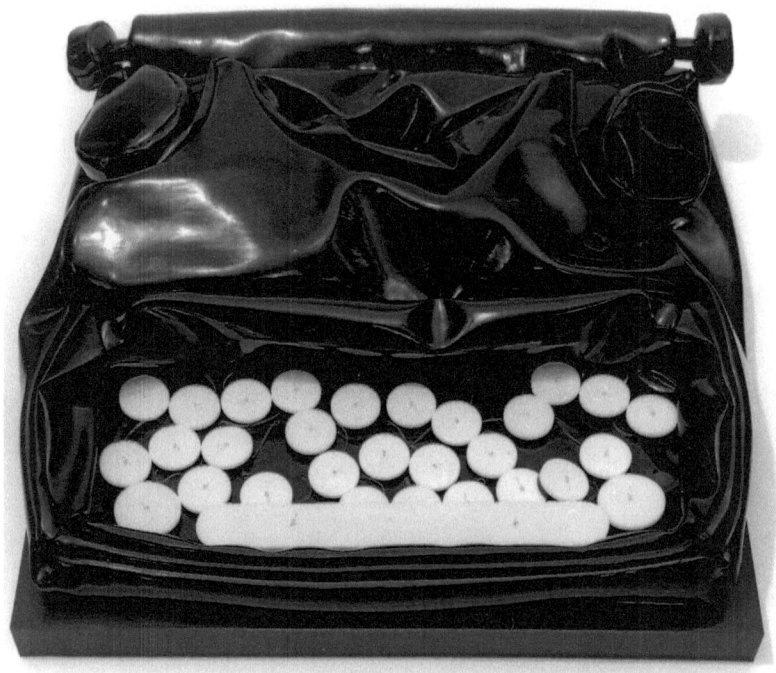

Figure 11.3 *Soft Typewriter*, 1963. Vinyl filled
with kapok, Plexiglas, nylon cord, 9 × 26 × 27½
in. (22.9 × 66 × 69.9 cm). Collection Esther
Grether, Basel. Photo: Geoffrey Clements;
courtesy the Oldenburg van Bruggen Studio.

fender or a crushed cab is considerable" (fig. 11.4). There is a certain
poignancy in the melancholy exhaustion of the droopy telephones and
unkempt tires. But to attribute human qualities and human feelings to
inanimate objects is to hold a pathetic fallacy. Such a pathetic fallacy,
however, which sees objects as tired and as scarred as people, is central
to Oldenburg's content. For it is a particular kind of world Oldenburg
is trying to describe, and a particular kind of accommodation between
man and his man-made nature that he is prescribing. In a passage reminiscent of the late Wilhelm Reich, Oldenburg writes: "Those who care
for the world at this time tend to undress and go naked rather than in
armor. I don't find anything metallic suited to this sensibility." If the
soft machines are unthreatening, friendly even, in that they are like us,

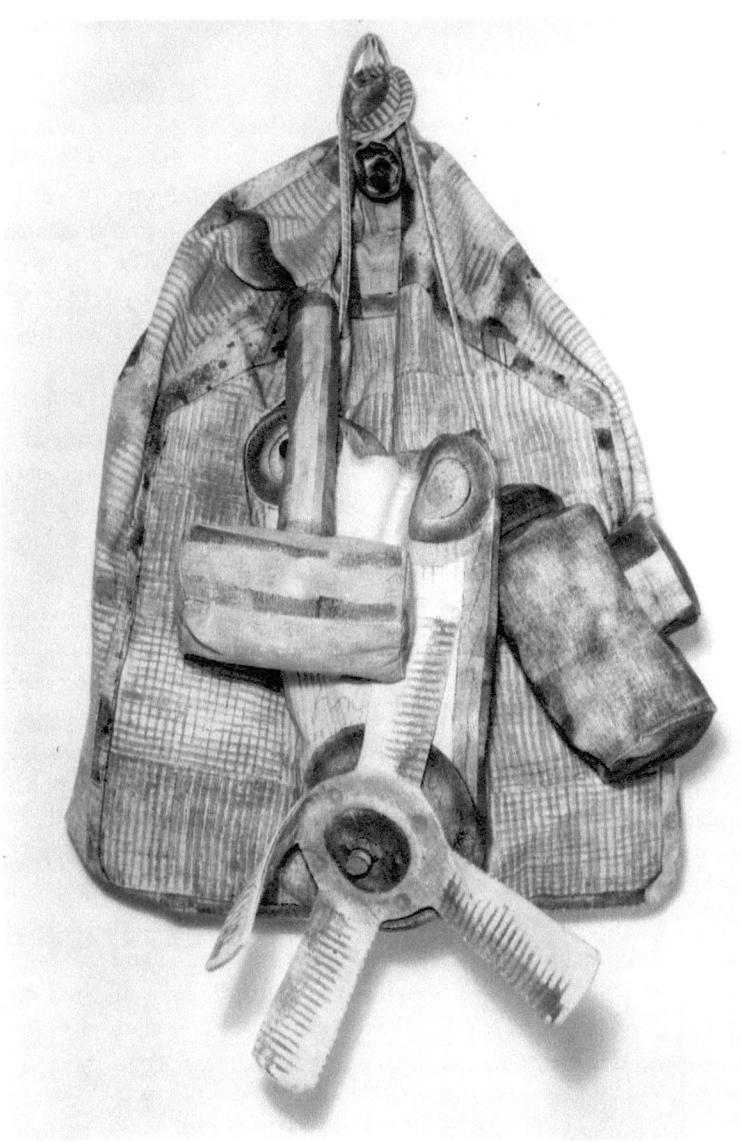

Figure 11.4 *Soft Engine Parts #1 (Radiator and Fan), Airflow, Scale 5*, 1965. Canvas filled with kapok, patterned with spray enamel, 32 × 24 × 18 in. (101 × 56 × 31 cm) installed. Collection The Art Museum, Princeton University; Lent by the Schorr Family Collection, Calif. Photo: Geoffrey Clements; courtesy the Oldenburg van Bruggen Studio.

we cannot consider them alien. And it is an end to the alienation of man from his industrial environment that Oldenburg, the post-Marxist and post-Freudian, prescribes. His is the message of the second half of the twentieth century, the message of such post-Marxist, post-Freudian thinkers as Norman O. Brown, whose *Life against Death* (1959) was obviously a profound influence on Oldenburg's thought and iconography.[4] Like Brown, Oldenburg sees the possibility of an end to the estrangement between man and the phenomenological world he inhabits.

"An object in the shape of the artist" is Oldenburg's description of his work. Relating sculpture to one's own body image can result in a kind of dislocated expressionism; and in one sense the soft sculptures are really a series of self-portraits. Many, like the gaping faucet-eyed washbasin or the phallic Dormeyer blenders, actually parallel specific features of the human physiognomy or anatomy. Thus, Oldenburg's images act as a surrogate for the human body. Oldenburg admits it is the same to him whether his image is a cathedral or a girdle, since "the contribution of subject matter is almost a side effect since what I see is not the thing itself but—myself—in its form."

As surrogates for the human body, the soft machines serve as totems, "a kind of figure representation in which the presence of a figure is evoked, as in a seance or hallucination." The image is individualized to the degree that one is convinced that "someone very particular is in the room with you." Like Klee and Dubuffet, Oldenburg seeks to call on the power of the primitive totem which manifests the charisma of submerged psychic forces. Like them, he reveres childhood and the innocent naiveté of the child's eye as well as the art of the sidewalks and the madhouse. And like their work, Oldenburg's works appear to play host to some primitive force or energy, an energy that often seems to have a specifically sexual charge.[5]

In certain respects Oldenburg's "presences" are like the mysterious, quasi-human personages that peopled surrealist painting. Other aspects of Oldenburg's imagination also link him with the surrealists, not in the sense of having been influenced by them, but in the sense of belonging to the same "family of mind." Like the surrealists, Oldenburg delights in the metamorphosis of one thing into another. The "hard," "soft," and "ghost" models of the typewriter, telephone, light switch, etc., show these objects in different states; the three daffy troll-like Silex juicits (fig. 11.5) reveal the object in different comic attitudes; and the series of

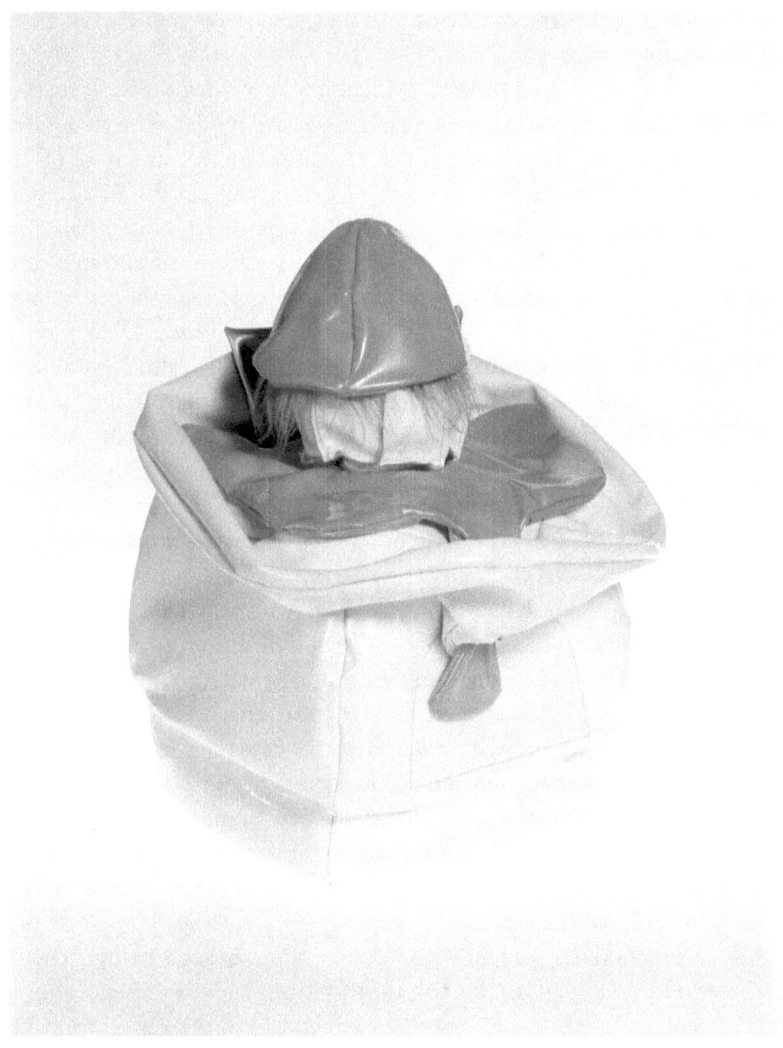

Figure 11.5 *Soft Juicit*, 1965. Vinyl filled with
kapok, fake fur, 20½ × 17 × 16 in. (52.1 ×
43.2 × 40.6 cm). Collection Shirley Blum,
Westport, New York. Photo courtesy the
Oldenburg van Bruggen Studio.

melting foods and partially eaten foods represent sequences that suggest the passage of time.

In a series of related objects, Oldenburg may alter the size, shape, form, substance, or state in time of each successive model. The alteration emphasizes the process of change; the state of the object in any of these series is always unstable, transitional, in flux: the objects are always in a process of becoming, rather than in any fixed, resolved, closed state. In the swimming pools, Oldenburg explores different forms of the same object. The interest in mutability is one he shares with a number of young abstract artists, most notably Morris, Stella, and Ron Davis. Oldenburg's investigations of the possibilities for new forms available from each object are often as exhaustive as the permutations of Morris, the spatial rotations of Ron Davis, or the systematic structural exploitations of Stella. At one point, for example, Oldenburg suggests treating the Airflow four different ways: interior, exterior, in sections, and finally whole. The presentation of an exhaustive and equally meaningful set of alternative solutions is common to the methodical thought of the younger generation. Announced in Johns's multiple presentations of the flag, it seems related to the discovery in the physical and social sciences that different types of coexistent models, each adequately accounting for the same data, are possible.

In keeping with his interest in metamorphoses, Oldenburg constantly sees analogies between dissimilar images which may assume, in his imagination, analogous forms.[6] Thus the relationship of Oldenburg's images to their prototypes is not literal nor even logical, but associative. Although Oldenburg claims that his approach is naive imitation, what he does with the objects he imitates is to "charge them more intensively" in order to maximize their power as contemporary totems. These totems, although functional, maintain their "magic" aura through being exalted by the artist's imagination into charismatic personages or presences.

Oldenburg explains the degree to which the image differs from its prototype: "If I alter, which I do usually, I do not alter for 'art' and I do not alter to express *myself*, I alter to unfold the object and to add to it other object qualities, forces. The object remains object, only expanded and less specific." Oldenburg's decision to remain an image-maker in a period when abstract art is ascendent seems based on his conviction that since allusion cannot be eliminated entirely, it must therefore be rendered redundant. He apparently believes that if one cannot eliminate the image, then one can at least render it meaningless or neutral by reducing all images to the common denominator of the body image.

The world, for Oldenburg, is constantly in motion. He is impressed above all by the movement of New York: "Objects previously still begin to move. The Pizza becomes Fan. The Fan chops. Fragments fly." Oldenburg has always conceived in terms of environments—in this, too, he has influenced current abstract sculpture which places so high a value on the relationship of the work to its environment.[7] Oldenburg sees the city as the artist's total environment, and suggests "a series of pieces treating New York . . . as an object sculpture." In fact, one of the most striking things about Oldenburg's imagination is his ability to conceive a complete personal universe and mythology. Oldenburg's objects do not constitute merely a string of related images, but a highly structured iconographical program, as coherent as the iconography of any old master, and as tied to a specific worldview—from the point of departure of the Airflow, for example. Oldenburg generalizes "a place with many different sized objects inside it, like a gallery, a butcher shop, like The Store." Later, Airflow becomes a metaphor for the space around objects, a space in which objects can be seen falling, floating, or flying, propped up, lying down, or suspended.

Although at the heart of Oldenburg's effort is a reversal of normal expectations—not as I have pointed out, our expectations about objects, but our expectations about art, specifically sculpture—irony is not a component of his work. In its total lack of irony, Oldenburg's work differs from the rest of pop art. But in place of the negative and pessimistic sense of irony, Oldenburg has substituted the cathartic force of humor, especially as it manifests itself in the tragic-comic. The sagging, clownish objects are, in their pathos and vulnerability, like the great oafish clown Oldenburg himself often impersonates in his happenings. Here, as the deadpan, baggy-pants ringmaster, the heir of Chaplin and W. C. Fields, Oldenburg directs the activities of his circus. And the metaphor of the clown is well taken. From Pagliacci to Pierrot to Picasso's and Fellini's harlequins, the clown assumes the role of the deracinated tragicomic hero of modern times, as earlier the fool had represented a persona of Everyman. Oldenburg's art belongs to the tradition of the satyr plays, and to that of the fool and the clown; like the other works of this tradition, its message is the fallibility and vulnerability of man. Oldenburg has claimed that he wishes "to present the geography of the human imagination with real mountains and cities." His content he describes as "always the human imagination both as historically constant and as universal among individuals." Oldenburg's faith in the redemptive power of the imagination is the guarantee that his innocence is genuine, even if it comes clothed in the most extreme sophistication and awareness. From the genuine innocence, vitality, and originality of his vision, he has extrapolated a new vocabulary of forms that has already enriched the history of art. This vision is both grandiose and optimistic; it bespeaks the expansiveness and generosity, as well as the generalizing intelligence of the large talent.

Notes

1. Oldenburg shows an unusual degree of objectivity about his work. For that reason, I have drawn to a great extent on his own notes, which seem to me by far the most intelligent things written about his work. All quotes in the text therefore are from Oldenburg's statements in the following: "Extracts from the Studio Notes," *Artforum* 4, no. 5 (January 1966), pp. 32–33, and *Claes Oldenburg Skulpturer och teckningar* (Stockholm: Moderna Museet, 1966). With his usual detachment, Oldenburg assesses himself: "My theories are not original, my execution is, and my distinction lies in my sensuality and imagination rather than my intellect."

2. Outside of Oldenburg's own writings, the most intelligent discussion of his work is Donald Judd's "Specific Objects," *Arts Yearbook* 8 (1965), in which Judd places Oldenburg within the general context of object sculpture, to which his work surely relates more closely than to pop art, the context in which it is normally considered. Reprinted in this volume.

3. The extent of Duchamp's influence on current aesthetic attitudes can scarcely be overemphasized. What is interesting, however, is that the focus has been shifted from *finding* to *making* in an open situation that affords *abstract* artists the same freedom from restrictive conventions as the original Dadaists claimed. The highly eccentric, noncanonical geometric art of today is as dependent on freedoms won by Dada and surrealism as abstract expressionism was. Not to acknowledge this aspect of current thinking is to falsify history.

4. So in tune with Norman Brown's thinking was Oldenburg that before *Love's Body* (1966), the sequel to *Life against Death* in which Brown uses the human body as a metaphor for all political, social, and economic organization, Oldenburg had already anticipated this line of thought by using soft sculpture as a body image surrogate.

5. In his interest in the mythic and the totemic, Oldenburg appears to be exhuming the lost surrealist content of abstract expressionism which was active in the early 1940s, but became submerged after World War II when the surrealists returned to Europe.

6. He notes such analogies as that between the square war monument and the square slab of butter in the baked potato, the giant frankfurter and Ellis Island, and the ironing board monument and the shape of Manhattan.

7. "My work makes a great demand on a collector," Oldenburg states. "I have tried to make it in every way so that anyone who comes into contact with it is greatly inconvenienced. That is to say, made aware of its existence and of my principles." One is struck by how close this statement comes to the intention of primary structures, another suggestion that the meaningful links are between the strongest, most advanced artists of the younger generation, rather than in terms of artificially created "movements" or "schools" such as pop or primary.

Object Lessons

Nadja Rottner

Softness could mean both a flowing together and flowing apart of definitions.[1]

—*Claes Oldenburg*

I want my work, my language to be as light as words and as changeable.[2]

—*Claes Oldenburg*

In the afternoon of October 5, 1962, art scene luminaries flocked into Dick Bellamy's Green Gallery in uptown Manhattan, a space quickly gaining a reputation for supporting a new generation of post-abstract-expressionist artists. There they witnessed an exclusive performance by sculptor and performance artist Claes Oldenburg. Turning his second exhibition of *The Store* (the first took place in his studio in the Lower East Side earlier that year) into a makeshift theatrical stage for *Sports*, Oldenburg had removed most of the new plaster and enamel food and clothing objects from display, while leaving the supersized, soft *Floor Burger* in situ to serve as a prop (figs. 12.1, 12.2). The crowd of about twenty-five attendees, including Andy Warhol,[3] Yayoi Kusama, Donald Judd, Harry Smith, John Chamberlain, Robert Breer, and Henry Geldzahler, lined up against one long wall of the exhibition space. Oldenburg had handed them, upon entry, the current edition of the *New York Daily News*, its headline announcing the 6–2 World Series win of the New York Yankees over the San Francisco Giants.

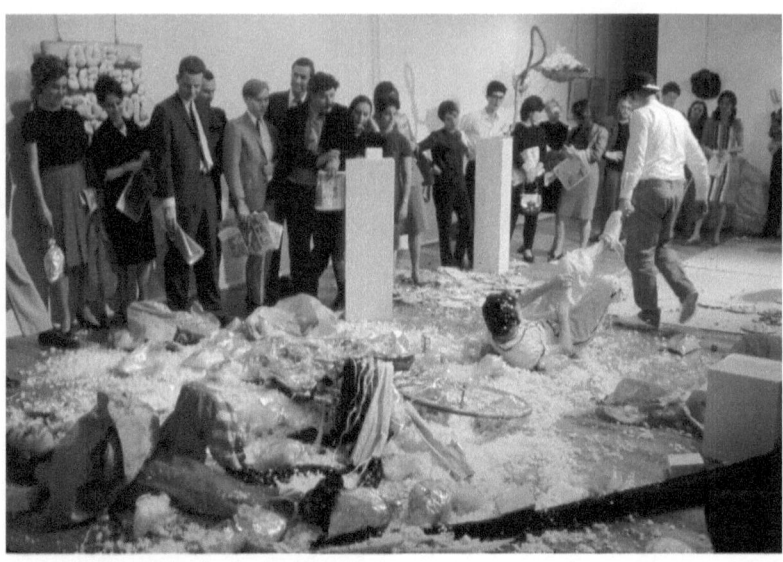

Figure 12.1 *Sports*, October 5, 1962. Green
Gallery, 15 West Fifty-seventh Street, New York.
Left to right: Patty Mucha, Lucas Samaras, Claes
Oldenburg. Photo © Robert McElroy/Licensed by
VAGA, New York, NY; courtesy the Oldenburg van
Bruggen Studio.

Sports deliberately unfurled a series of athletic exercises. While Patty
Mucha emerged from the inside of the *Floor Burger*, Oldenburg, as the
"operator," stacked a range of food props, made from painted plaster,
onto white pedestals customarily used to display high-end sculpture.[4]
Over the next twenty minutes the pace of the performance became
increasingly turbulent, culminating in a frenzy of destruction that cli-
maxes in a final display of trashed goods and "dead" performers, played
by Mucha and Lucas Samaras—two key performers from Oldenburg's
Ray Gun Theater, a series of ten performances staged in the back of the
original *Store*. *Sports* ended when Oldenburg placed Mucha back inside
the giant *Floor Burger* and dragged Samaras offstage. Recursively structured, the performance ended where it began, except for the disorder
and chaos Oldenburg had orchestrated inside his own exhibition (see
fig. 12.1). The floor was strewn with blue-rimmed white paper plates;
small pink and yellow balls of plaster "food"; large sheets of brown packing paper; long strands of beige string; an old bicycle; Chinese take-out

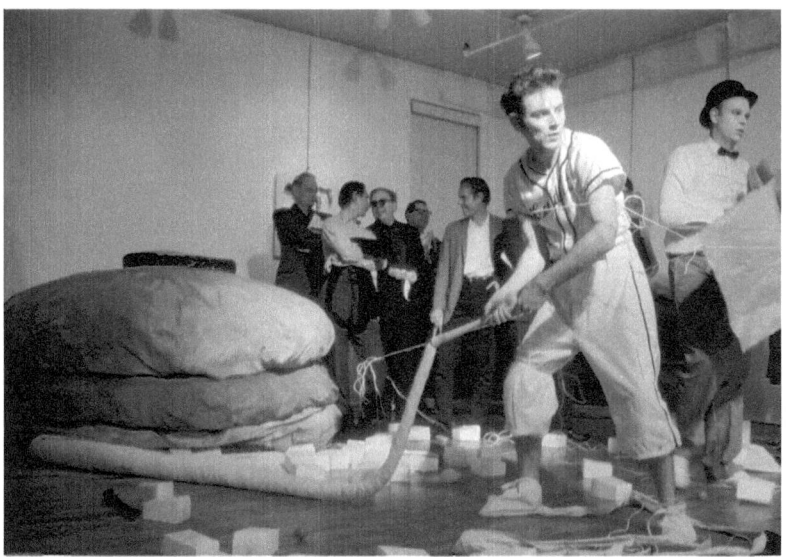

Figure 12.2   *Sports*, October 5, 1962. Green
Gallery, 15 West Fifty-seventh Street, New York.
Pictured: Lucas Samaras, Claes Oldenburg. Photo
© Robert McElroy/Licensed by VAGA, New York,
NY; courtesy the Oldenburg van Bruggen Studio.

boxes; several large, silver aluminum bags; and a profusion of small, white
foam pieces—the filling material for the bags, which had been ruptured
during the proceedings. Resembling later mid-1960s trends in process-
based installation art, where "form" in sculpture is determined by the
behavior and chance arrangement of matter, the leftover sea of scatter
and spill in *Sports* is dominated by white Styrofoam pieces and take-out
boxes. The very same material was used as a stuffing for the oversized
and malleable food sculptures of the *Floor* series: the *Floor Burger*, the
Floor Cone, and the *Floor Cake*, all of which were sewn by hand, painted,
and filled in the empty Green Gallery over the summer. Two soft props,
made specifically for *Sports*, took center stage as agents of destruction: a
set of extra-long black and white baseball bats for Samaras and bulging
beige boxing gloves for Mucha. For Oldenburg, softness in sculpture is
both reactive—it responds to touch and gravity—and active—it exerts
influence onto its surroundings.

In *Sports*, performers ritualistically destroy objects "as if" they were
art (see Samaras in fig. 12.2). *Sports* consummated the underlying anti-art

attitude of *The Store*, and, more importantly, performatively enacted the epistemic power of soft sculpture—a new sculptural idiom whose idiosyncratic mode of address, unique to Oldenburg's art, forms the topic of this essay.

As Rosalind Krauss has shown, Oldenburg's soft sculptures share much with his contemporary performance art—rewriting conventions of viewing in art and reality, and pushing static media toward a durational and intersubjective mode of theatricality in which meaning is not determined a priori, but rather created in the extended moment of the viewer's individual response. And thus soft sculpture "performs its own drama of experience."[5] Krauss concluded that the soft object debunks an older model of idealist sculpture (and a Hegelian dynamic of form and content in which matter is sublimated into conceptual content) with a more contemporary phenomenology of viewing; furthermore, it makes the viewer aware of this paradigm shift. A traditional dialectical formalism cannot account for the durational experience of viewing the soft object.[6] The *Floor Burger* is not supposed to be experienced as a static and preconceived entity to be understood in a flash: when one looks at the work, one does not "forget" technique, material, and internal structure (matter) in favor of an experience of formal unity; instead, these aspects are foregrounded. More specifically, Krauss argues that the soft object conforms to a model of "physical shock" in the tradition of Antonin Artaud, with gigantism and softness sensorially assaulting the viewer. Once the spectators' latent emotions are brought to the surface by "shock," they should come to recognize that withholding these repressed feelings can be dangerous and destructive, potentially leading to hatred and violence in everyday life. For Artaud, "a state of deepened and keener perception" can combat this condition;[7] his theater was designed to wrench the viewer out of her habitual contact with the world. Likewise, Oldenburg's theater (like his soft sculpture) presents an experience of heightened physicality and seeks, as the artist put it, to make the viewer "receptive to a new way of looking at things."[8] Oldenburg's anti-interpretive stance is part of a larger postwar move toward a "recovery of the senses" through art which eluded definitive interpretation—famously diagnosed by Susan Sontag in 1965 as the key impetus behind interdisciplinary performance art in the 1950s and 1960s.[9] Yet while Oldenburg's work participates in the postwar legacy of "therapeutic" art, the heightened sensory experience it creates provides the basis for an alternative ontology of the image that neither partakes in a phenomenology of literalist immediacy often attributed to minimalist sculpture and dance, nor is explained by Artaud's cathartic production of emotionally resonant meaning.

I shall elucidate an alternative historical path through an analysis of Oldenburg's relationship with language, a relationship which suggests that soft sculpture should not be considered in the context of word-less Artaudian theater and its collapse of content into form; rather, it embodies a different critique of iconicity in representation. The image in soft sculpture is not secondary and accidental nor anarchic, as in Artaud's conception of a cathartic purge through an anti-interpretive un-leashing of sensory assault, but enters into an incessant dialogue with form. Seen in a new light, the image in soft sculpture reveals some-thing unique about the structure of human thought, with the structure of imagistic form standing as an analog for the structure of the mind. In order to understand the "content" of Oldenburg's *Floor Burger*, its unique morphology, and its critique of both verbal and visual iconicity, an alternative, performative conception of formalism is needed. Henri Focillon's theoretical text on the internal workings of form, structure, and experience, *The Life of Forms in Art* (1934), was an important book for Oldenburg during his years as an English major at Yale University in the early 1950s, informing his deeply rooted belief in the expressive relevance of nonformal elements in art.[10] By this he meant elements of form or content that cannot be reduced to exegesis. *The Life of Forms in Art* was not only an early catalyst for Oldenburg's faith in the ultimate restorative potential of art, anchored in the belief that meaning in art should be inaccessible through linguistic analysis, but it provided a valid model of form. About a decade before Artaud became a household name in the performing arts scene, Oldenburg was considering how art might expose the limitations of language; and Sontag's Artaudian dictum of anti-interpretive art was aligned with a larger postwar turn in the experimental arts toward theater.[11]

Henri Focillon's conception of form asserts the importance of pro-cess, material, and context, and theorizes a triadic interplay between form, matter, and viewer. Focillon, like Oldenburg, firmly believed in the irreducibility of art to interpretation; he argued that words and plastic forms had become mere signs for experience and, as such, only distorted reality, presenting viewers with a limited, preconceived, intellectual idea of objects. Instead of finding signification only in iconicity, but without forfeiting the power of images, Focillon attributes meaning to the expres-sivity of plastic forms. Meaning could be derived not only from what artworks represented but from their very forms themselves, removed from any representational content.

Sports

Reading Oldenburg in Focillonian terms reframes the discussion of soft sculpture around the parallelism of words and forms in art, shifting to an understanding of materiality as a signifying force in its own right. On initial perception, the imagistic *Floor Burger* appears simple. The viewer doesn't doubt her experience of the work as a burger; the work is not semiotically elusive (she can state that she sees a Brobdingnagian sculpture of a hamburger) or characterized by information loss, as in modernist abstraction. And yet the viewer's experience is so rich and complex that when she attempts to verbalize the precise sensory effect, language seems to fail her, creating an awareness of the limitations of verbal communication. As dramatic stagings of defamiliarized food and household items, soft sculpture's theatricality is anchored in the complication of both the viewer's affective and intellectual experience of the work. The viewing experience resists any easy resolution, as the object presents a new, alternative way of reading the alignment of form and content. Form contributes to content without being sublimated into it. The ideality of the image and the verbal expression of content are undermined by the nonformal (nonconceptual) expressivity of matter. Matter, in the *Floor Burger*, is not formless, but takes shape in the form of a "deformed" image. The shape of the burger stands in the way of visual iconicity and, by the same token, matter is formed by the image. Furthermore, both the word "burger" and the immediate visual identification of a burger's shape stand in the way of an unmediated sensory experience of *Floor Burger*. To impose (either visually or verbally) the concept "burger" onto the sculpture is to limit one's experience.

Oldenburg follows minimalism's convention of literalist titling by directly referring to the consumer objects and food items that he represents in his art. He does so, he explains, only to distance himself from this trend, declaring that calling the *Floor Burger* a burger is a "perversity of mine . . . like a red herring to throw you off; or to raise a question."[12] Such a title widens the gap between the viewer's expectation of a truthful representation of a burger and its actual sculptural manifestation. He uses the denotative function of language to contextualize the viewer's experience, only to sculpturally undermine her expectations by considerably exaggerating scale and physicality. This exaggeration is not enough, however, to break away from the iconic identity of the work as a "burger." The physicality and "floor-ness" of the object actively undermines the iconicity of the burger. When the artist exploits the denotative power of traditional language by calling the work "a burger," he evokes not only the shape of the ideal burger but also suggests its function. Discussing the *Floor Cone*, for example, Oldenburg stated: "the name of a thing is a verbal shape of it, used that way, to call up shape[s] easily. [A n]ame . . . is an abstract as well: cone, for example."[13] And, the "name of the thing tells you how to grab it."[14] Similarly, the Ray Gun Theater is scripted by breaking the link between objects and their role in everyday life, a link simultaneously reflecting conventions of everyday speech and the quotidian function of task-based objects. "I now attack the abstraction of language" is a rallying cry that applies to Oldenburg's sculpture and performance art, as is manifested in *Floor Burger* and its dual role as both independent sculpture and prop.[15]

Several inversions between categorical hierarchies are performed in *Sports*, one of which is to treat sculpture "as if" it were a disposable prop. Soft sculpture's first incarnation occurred in the form of "residual objects," as Oldenburg came to view fabric props left over from the Ray Gun Theater as independent sculptural objects.[16] Another such reversal opens up a complex, flippant interplay of agency between subject and object, the understanding of which depends on the viewer's frame of reference. In *Sports*, the *Floor Burger* performed its lost functionality of being handled, eaten, and digested in a humorous inversion; it was now the human who was "ingested," as Mucha emerged in the first few minutes of the performance from underneath the top layer of the *Floor Burger*. She concealed herself between the "bread" and the "meat patty" before viewers entered the gallery, and was placed back into the burger at the conclusion of the performance. *Sports* and its playful reversal of the relationship between human and burger introduces a second layer of dissociation, on top of the first, reflexively recalling the original act of defamiliarization in which the food item, an object meant to be consumed, was reproduced as a sculpture larger than life-size. The jarring contrast between the actual shape of the sculptural object and the imagined ideal of the burger's form activates thoughts about the process of making art and the activity of eating, as seen simultaneously from the vantage points of both the object and the subject. It is in the eye of the beholder, as the artist programmatically refuses a resolution.

Oldenburg created performances to both supplement and complicate viewers' experience of his sculpture as early as 1960, in connection
with his installation *The Street*.[17] As a continuation of this tradition, *Sports*
demonstrates an interesting conceptual shift between the mechanics of
experience set in place in the first and second *Store* exhibitions. When *The
Store* moved from a small studio space in the Lower East Side uptown to
the Green Gallery, the work's play on the relations between art and commerce was altered. The earlier downtown installation, in the small space
of a former dinette, exerted a constant intellectual push and pull between
annihilating art (viewers were instructed to handle the art object "as if" it
were an everyday commodity) and enforcing aesthetic distance (unlike a
mass-fabricated item, the artwork was precious, unique and handmade).
The ideal viewer looked upon the first installation as *both* a work of art *and*
a commercial display, thinking through how these perspectives were inter-
related and interdependent, modifying each other in turn.[18] The first *Store*
enacted two antithetical conceptions of objecthood and modes of viewing:
the controlled, distanced, and contemplative experience of art, and the
free "hands-on" browsing through goods in the commercial sphere.

At the Green Gallery, however, viewers were no longer able to experience an interactive atmosphere and handle the objects "as if" they were
commodities. Instead, the new line of soft sculpture now pushed and
pulled viewers between two different visual techniques of modern art:
cognitive distantiation and physical estrangement, and empathetic affect
and emotional proximity. Soft sculpture employs a formal defamiliarization of scale and physicality that catapults the object out of normal
relations with human scale and, simultaneously, relies on the affect of
pliable softness to shrink distance and pull the object back into the realm
of the human body. Cognition and affective perception are ineluctably
linked in soft sculpture in an eternal push and pull between intellectual
measure (objective knowledge) and affective charge (subjective experience). Form, in the soft object, is made up of elements both formal
(the recognizable image of a burger) and nonformal (the expressivity
of the matter out of which the form was constructed). Hence, content
is the active staging of the interaction of both formal/conceptual and
nonformal/nonconceptual forces; the object simultaneously invites an
intellectual reaction to the form (of a burger, a cake, or a cone) and
provokes an intangible, emotional response to the material's pillowy, sagging appearance, which in turn is linked inevitably to representational
content, which links back to form, and so on and so forth. Soft sculpture

has frequently been viewed as anthropomorphic because it evokes the image of the human body (or parts of it), and creates an uncanny feeling of dead organicity come "alive." However, by the same token, the "body" is objectified and encapsulated in the image of the commodity object in a grotesque and humorous way that defies linguistic description.

Oldenburg rejected both simple discursivity and a simple phenomenology of viewing in favor of a circular experience of internal tension and structural ambiguity enacted in the viewer's perception of the work. Form, for Oldenburg, is not the limit of meaning, but the gateway to an unconstrained realm of signification beyond the grasp of standard analysis. He values participatory response to his art and incorporates the contingencies of perceptual experience—now conceived as a vehicle itself of becoming, relaying a form of knowledge that resists classification.

Toward a Metamorphosis of Form

Focillon's formalism allows the perceptual processes of sight and the experience of both the artist and the viewer to become part of the conception of the art object. In other words, the artwork's meaning incorporates elements of the work's production (the process of the object's making is legible in the final product) and reception (meaning is created, and not just received, by the viewer). Hence, the artwork, which now encompasses elements of time, is located at the intersection of the intellectual genesis of form in the artist's mind, the actual conditions of production (material and technique, the hands of the artist, and forces of nature such as gravity), and the reception of the form in the eyes of the viewer. In short, the challenge Oldenburg posed for himself was how to express something so outside the bounds of representation that it might never be captured: the dynamic character of experience itself. The drama of Oldenburg's formalism in the soft object is intrinsically related to both his and the viewer's processes of projective vision: perspectival vision that changes when the body of the viewer moves through space. Space, for Oldenburg, is both projective and multifocal. He frequently mixes different viewing points and angles in his installations and sculptures as traces of artistic process.

In the original *Store*, Oldenburg sought to incorporate into his handmade plaster reliefs of food and clothing items both the commodity object *and* his experience of seeing it (a major departure from the Duchampian conception of the readymade). In preparatory drawings, Oldenburg sketched commodities as he perceived them, incorporating

perspectival distortions such as an intervening glass window, or the blur
of motion as he passed a shop. The final installation also sought to preserve the contingencies of his experience in the arrangement of the objects, further complicating the issue of perspective: "The store windows
I see now serve as models for clusters—eye clusters—[a] formal model
for a kind of visual experience: fragmentation, simultaneousness, superimposition, which I wish to recreate in clusters."[19] As a re-creation of
Oldenburg's experience of the city, *The Street* is similarly characterized
by changes of scale and the amalgamation of the different vantage points
from which the paper and cardboard reliefs are drawn, to the point of
logical incompatibility.[20]

As the viewer moves through the space of Oldenburg's installations,
she establishes multiple centers of focus that do or do not match the ones
engrained in both the single reliefs and their installation, transcending
the simple focus of the phenomenological subject. The installations have
multiple entrance and exit points, and there is no single "center" toward
which all works are oriented (the subjective "center" of the viewer herself is pointedly set within the awareness of incompatibility as a measure
for disorientation). As a historical point of reference, John Cage's multifocal theater in the early 1950s similarly explored new seating arrange-
ments that guaranteed each viewer a unique experience by prohibiting
a single or total view; no viewing point was inherently more revealing
than any other. In Oldenburg's theater, as in Cage's, the multifocality and
simultaneity of the viewing experience lead to what Focillon referred to
as a "polycentric" and "labyrinthine" experience of space.[21] Glossing over
the considerable differences of their conceptions of space and process,
they take part in the same postwar moment captured in poststructuralist thought by the metaphor of the labyrinth, which refers to artworks
where meaning is rather open and indeterminate, dependent on the individual viewer and her "composite" impression.[22]

Likewise, scale in Oldenburg's soft objects is polycentric, relative,
and relational, albeit with a twist. He programmatically confuses subject-
centered and object-centered perspectives, alternately focusing on his
experience of space from the point of view of his body and the "body"
of the commodity object. Supersizing the *Floor* series was, in part, a response to the changing architectural landscape of Midtown skyscrapers
(the Green Gallery was located on Fifty-seventh Street), and the more
residential areas of the Lower East Side, which he noted on his daily
commute to the gallery during the month of August—the time of

production for the *Floor* series. (Process is key in Oldenburg's art. This important period of creation is indexed in the soft *August Calendar*, which shows the days of the month of August, with Sundays marked in red; it is visible in the background of fig. 12.1.) Furthermore, the scale of the *Floor Burger* was created on the scale of the Steinway pianos on display in a large showroom, located in the same building as the gallery,[23] which, in turn, became a reflection of the towering height of Midtown architecture. A phenomenological, embodied perspective (the artist walking, for example, looking at skyscrapers) and an object-centered perspective (the artist looking at space from the vantage point of the piano and its relation of scale to the showroom) both inform the soft object's gross enlargement of scale. Oldenburg expressed his concern with the mutability of projective vision poignantly: "Scale is relative. I'm fascinated with vision, the relation of the tangible to the visible. . . . And that is why I get involved in these perspective things where I construct things according to my own perspective."[24] According to the rules of one-point perspective, the object very far away is very small, and the one right in front of us is very large. If we "undo" this learned geometricity and set aside the rules of "real" reality, the object far away becomes gargantuan.[25] Oldenburg's art incorporates his own perceptual experience, imbued by the forces of his artistic imagination and the "as if."[26] Tied to the artist's experience of projective vision is the enhanced physicality of the sculptural object (the larger an object, the more visceral the viewer's experience). Oldenburg's art is situated at the intersection between the perceptual question of how we see (always aware that there is no transparency of vision) and the ontological mystery of what reality is really like. The viewer, in the postwar tradition of indeterminate art (first popularized by Cage's theater in the early 1950s), is freed from discovering the work through monofocal perspective and by deciphering the artist's intentionality, and is forced to become more actively engaged in the formation of her own viewing point and understanding. Formal intuition and creative imagination envisioning the impossible—a reality and an art without mediation—are both faculties located at the limit of thought in Oldenburg's soft sculptures, and he seeks to actively propagate these faculties in the experience of his art.

The Third Object

Oldenburg's conception of art is that of a third reality where the art object becomes the physical interlocutor between mediated perception (formalist art) and unmediated reality (the experience of the viewer and of the artist), and with the sculptural object actively staging this drama. Similarly, in Focillon's terms, art becomes a third realm of reality—activated in the experience of the viewer—distinct from both material reality and mental life, taking part simultaneously in the physical reality of matter and the life of the mind.[27]

Historically, Oldenburg's "objective expressionism,"[28] as he named the new style of his soft sculptures, links two antithetical traditions of postwar art: process art (with its rhetoric of unmediated experience and embodied nature)[29] and neo-Dada found object art (with its mediated, secondhand pop objects and imagery). His statements exemplify a popular 1950s rhetoric (also found in the writings of Jackson Pollock, John Cage, and Allan Kaprow) of experience-based art as an art of "nature," celebrating immediacy, spontaneity, and improvisation. At the same time, Oldenburg confronts the secondhand reality of consumer culture in a critique of reified experience shaped by technologies. In an interview with Robert Pincus-Witten, Oldenburg stated: "we are all victimized by stereotypes in the films and in the comics, and the artist is forced to deal with clichés."[30] He seeks to combat what he calls the "clichés" and "stereotypes" of the media landscape. The soft works were fashioned after advertisements in the print media, rather than drawn from reality. Treating the media landscape as the new nature, he sets mediated images alongside acts of chance and improvisation, and hence imbues them with a new, physical and emotive force in an art of restoration.[31]

Like his soft sculpture, which emerged out of the context of the Ray Gun Theater in 1962, his performances are marked structurally by the occurrence of irreducible dualities—the universal and the personal, objective and subjective experience, nonsymbolic and symbolic acts, dream reality and waking experiences, etc. In the artist's words, on the one hand the Ray Gun Theater supported a theater of "silence . . . accepting the world," which is, in the tradition John Cage's theater, a "rational and objective theater anchored in empirical observation"; on the other hand, it referenced an "expressionist" theater that created "very engaging and emotional sequences," in the tradition of Red Grooms.[32] The viewer can sometimes distinguish one scene (or event or tradition) from another, but she can never resolve them into a single unified whole. Both Oldenburg's soft sculpture and his performance art in 1962 are situated at the intersection between unmediated and mediated experience: "My theme is the relation of natures—nature and mannature."[33] The following statement conclusively encapsulates the artist's conception of an art of the "third object":

> It [the brain-body duality] is a bizarre distinction: since [the] brain is also nature. [I]t is hard to think of anything that is not nature, it is a problem of language—referring traditionally to separate things, I use them [the brain and the body] consciously in the work as [a] dynamic, [between the] representation of conceptual versus [the] representation of [the] natural/physical. [M]y work is not philosophical, I do not represent unity, my object is the third object. . . . [I]f I would resolve it my work would not have a dynamic. . . . [M]y work is the confrontation between brain and body, nature and the interpretation of nature/handling of nature.[34]

Soft sculpture, then, as the third object, actively stages this brain-body dynamic, which depends on the viewer to be actualized. The *Floor Burger* presents viewers with an image of a burger whose formation as a three-dimensional object is process-based, depending on chance and gravity as form-giving forces. Yet the "formless" and soft shape is based on a "hard" geometric cardboard image that serves as the pattern for the *Burger*'s soft canvas skin. Soft sculpture simultaneously demonstrates the geometrification of organicity and the organic softening of geometric simplicity,[35] as becomes apparent when Oldenburg's working method is explicated.

The genesis of *Soft Toilet* (1966) best exemplifies Oldenburg's artistic process (figs. 12.3–12.7). First, he felt aesthetically attracted to a real toilet, observing it "as if" it were a sculpture.[36] Over the next two years, in the manner of a media archaeologist, he worked on a composite image of a toilet after images in the media (billboards, magazines, newspapers), creating what he called the "universal shape" of the toilet. (Figure 12.3 shows one such image clipping.)[37] The final prototype preserved the dramatic vantage point and oblique angle of commercial photography, in which the object is pushed toward the viewer (almost as in reversed perspective)—a popular convention in contemporary advertisement to enhance the immediacy of the appeal (fig. 12.4). All-importantly, the drawing of the *Blue Toilet* (1965) shows in the upper right-hand corner a small outline of a toilet seen from the side and rotated 90 degrees counterclockwise; the projection into space is undone in the diagrammatic incarnation, pointing to Oldenburg's constant play with spatial vision and

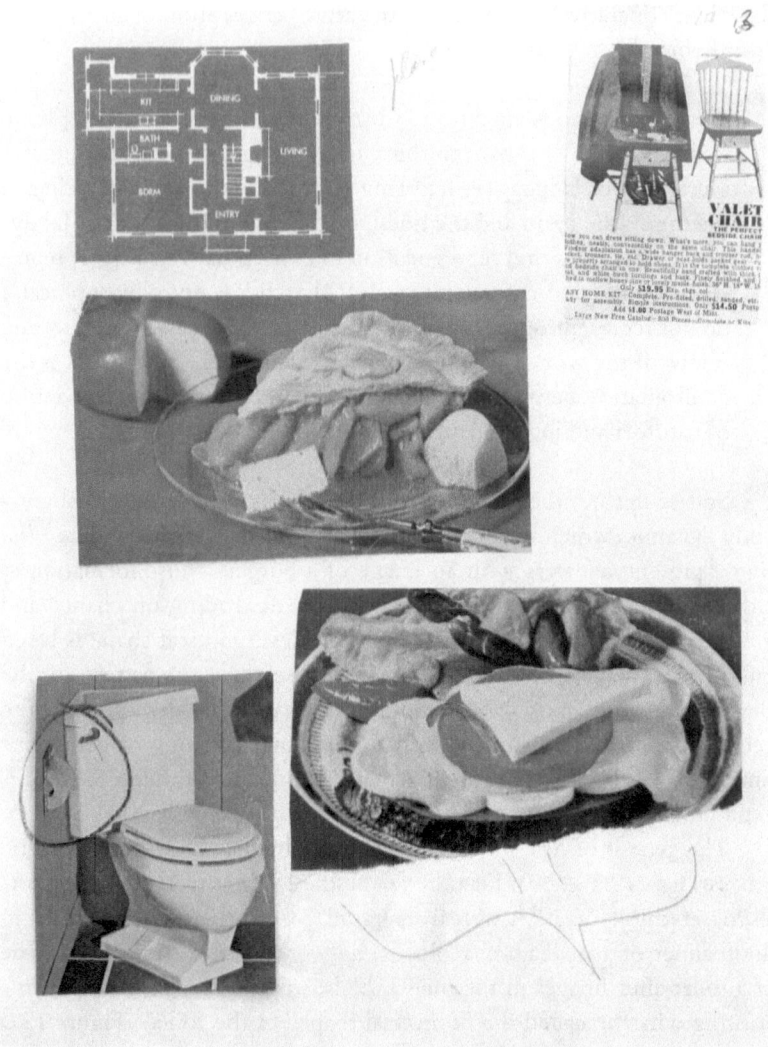

Figure 12.3   *Notebook Page: Los Angeles Details,*
1963. Clippings, 11 × 8½ in. (27.9 × 21.6
cm). Collection Claes Oldenburg and Coosje
van Bruggen. Photo: D. James Dee, New York;
courtesy the Oldenburg van Bruggen Studio.

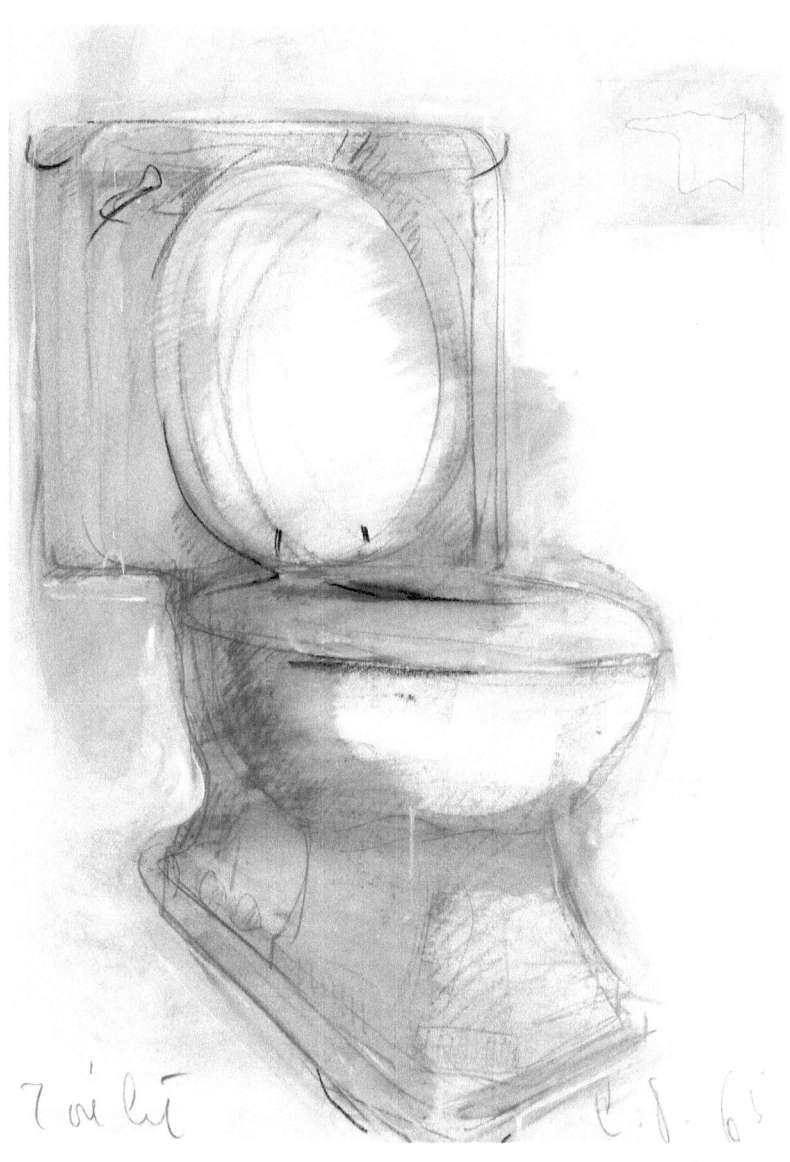

Figure 12.4 *Blue Toilet*, 1965. Crayon,
watercolor, collage, 29¾ × 21¾ in. (75.6 × 55.2
cm). Collection Museum Boymans-van
Beuningen, Rotterdam. Photo courtesy the
Oldenburg van Bruggen Studio.

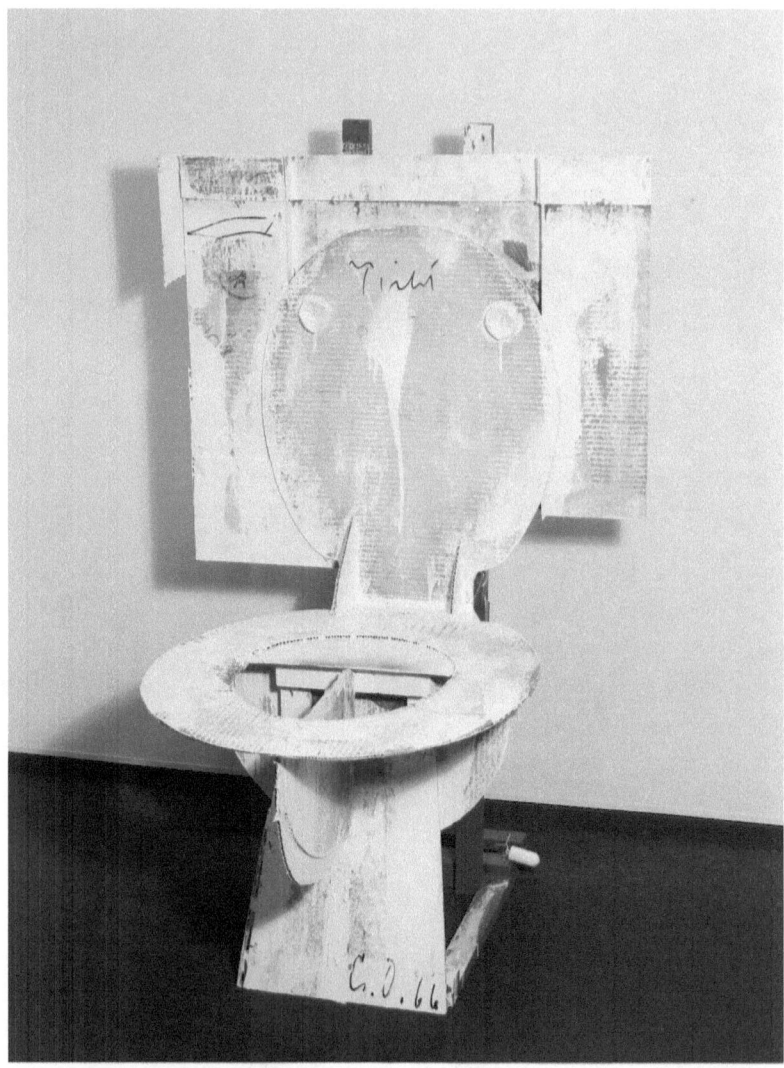

Figure 12.5 *Toilet—Hard Model*, 1965–1966.
Enamel, spray enamel, and felt pen on cardboard,
wood construction, 45¼ × 28⅜ × 33⁷⁄₁₆ in.
(115 × 72 × 85 cm). Collection Museum für
Moderne Kunst, Frankfurt. Photo courtesy the
Oldenburg van Bruggen Studio.

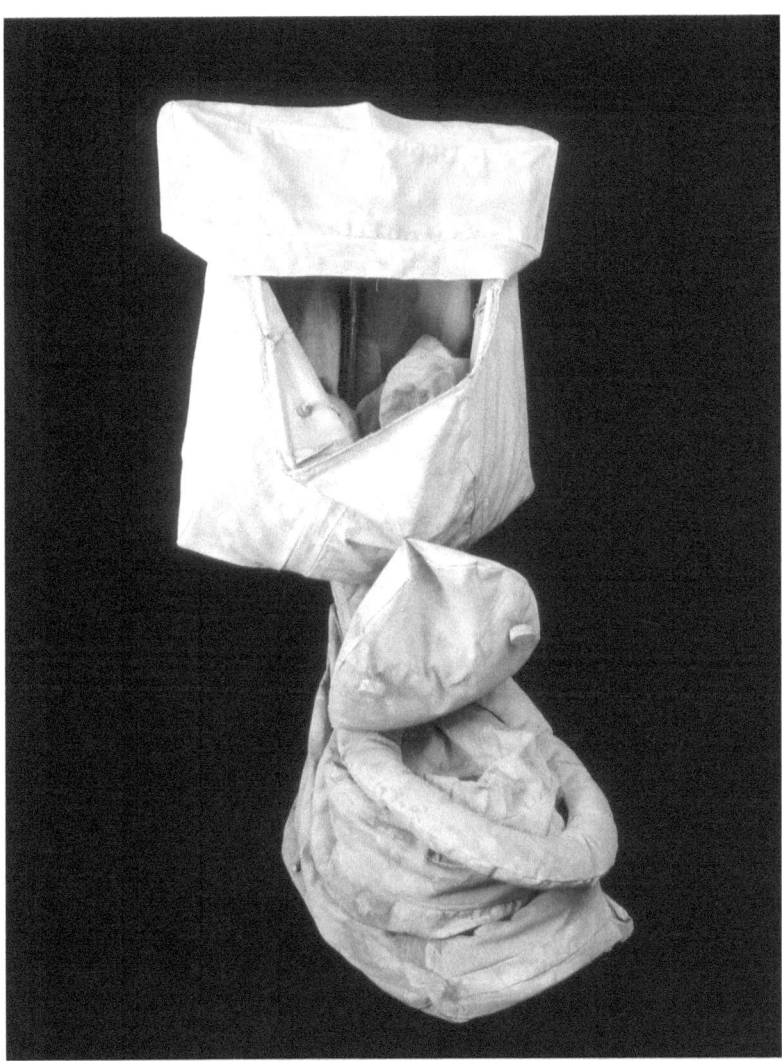

Figure 12.6 *Soft Toilet—Ghost Version*, 1966.
Canvas filled with kapok, painted with acrylic,
on metal stand and painted wood base; toilet:
51 × 33 × 28 in. (129.5 × 83.8 × 71.1 cm); base:
10 × 16 × 16 in. (25.4 × 40.6 × 40.6 cm). Private
collection. Photo courtesy the Oldenburg van
Bruggen Studio.

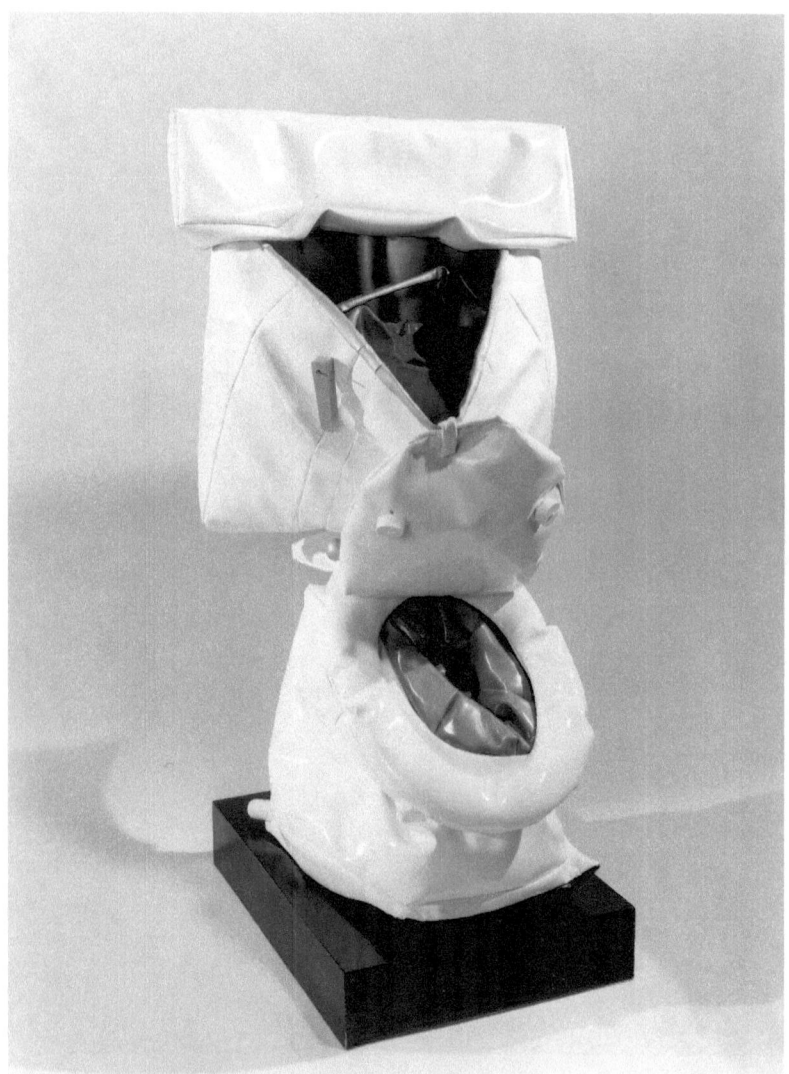

Figure 12.7 *Soft Toilet*, 1966. Vinyl filled with
kapok, wire, Plexiglas, on metal stand and
painted wood base, 57¹⁄₁₆ × 27⅝ × 28¹⁄₁₆ in.
(144.9 × 70.2 × 71.3 cm). Collection Whitney
Museum of American Art, New York, 50th
Anniversary Gift of Mr. and Mrs. Victor W. Ganz.
Photo courtesy the Oldenburg van Bruggen
Studio.

the interrelation between geometry, the body (of the subject or object), and sight. The *Blue Toilet* is the basis for a life-size cardboard model with a fair degree of abstraction as the curvilinear shape is broken down into geometric units (fig. 12.5). This "hard" version, in turn, provided the stencils for all future incarnations in the pliable materials of canvas or vinyl (figs. 12.6, 12.7). Oldenburg was attracted to iconic, rather than leading-edge, commodity objects because they best enabled the generation of a universally recognized shape.[38] The structural ambiguity of the generated shape between flat form and three-dimensional volume, then, is not akin to the (unmodified) surrealist fetish object from the flea market, with a psychic force imbued by history and projected onto it by its owners, nor is it representative of the planned obsolescence of commodity design.

Interestingly, in the two different malleable versions—the white "ghost" model is made of painted canvas and the shinier final soft object is vinyl (both are stuffed with kapok, an organic material found in life vests from the 1960s)[39]—meaning remains the same; a change in material does not lead to a substantial change in content. If the *Soft Toilets* were to be "deflated" by removing the filling, there would be congruence between armature and shape. Meaning is located in the internal structural interplay between flat and three-dimensional, hard and soft.

For Oldenburg, the importance of the soft skin lies in its capability of sustaining both pictorial (in its flattened and deflated state) and sculptural qualities (when stuffed): "Sewing is interesting as a technique because there is a constant relation of scheme to actuality, plan to life, flat to agitated and in the same material. I am still working on canvas, that is, still a painter trying to inflate the plane . . . the deflated state of sculpture is a plane."[40] Soft sculpture is simultaneously flat and three-dimensional, painterly and sculptural, abstract and representational. Rather than conceiving of the stuffing of the object as a process of "deforming" form, Oldenburg described it in biological terms—as an organic process of swelling or inflating.[41]

Programmatically confusing object and subject positions, he declared that *Floor Burger* (or any soft sculpture) had a "living quality," as "it seems stopped in sort of organic motion and that's something I like very much, that feeling of organic motion."[42] In the tradition of twentieth-century process philosophers, who identify reality with change and dynamism, Focillon advocates a conception of form in a constant state of becoming rather than being.[43] The soft object embodies such a state of becoming in its "final" form, with the process of stuffing arresting form, yet with the potential of changing shape when moved and touched. The actual shape is also contingent upon processes of chance in the activity of stuffing, the choice of materials used, and gravity's pull on the object. In the soft object, then, the "swollen" expressivity of form disturbs an easy recognition of the image as an accurate representation (of a burger, for example). In turn, the simplified geometricity of the image imposes shape upon matter. It is not only given plastic form but imbued with the nonformal expressivity of matter, which complicates easy image recognition. This is the drama of soft sculpture.

Rather than simply celebrating the revival of touch and physicality (and eroticism) in art, Oldenburg's formalism is performative, enacting an epistemological insight into the complexities of human experience as a dynamic that, from a "felt" point of view, lacks sharp intellectual distinctions between intuitive and discursive thought, perception and cognition, feeling and thinking, nature and culture, hard and soft, industrial and artistic, vision and reality. As soon as the viewer thinks about the nature of her experience, she is trapped in the dichotomous world of Western rationalism. The crux of the soft object's position is that it does not resolve the split between body and mind, being and perceiving, but actively stages the limitations such an intellectual position places upon daily reality; and hence it perpetuates the very distinctions it throws into question. However, for the duration of the viewing experience, the joy of looking and feeling is coupled with an ensuing awareness of how the mind always needs to structure reality.

My reading moves away from identifying soft sculpture with either an emotive pathology of the erotic fetish, in which a person is aroused and projects feelings onto a physical object, or the objectification of human relations in the tradition of the commodity fetish; the erotic appeal of the soft object is an often-noted feature of Oldenburg's art. What Walter Benjamin termed the "sex appeal of the inorganic"—the consumer's erotic feelings toward the fetishized commodity—is only half of the equation, as I have pointed out above.[44] Hal Foster, in discussing Richard Hamilton's conflation of the female body with the body of a car in works such as $he (1958–1961), points to the merger of the sexual and the commodity fetish as a form of "super-fetishism" in pop art.[45] The *Floor Burger*, by contrast, does not merge the outline of a subject (women) and object (burger) into a new, shared hybrid contour line that mimetically belongs to both. Instead, contour in the soft object belongs to either the flat and two-dimensional body or the three-dimensional volume, and it is the drama of their intuited unity and intellectual separateness that the soft object enacts, always depending on the viewer's active participation. Among representations of commodity objects in states of "melting" softness, yet another, older model warrants consideration.

Weary of psychoanalytic interpretations of his art in general, Oldenburg distanced his soft sculpture explicitly from the representational, paranoiac surrealism of Salvador Dalí's soft watches. A soft object such as the *Soft Toilet*, as I have shown, was not based on a dream image, but was the result of conscious choices regarding form, structure, technique, and material.[46] This does not mean, however, that human psychology and the field of psychoanalysis are of no importance in understanding his art.[47] Focillon's theory of form does allow for the inclusion of psychological experience in art; or, as Oldenburg phrased it, "the psychological is not verboten."[48]

A "rupture" of the unconscious into consciousness can occur during the experience of a soft sculpture.[49] Focillon's conception of the "aura" of a work of art (its ability to evoke in the viewer a proliferation of images) was developed around the same time that Walter Benjamin published his famous 1934 "Work of Art" essay,[50] in which he mourns the loss of an authentic experience of the art object in the age of technological reproduction, and argues that the overstimulation of visual experience represented a danger to the individual—a view far removed from Focillon's celebration of images' multivalence. For Benjamin, in the moment of "physical shock," the forces of history and memory rupture the consciousness of the viewer in the flash of an image. During "the event"[51] (Focillon's term for the duration of the viewer's intersubjective experience, which differs from the instantaneity of Benjamin's "shock"), the viewer (and for that matter the artist) may foster multiple associations in the form of allusions—a rhetorical form of indirect reference, anchored in previously acquired experiences of both conscious and unconscious "knowledge." The motor that drives allusion, for Focillon, is formal. Visual analogy is its generator and, for Oldenburg, structural ambiguity is its guiding principle.

Notoriously, Donald Judd has read soft works such as the vinyl *Soft Light Switches 1/2* (1964) in a sexual context by claiming that is what the artist "felt" during the production process. Struggling to reconcile what he considers the literalism of the soft object's materiality and its "simple" image status (by which he means a Gestaltist experience of wholeness) with its affective psychic charge and sexual resonance, he clarifies that while the sculpture's overall form does not visually resemble two breasts in its shape, the two prominent switches alone indirectly evoke two nipples.[52] Hence, Judd rightfully concludes, due to the lack of complete visual resemblance the work is not metaphorical or anthropomorphic in a traditional sense. When Oldenburg cut an image of hanging breasts from an advertisement and pasted it in his notebook next to a drawing and clipping of what would later become the soft sculpture *Dormeyer Mixer* (1965), he makes a similar statement about the work's sexual connotations (fig. 12.8). The two clippings at the bottom of the notebook page show breasts both openly and suggestively, directly and indirectly. Importantly, only the mixer's two beaters resemble breasts rather than the whole body of the sculpture, keeping the ambiguity between subject and object purposefully open and alive. This also holds true for the *Soft Light Switches*.

Dario Gamboni, in his history of the role of ambiguity in twentieth-century art, makes an important distinction between hidden and potential images in art.[53] He describes a "hidden image" as one that is planted unconsciously by the artist and reveals a repressed and unresolved (sexual) tension slumbering unrecognized beneath the surface of awareness in an artwork, while a "potential image" is established consciously by the artist and depends on the beholder for realization. Some of Oldenburg's soft objects are arguably more directly sexual in their allusion to male or female body parts (such as the *Soft Light Switches* or the *Dormeyer Mixer*) than others (such as the *Floor Burger* or the *Soft Toilet*). What neither Judd nor Gamboni account for is the structural ambiguity inherent in Oldenburg's notion of the image, where each image is both potential and hidden and sexual and objective at the same time. Judd's interpretive problem is that the soft object's materiality is not modernist and literalist (or symbolist); it is outside the tradition of modernist formalism and is performative and metamorphic.

The sexual implications in Oldenburg's art are foundational—"the erotic or sexual is the root of art; its first impulse"[54]—yet they only indirectly influence the genesis of sculptural form and morphology of the soft works.

A Poetry of Form / A Poetry of Words

My art is very much a language, in which some characters are fixed, some floating, some obvious, some secret hidden even to me (or especially to me).[55]

—*Claes Oldenburg*

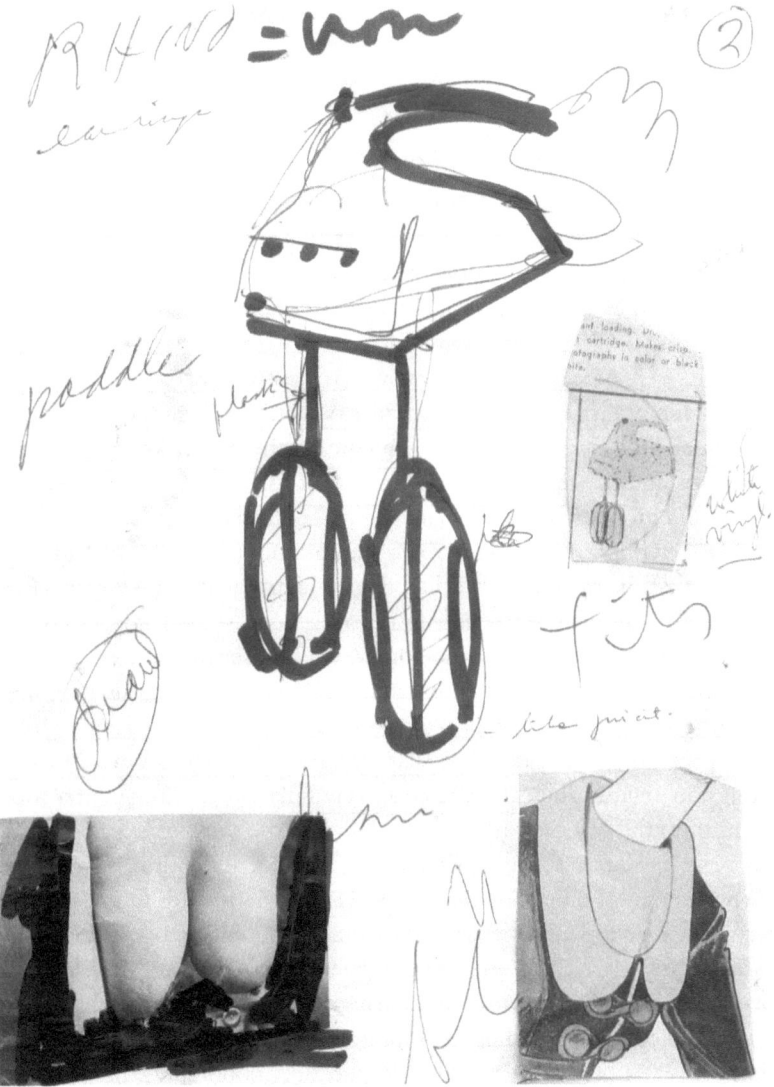

Figure 12.8 *Notebook Page: Dormeyer Mixer*,
1965. Felt pen, ballpoint pen, clippings, collage,
10⅝ × 8 in. (27 × 20.3 cm). Collection Claes
Oldenburg and Coosje van Bruggen. Photo:
D. James Dee, New York; courtesy the Oldenburg
van Bruggen Studio.

A city is all words—a newspaper, an alphabet.[56]

—*Claes Oldenburg*

Oldenburg reveals his visual reasoning for the soft sculptures in a series of diagrammatic charts, the first of which was generated in 1962 (fig. 12.9). In these diagrams, soft works are connected not through their utility function as objects in daily life, or their sexual and erotic connotations, but by formal, geometric permutation. Considering an advertisement's image of a hamburger in purely formal terms, Oldenburg saw not the image or figure of a burger but "two soft circles with one soft circle in the middle."[57] He perceived, in his own words, "a structure or a form that has taken a temporary life in this particular object."[58] Oldenburg's imagistic and procedural formalism is morphological as he breaks form down into structure, and the result is a "vocabulary" of form organized in pictorial charts and grouped by visual analogy. His "alphabet" is derivational.

For example, the cipher for a hamburger (*Floor Burger*) equals a mouth that, in turn, equals a hot dog, which equals a newspaper (see fig. 12.9). The hamburger equals a mouth because both shapes consist of three layers, one on top of the other, with either the bottom layers or all layers curved. On the same chart, an ice cream cone equals a fuselage since both shapes can be broken down into a cone (a triangle and a circle) seen from the side. This chart represents frontal and profile views alongside oblique angles, and retroactively links his previous plaster food items from the first *Store* (the banana split and the ship, for example) with his new line of soft works. Oldenburg's projective vision is operative even in the most schematic of systems. Paving the way for future soft objects, this drawing marks a seminal turning in his career as a sculptor: the *Floor Burger*, *Floor Cake*, and *Floor Cone* were the first works to actually be broken down into simple geometries with separate parts and layers to be assembled and stacked upon completion. Toward the latter part of the decade, when producing large-scale outdoor monuments, he began to create more systematical blueprints, like an engineer or architect, focusing again on outlines and structure.

What Oldenburg refers to as his "visual grammar" is thus a system of food and commodity objects linked to each other by morphological resemblance. His artistic agenda can be compared to a strategy of visual rhyming in poetry, where typographic connections connect otherwise unrelated words (such as "rough" and "through," or "laughter" and

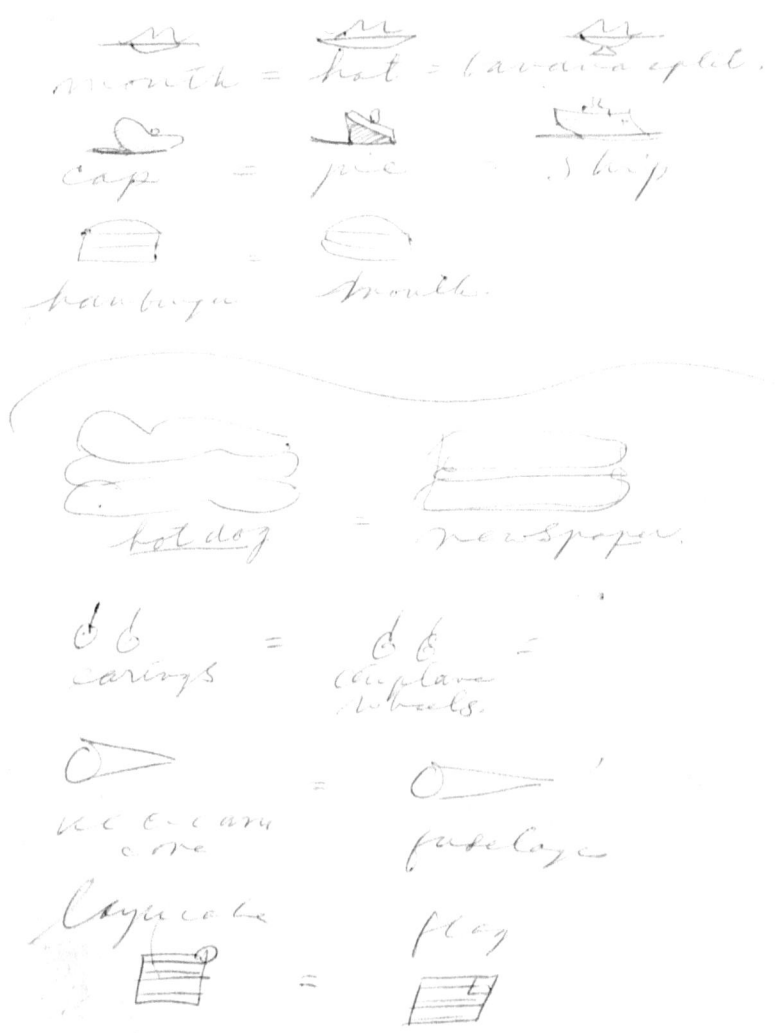

Figure 12.9 *Notebook Page: "mouth = hat = banana split / cap = pie = ship / hamburger = mouth / hot dog = newspaper / earings = airplane wheels / ice cream cone = fuselage / layercake = flag,"* 1962. Ballpoint pen, 11 × 8½ in. (27.9 × 21.6 cm). Collection Claes Oldenburg and Coosje van Bruggen. Photo: D. James Dee, New York; courtesy the Oldenburg van Bruggen Studio.

"slaughter") into chains of visual similarities of a different order. For Oldenburg, as for Focillon, forms evolve in a way analogous to words through plastic rhyming; that is, the different plastic forms are "words" related to each other as visual synonyms, and are considered "equals."[59] Oldenburg's writings about the importance of form in his art contain frequent analogies to language. The artist succinctly remarked that he "consider[s] visual art as poetry, a form of writing, or writing a form of visual art."[60] These chains of visual synonyms are not organized according to a minimalist logic of simple or complex mathematical permutations, as Barbara Rose argued,[61] but follow an evolving experimental logic of structure that is purely formal and shaped by the artist's intuition and creative imagination: "I don't see a plug so much as a certain kind of structure. It has to do with the way I see my work." Oldenburg further clarifies that for "a vocabulary of structure I used Roget's Thesaurus."[62] Asked about the use of a dictionary, the artist responded, "it's maybe that you look up something and then you have another one with a similar structure, like synonyms."[63]

As in language, an "etymology" of form in Oldenburg's graphic system of structure leads to the discovery of what he called "ur-types" of form.[64] The most important "structure" is the Ray Gun (two straight lines at a right angle).[65] The psychological aspects of Oldenburg's work surface in these "archetypes" of form:

> I like to believe that there is a set of forms that each individual carries and he reads the world through these forms. They're sort of the imprint of his mind and sensibility. And this constitutes his style. Everyone can find out what these forms are if they study themselves and practice creating forms. . . . So this is something that one is seeing and then the superimposition of an object across these forms you see this image [sic] that you want to see enshrined in some kind of object, incorporated in some sort of form.[66]

By his own admission, the Ray Gun (the right angle that, the artist contends, lies at the origin of the universe)[67] is a phallic form, and the "umbrella and disk shape with a leg"—a secondary derivation of the basic right angle—is its female extension. But it was only later, after he had been attracted to the formal and structural qualities of objects, that Oldenburg discovered the underlying sexual implications of his formal motif. His charts, and, by extension, the sculptures, oscillate between the two poles of universal geometric intelligibility and a deeply personal, cryptic psychology of feeling tied to forms and structure. Instead of negating each other, however, these poles of human existence constantly inform and reinforce each other in Oldenburg's metamorphosis of form.

Recent scholarship on pop art has moved away from iconographic interpretations of subject matter and symbolic content, toward readings that complicate the legibility of the image. Scholars in this tradition focus on how the work operates and what it can do for the viewer, rather than solely on what it depicts.[68] What distinguishes soft sculpture from other object sculpture in pop art is the work's affective charge—its strong appeal to the sense of touch and the erotic—and its simultaneous address to thought through structural ambiguity. Though drawing on different historical trajectories and theoretical frameworks, scholarly analyses of Oldenburg's soft sculptures have one common and particular characteristic: the understanding of these works as ambiguous and paradoxical. Scholars frequently resolve this ambiguity by turning to psychoanalysis, explaining the contradictory workings of the soft object along the lines of Freudian dream reality and the workings of the psyche.[69] I contend that soft sculpture does not resolve the dualisms between form and matter, figuration and abstraction, thinking and feeling, mind and body, conscious thought and the unconscious, nature and culture, vision and reality, but instead actively stages these dualities (anchored in the sculpture's morphology between pure geometry and chance-based, gravity-driven form) as unresolved structural ambiguities in lived experience: their perception depends on the perspective of the viewer. In other words, the soft object does not simply offer a critique of commodity culture by returning to a subjectivist experience of eroticism and sex, but seeks to carve a niche for human experience within and alongside mediated everyday reality.

Oldenburg's soft sculptures make the viewer aware that human experience, when lived directly rather than filtered through linguistic expression, cannot be reduced to the dichotomies of Western thought. The reality of the soft object is not objectively defined through the either/or, but follows the logic of both/and decided upon by the participatory experience of the viewer. By the same token, a productive discussion of Oldenburg's art cannot be confined to the historical configurations of form–content and matter–form, which epitomize rational and linear thought. In Focillon's antideterministic take on the dialectics of the image in art, matter and form are not predetermined and antithetical entities to be resolved in the static unity of the work; instead, content and form are two dualities experienced as lived entities in an incessant exchange whose "content" is decided by factors of both production *and* reception.

In Oldenburg's work, this structural tension, modeled after Focillon's take on form, leads to a spectatorial effect of ambiguity, one that ultimately sets his art apart from a poststructuralist openness of form. Cleanth Brooks (one of Oldenburg's teachers at Yale University) confirmed the importance of the structural ambiguity of form in poetry, one of the tenets of New Criticism, a then-popular method of interpreting literature. Brooks and other New Critics believed that poetry is deeply ambiguous, and that ambiguity comes alive in the experience of the reader without being resolved, animating the poem continuously from within through the reader's intellectual engagement.[70] Before Oldenburg encountered approaches to indeterminacy in performance art of the late 1950s (his experience of Cage was rather delayed) and arguments for minimizing the importance of authorial intention in a work's reception, he studied the work of two other advocates of New Criticism, Monroe C. Beardsley and W. K. Wimsatt Jr., including their theory of the intentional and affective fallacies.[71] These authors posited that poetry must transcend the intentions (and feelings) of the poet (the intentional fallacy); similarly, the content of poetry transcends the effects that it carries to the reader (the affective fallacy).[72] Oldenburg's soft sculptures attempt to avoid the Scylla of the intentional fallacy and the Charybdis of the affective fallacy, and draw their meaning simultaneously from the artist's conceptualization of experience and his feelings and the viewer's active affective and cognitive participation.

While Focillon's theories of form are elusive and at times esoteric, he nonetheless provides a framework for considering Oldenburg's soft sculpture. Focillon's approach enables us to reevaluate issues discussed in the critical literature on Oldenburg—ambiguity and paradox, anthropomorphism, and psychological interpretations—from a fresh perspective, opening the work onto a different set of questions: How are forms generated and connected? How is "content" communicated, and whose content is it? Instead of asking what the work represents, we ask what the *structure* of the work sets in motion—or, as the artist phrased it so succinctly, it is irrelevant to him whether an image represents a cathedral or a girdle.[73] As T. S. Eliot (the poet whose work dominated the literature classroom during Oldenburg's time at Yale) wrote, the poet's duty "is to his language, first to preserve, and second to extend and improve. In expressing what other people feel he is also changing the feeling by making it more conscious; he is making people more aware of what they feel already, and therefore teaching them something about themselves. . . . [In addition, he] can make his readers share consciously in new feelings which they had not experienced before."[74]

Discussions of Oldenburg's relationship to language are usually confined in the literature to the role of Artaudian theater and its importance for the wordless experimental artists' theater of the happenings, in which meaning was conveyed by sensory experience rather than by speech. I have attempted to complicate this discussion, in part by emphasizing Oldenburg's affinity with American poetry. Oldenburg's soft sculptures stake a claim for the restorative role that structural ambiguity can play in art, shifting the focus toward an overlooked anti-interpretive legacy for the postwar arts, one which supports a newly reconfigured parallelism between words and plastic forms.

Like Eliot, who straddled the divide between feeling and thinking, Oldenburg's formalism not only crosses the boundaries of disciplines (a characteristic ambition of performance-based art in the 1950s) but seeks to actively engage with cultural and social experience. Tracing Oldenburg's belief in art's ability to restore an experience of reality enhances our conception of pop art, offering an enriched image of this historical moment and its complex intellectual concerns. In Oldenburg's soft sculpture, subject matter and sexual allusions do not form the core of the work's content.

Notes

1. Claes Oldenburg, interview by Barbara Rose, 1968, transcription of cassette tape C-90, Track 01, April 29, 1968, Barbara Rose Papers, 1940–1993, Getty Research Institute, Los Angeles. Transcription mine.

2. Claes Oldenburg, "Notes, New York, 1965–1966," quoted in Coosje van Bruggen, "The Realistic Imagination and Imaginary Reality of Claes Oldenburg," in *Claes Oldenburg: Drawings* (Valencia: Instituto Valenciano de Arte Moderno Centre Julio González, 1989), p. 33.

3. Warhol's installation of helium-filled floating *Silver Clouds*, developed in collaboration with Billy Klüver and Bell Laboratories for an exhibition in 1966 at Leo Castelli Gallery, appears to have been inspired by the silver bags attached to a silver bicycle used in *Sports*.

4. Oldenburg explained his role as "the operator" in an interview with the author, May 21, 2010.

5. Rosalind Krauss, *Passages in Modern Sculpture* (Cambridge, Mass.: MIT Press, 1981), p. 230.

6. Yve-Alain Bois, "Introduction: The Use Value of Formless," in Yve-Alain Bois and Rosalind Krauss, *Formless: A User's Guide* (New York: Zones Book, 1997), pp. 24–26. Bois sets up these four categories of anti-form in response to the normative (dialectical)

formalism of Clement Greenberg. Oldenburg's conception of metamorphic form parallels the four antimodernist rubrics of the "formless," an alternative conception of performative form developed by Bois and Krauss, following Georges Bataille's critique of representation. Like Bataille, Focillon developed his alternative view of the dynamic between form and content in the 1930s. For Bois and Krauss, Bataille's theory of "deformation," where form actively undermines content, is characterized by horizontal vision, base materialism, time as pulse, and art's entropic loss of information. In Focillon's view, vision is polycentric; materiality is expressive and metamorphic; visual experience is durational and intersubjective; information is silenced; and art is opened up toward ambiguity.

7. Antonin Artaud, "First Manifesto," in *The Theater and Its Double*, trans. Mary Caroline Richards (New York: Grove, 1958), p. 91.

8. Oldenburg, quoted in Robert Pincus-Witten, "The Transformation of Daddy Warbucks: An Interview with Claes Oldenburg," *Chicago Scene* 4, no. 4 (April 1964), p. 36; reprinted in this volume.

9. Susan Sontag, *Against Interpretation and Other Essays* (New York: Farrar, Straus, and Giroux, 1962), p. 301. Sontag's reading of contemporary performance art is anchored in an Artaudian conception of theater. Similar critiques of language's inability to capture the fullness of human experience—American process philosophy, French phenomenology, American pragmatism, and Norman O. Brown's psychoanalytic reading of American literature—were intellectual landmarks in a larger history of the postwar rise of experience-based performance art.

10. Henri Focillon, *The Life of Forms in Art* (1934; repr., New York: Zone Books, 1989). Focillon taught at Yale between 1933 and 1943, and Oldenburg was part of the Yale class of 1950. It is likely that Oldenburg took an art history class with George Kubler, Focillon's intellectual heir at Yale. Oldenburg's interests shifted from drama (he studied and acted in Elizabethan and pre-Elizabethan theater) to art only in his last year, and he graduated with a B.A. in English. Claes Oldenburg, interview with Paul Cummings, 1973–1974, tape recordings, Archives of American Art, Smithsonian Institution, Washington, D.C., transcript, p. 29. Courtesy Claes Oldenburg. (Hereafter abbreviated PC.) About Focillon, he said: "It [Henri Focillon's *The Life of Forms in Art*] was my textbook in art history when at Yale. I think it had a great influence in my thinking" (ibid., p. 397).

11. Susan Sontag, "Happenings: An Art of Radical Juxtaposition," in *Against Interpretation and Other Essays*, pp. 263–274.

12. PC, p. 399.

13. Claes Oldenburg, quoted in Barbara Rose, "Claes Oldenburg's Soft Machines," *Artforum* 10, no. 5 (June 1967), p. 32; reprinted in this volume.

14. Ellen H. Johnson, "Oldenburg's Poetics: Analogues, Metamorphoses, and Sources," *Art International* 54, no. 4 (April 1970), p. 43; reprinted in this volume. Johnson points to the important role metamorphosis—and, in particular, literary metamorphosis—plays in Oldenburg's art. An iconic example of literary metamorphosis can be found in Franz Kafka's *Die Verwandlung* (1915) when the protagonist Gregor Samsa transforms into a large, grotesque insect-man. The concept of metamorphosis that this essay develops, however, is different.

15. Oldenburg, quoted in Johnson, "Oldenburg's Poetics."

16. Claes Oldenburg, quoted in *Claes Oldenburg: An Anthology*, ed. Germano Celant (New York: Guggenheim Museum Publications, 1995), p. 143. The fact that the collector David Hayes looked at props such as *Freighter and Sailboat* "as if" they were independent sculptural objects was a breakthrough moment in Oldenburg's thought process. By the

same token, the bats from *Sports* were turned into an independent sculpture. For a discussion of the occurrence of softness before 1962, see Coosje van Bruggen, "Soft and Hard," in *Nur ein anderer Raum (Just Another Room)* (Frankfurt am Main: Museum für Moderne Kunst, 1991), pp. 85–107.

17. The sensory impact of the flat cardboard and paper reliefs of scenes from daily life in *The Street* was intensified in the cathartic performance *Snapshots from the City* (staged inside *The Street* at the Judson Gallery on February 29, March 1, and March 2, 1960), which acted out the violent nature of city life only indicated visually in the installation. The two main performers—the artist and his wife—played a city bum and a prostitute. The performance's level of sensory assault (bright lights were turned on and off rapidly at irregular intervals) reflected the influence of Artaud's conception of theater. Artaud's influence on New York's wider art scene has been duly noted in scholarship on the happenings. For a recent discussion of the relevance of Artaud for Oldenburg and his theater, see Judith Rodenbeck, "Madness and Method: Before Theatricality," *Grey Room* 13 (Fall 2003), pp. 55–79. For Oldenburg's later *Store* projects, however, Henri Focillon's critique of iconology provides a more apt structural model for the formalism of the soft object, as I have argued in this paper.

18. A similar view is presented by Cécile Whiting, *A Taste for Pop: Pop Art, Gender, and Consumer Culture* (Cambridge: Cambridge University Press, 1997), pp. 26–27; part of chapter 1, "Shopping for Pop," is reprinted in this volume as "Oldenburg's *Store*."

19. Claes Oldenburg, *Store Days: Documents from The Store (1961) and Ray Gun Theater (1962)*, ed. Claes Oldenburg and Emmett Williams (New York: Something Else Press, 1967), p. 14; excerpts reprinted in this volume.

20. More specifically, the cardboard reliefs from *The Street* (1960) were, in Oldenburg's words, "the concrete realization of vision, passing from one item to another in a multitude." Oldenburg, quoted in Barbara Rose, *Claes Oldenburg* (New York: Museum of Modern Art, 1970), p. 69. As with Jackson Pollock's drip canvases, viewers of *The Street* were not meant to literally trace the physical (and perceptual) movements of the artist; rather, the work indirectly sought to evoke just that idea.

21. Focillon, *The Life of Forms in Art*, p. 67.

22. For a reference to the labyrinth as garden, see Umberto Eco, *A Theory of Semiotics* (Bloomington: Indiana University Press, 1976), p. 275. Eco modeled his conception of the open work after the arbitrary relationship between musical scoring and performance in Karl Heinz Stockhausen and Pierre Boulez, both of whom freed the performer from interpreting the work in the way the artist had intended; this tradition continues in the music and theater of John Cage. Umberto Eco, *The Open Work* (Cambridge: Harvard University Press, 1989), pp. 38–39.

23. Van Bruggen, "Soft and Hard," p. 93.

24. Claes Oldenburg, interview with John Jones, tape recordings B6, Archives of American Art, Smithsonian Institution, Washington, D.C., transcript, p. 9. Courtesy Claes Oldenburg.

25. Oldenburg, interview with the author, February 9, 2011.

26. See, for example, Oldenburg in 1963, quoted in Rose, *Claes Oldenburg*, p. 192: "[T]he human imagination does not obey any proprieties, as of scale or time, or any proprieties whatsoever."

27. Focillon's conception of thirdness is derived from Karl R. Popper's ideas on "objective knowledge." Reality, according to Popper, is divided into World 1 (physical states) and

World 2 (conscious and unconscious mental states); art, as an "object of our own making," belongs to World 3 (the realm of the content of thought and the products of the human mind). Karl R. Popper and John C. Eccles, *The Self and Its Brain* (New York: Springer International, 1977), pp. 36–43. The relationship between Focillon and Popper is established in Jean Molino, introduction to Focillon, *The Life of Forms in Art*, pp. 12, 20, 29.

28. Oldenburg, quoted in Rose, *Claes Oldenburg*, p. 193.

29. Two different postwar conceptions of process art come together in Oldenburg. In the tradition of Jackson Pollock, the physical performance of the artist and its inscription into the materiality of the paint (of canvas, etc.) opens the work toward meaning. Capturing the movements of the artist-performer, the painting is viewed as a "document" that traces its own making. Arguing against the subjectivity of the author and her inscription into the expressive work, John Cage proposes that the work of art is process-based if it engenders an awareness in the viewer of her own subjective experience of time as duration. To Cage, the structure of a work, the way it unfolds in time and space, is most important; meaning is a product of how this form is perceived differently by each viewer, not the result of a preinscribed text or authorial intention.

30. Pincus-Witten, "The Transformation of Daddy Warbucks," p. 38; reprinted in this volume.

31. Interview with the author, April 22, 2010. Oldenburg stated: "my stereotype in soft sculpture is on top of that stereotype that exists in reality. My sculpture is the definite version of it."

32. Oldenburg, quoted in Richard Kostelanetz, *The Theater of Mixed Means: An Introduction to Happenings, Kinetic Environments, and Other Mixed-Means Performances* (New York: Dial Press, 1965), pp. 135–136.

33. Claes Oldenburg, "Notes, New York, 1965–1966," quoted in van Bruggen, "The Realistic Imagination," p. 40.

34. Claes Oldenburg, "Extracts from the Studio Notes (1962–1964)," *Artforum* 4, no. 5 (January 1966), p. 32. With regard to the categorical distinctions between abstract and figurative representation, he declares: "Fig/non fig is a moronic distinction. The challenge to abstract art must go much deeper." Oldenburg, *Store Days*, p. 101.

35. Oldenburg, "Extracts from the Studio Notes," p. 32.

36. PC, pp. 73, 207. He started to think about making a toilet sculpture in 1963, when he visited the house of Virginia Dwan in Los Angeles.

37. Oldenburg, interview with the author, April 22, 2010.

38. Oldenburg, interview with the author, May 20, 2010.

39. Oldenburg, interview with the author, February 9, 2011. The material was bought in an outlet for industrial leftovers called Lincoln Fabrics in Los Angeles. This is also where he bought the vinyl and fake fur.

40. Oldenburg, quoted in van Bruggen, "Soft and Hard," p. 94.

41. Van Bruggen, "Soft and Hard," p. 97. In his preparatory drawings for *The Store*, Oldenburg created images of people blown up like balloons. Courtesy Claes Oldenburg.

42. Oldenburg, quoted in "Claes Oldenburg Talking with Paul Carroll," January 22, 1963, unpublished interview, transcript, p. 3. Courtesy Claes Oldenburg.

43. Andrei Molotiu, "Focillon's Bergsonian Rhetoric and the Possibility of Deconstruction," *Invisible Culture: An Electronic Journal for Visual Studies* 3 (2000).

44. Walter Benjamin, quoted in Hal Foster, "On the First Pop Age," *New Left Review* 19 (January–February 2003), p. 102.

45. Foster, "On the First Pop Age," p. 102.

46. PC, p. 268.

47. PC, p. 200. He stated: "Fetishism is an extremely important thing to me both in the object-making and in the Happenings. Fetishistic behavior—that book, *Sexual Aberrations* by Stekel . . . is so important to the Happenings."

48. Oldenburg, interview by Barbara Rose, 1968, cassette tape C-91, Track 01, April 29, 1968, Barbara Rose Papers. Transcription mine.

49. Molino, introduction to *The Life of Forms in Art*, p. 16.

50. Walter Benjamin, "The Work of Art in the Age of Mechanical Reproduction," in *Illuminations: Essays and Reflections*, ed. Hannah Arendt, trans. Harry Zohn (New York: Schocken Books, 1968), pp. 236–240. The connections between the writings of Benjamin and Focillon are manifold, as Benjamin was influenced by Focillon's conception of aura. This subject, however, exceeds the topic of this essay.

51. For Focillon, see Molino, introduction to *The Life of Forms in Art*, p. 20. For Benjamin, see "The Work of Art in the Age of Mechanical Reproduction."

52. Donald Judd, "In the Galleries," *Arts Magazine* 38, no. 10 (September 1964), p. 36; reprinted in this volume as part of "Reviews and Writings."

53. Dario Gamboni, *Potential Images: Ambiguity and Indeterminacy in Modern Art* (London: Reaktion Books, 2002), pp. 17–19.

54. Oldenburg, quoted in Van Bruggen, "Soft and Hard," p. 90.

55. Claes Oldenburg, *Raw Notes: Documents and Scripts of the Performances* (Halifax: Press of the Nova Scotia College of Art and Design, 2005), pp. 7–8.

56. Oldenburg, quoted in Johnson, "Oldenburg's Poetics," p. 43.

57. Oldenburg, interview with the author, May 20, 2010.

58. PC, p. 397.

59. Oldenburg, interview with the author, February 9, 2011. The term "equivalents" is used by Johnson, "Oldenburg's Poetics," p. 48. It has been taken up by Robert Haywood, who interprets Oldenburg's connections between otherwise unrelated consumer objects and parts of the human body (an ice cream cone equals a turd equals a cathedral) as a leveling effect with political implications. Robert Haywood, "Claes Oldenburg," *Notre Dame Review* 9 (Winter 2000), p. 2. Haywood argues that the abject qualities of excrement "dismantl[e] hierarchies of power." The implications of this theory, however, are not explored in his text, nor does he cite additional examples that would sustain such an overarching theoretical approach.

60. Oldenburg, quoted in Johnson, "Oldenburg's Poetics," p. 42.

61. Rose, *Claes Oldenburg*, p. 128.

62. PC, pp. 183, 184.

63. Oldenburg, interview with the author, April 22, 2010.

64. PC, p. 208.

65. Ibid., p. 209.

66. Ibid., p. 208.

67. Oldenburg, interview with the author, February 9, 2011. This system of equations, with the universal form of the Ray Gun as the beginning, is intuitive, rather than systematic. There are sculptures in his art that do not directly emerge from or cannot be confined to this system.

68. I am thinking, for example, of Michel Lobel's book *James Rosenquist: Pop Art, Politics, and History in the 1960s* (Berkeley: University of California Press, 2009); and Joshua Shannon's essay "Claes Oldenburg's *The Street* and Greenwich Village, 1960," *Art Bulletin* 86, no. 1 (March 2004), pp. 136–161, reprinted in this volume.

69. For example, Alex Potts in his 2004 essay on the issue of tactility in postminimalist process art detects an ambiguity between what he calls the literal and virtual states of form (the idea of the form before it is "destroyed"). Form is "unformalized" because any structural cohesion of form is destroyed in the act of making, and we confront an "unhinging of [phenomenological] tangibility from plastic form" in the tradition of modernist literality. For Potts, this split in the image is resolved by attributing a dream logic of condensation to the soft object. See Alex Potts, "The Interrogation of Medium in the Art of the 1960s," *Art History* 27, no. 2 (April 2004), p. 289.

70. Cleanth Brooks taught English at Yale University between 1947 and 1975. Oldenburg especially mentioned his textbook on T. S. Eliot's *The Wasteland*. PC, p. 26.

71. PC, pp. 26–27.

72. See W. K. Wimsatt Jr., *The Verbal Icon: Studies in the Meaning of Poetry* (London: Methuen, 1954), pp. 3–40.

73. Oldenburg, quoted in Rose, "Claes Oldenburg's Soft Machines," p. 32.

74. T. S. Eliot, "The Social Function of Poetry," in his collection of selected writings *On Poetry and Poets* (London: Faber and Faber, 1957), pp. 15–25. In PC, p. 26, Oldenburg revealed that "I was terribly influenced by *The Waste Land* which was one of the first things I got to read. . . . The analysis of *The Waste Land* still fascinates me."

Index of Names

www.ingramcontent.com/pod-product-compliance
Lightning Source LLC
Chambersburg PA
CBHW020902180526
45163CB00007B/2594